SURVIVING IN TWO WORLD

Contemporary Native American Voices

CLINTON JR. COLLEGE LIBRARY

SURVIVING IN
TWO WORLDS

Contemporary Native American Voices

Lois Crozier-Hogle and Darryl Babe Wilson

Photographs by Giuseppe Saitta

Edited by Jay Leibold

Assistant interviewer, Ferne Jensen

Foreword by Greg Sarris

University of Texas Press, Austin

Requests for permission to reproduce material from this work should be sent to Permissions, University of Texas Press, Box 7819, Austin, TX 78713-7819.

∞ The paper used in this publication meets the minimum requirements of American National Standard for Information Sciences—Permanence of Paper for Printed Library Materials, ANSI Z39.48-1984.

Library of Congress Cataloging-in-Publication Data

Surviving in two worlds : contemporary Native American voices /
    [compiled by] Lois Crozier-Hogle and Darryl Babe Wilson ;
    photographs by Giuseppe Saitta ; edited by Jay Leibold ; assistant
    interviewer, Ferne Jensen. — 1st University of Texas Press ed.
        p.   cm.
    Includes bibliographical references (p.).
    ISBN 0-292-74694-6 (cloth : acid-free paper). — ISBN 0-292-74695-4
(pbk. : acid-free paper)
        1. Indian philosophy—North America. 2. Indians of North America—Attitudes.
3. Indians of North America—Social life and customs. I. Crozier-Hogle, Lois, 1913- .
II. Wilson, Darryl Babe, 1939- . III. Leibold, Jay.
E98.P5S87   1997
305.897—dc20   96-25378

DEDICATION

To all of my children, to all children of every Native nation of the western hemisphere, to all children throughout the world, and to the mothers and fathers and grandmothers and grandfathers of these children.

To my people of wisdom and culture, of tradition and ceremony. To the dreamers, and those yet practicing our languages. To that amazing spirit moving earth in the balanced arc, keeping us just close enough to sun so life is mostly beautiful.

Finally, to June LeGrande, Cherokee, full of fun, excited about this life, who began this journey with us, but is now a spirit. She flows with that Great Power that moves the universe in a vast cycle. Those of us who knew June can assure others that she is encouraging our journeys; journeys appointed when first the vastness was sprinkled with stars, and happiness spread in a sparkling pattern between them each.

—DARRYL BABE WILSON

To all the above and to my own children, Allan, Stephen, and Francie Hogle Kelley, whose patience has flowed eternally as their mother became engrossed in yet another project.

Finally, to Hella Adler of London, who helped to deepen my search as together we lamented the loss of so much of the spiritual and numinous quality of American life.

—LOIS CROZIER-HOGLE

CONTENTS

The Best Way We Know How

One spring day, as I was driving renowned Pomo medicine woman and basket weaver Mabel McKay back to the Rumsey Reservation from Stanford University, I commented on an immense new housing tract just outside the Bay Area, north of Berkeley.

"Gee," I said, "nothing left of the big oak trees that used to grow there."

"Yeah," Mabel answered, looking out the car window. "Spirit said when the land is filled up with houses, when it's all covered over, that's a sign the end of this world is near."

Immediately my mind began to spin. First, I thought of a question a student at the university had asked her earlier. "If you are the last Dreamer among the Pomo people, what is going to happen to the spirit when you die?"

It was the same question I had asked, albeit in a different way, several years before, when I was concerned about the future of my own Pomo family and our traditions. Mabel gave the student essentially the same answer she had given me. "Nothing," she said. "Nothing will happen to the spirit. The spirit won't go away. It won't disappear or hide someplace. It's everlasting."

Could the oak trees and all that once lived in this valley be everlasting, too? I wondered. Could the people living in the new tract houses ever know about the land they live on? Could they ever know a way to hear its voices, its rules?

Next, I found my mind traveling back to what Mabel had just said about the world ending. If the world was going to end because of greed and violence, was there any use continuing to work so hard in the hope that things might be different, might turn around?

"Mabel," I said, "if the world is going to end, what should we do, how should we live?"

She looked at me and laughed. "The best way you know how," she answered. Of course, what else? I thought. The answer was obvious.

The spirit of a place, be it a valley or mountain, like the larger Great Spirit of which it is a part, does not change, it does not hide or go anywhere. It is our lot in life to know this spirit and live the best way we know how. No matter what Mabel and I talked about—and we talked about many things for over thirty years—our discussions always seemed to come back to these two important notions: the Great Spirit and the right way to live in its presence.

Many of us, Indian and non-Indian, have forgotten what we knew, or what our ancestors knew, about living in a way that reflects the world and ways of the spirit, of the land. Some of us may never have known.

The multitude of rich and varied American Indian voices in this collection of interviews serves as a reminder. The speakers, young and old, men and women, call like the birds that once lived in those old oak trees and now inhabit our rooftops. They call, reminding us not only of the great trees that once grew, but of the life that still exists and so badly wants to be heard.

And in these voices are lessons: lessons about what has gone wrong, what is right and healthful, and what we must do to connect with and remember what is right and healthful. They seem to keep coming back to the same things: the Great Spirit and the right way to live in its presence.

They keep coming back to talk to us. Hear them. Know them. Learn. Remember. They aren't going away. They aren't going to disappear or hide someplace. They tell of the everlasting.

—GREG SARRIS

PREFACE

They have spoken.

We present the voices of twenty-six Native Americans who share their insights, experiences, and emotions, as well as their pain, hope, and dreams for the future. In their own voices, they describe the survival of their cultures and the struggle to take their rightful place in the fabric of our nation. I hope this book will help to bring American Indians out of often-stereotyped dusty museum cases, beyond their tragic history, and onto the living stage of American life.

A renaissance is occurring among educated Native Americans today. Without forgetting those who remain in poverty and degradation on the reservations and in American cities, we want to bring attention to those who have discovered that to survive in contemporary America requires an ability to live their own values astride two cultures. They have suffered the tragedies and hardships of their ancestors, yet with amazing trust and astonishingly little bitterness they have moved on to *overcome*.

The germ of the idea for this book began with the quincentennial of Columbus's arrival in the New World. I realized that Native Americans would not be joining in this celebration. After all, they had been living on this continent for thousands of years, and Columbus's intrusion upon their comparatively peaceful life brought devastation.

The feelings evoked by the approach of the quincentennial were deepened by my own thirty-five-year battle to help preserve the earth. Upon returning to my native California after eighteen years away, I was shaken by the loss of orchards and open space to the unplanned, ugly sprawl of industry and residential ticky-tack. The hills, bay, and beaches were seriously threatened. Battles loomed everywhere, and I felt inundated. How could mankind be so consumed with greed and *outer* growth? How could he have lost his connection with earth and all nature? It was at this time that I came upon the words attributed to Chief Seattle:

> *Every part of this country is sacred to my people. Every plain and grove has been hallowed by some fond memory or sad experience of my tribe.*[1]

The question arose: What is it within the heart and soul of the Native American that could sustain this sense of sacredness for our earth? I wanted to find out.

I discovered that the Original Americans have lived the "web of life" for thousands of years. One Indian said to me, "If it isn't of the spirit, it isn't Indian." Whence comes this sense of connectedness with all living things and a belief that everything has spirit? The interviews in our book speak to these questions.

The process of finding our interviewees was long and varied. I had been warned that it might take months before those we approached would trust us enough to share their feelings and experiences. It didn't. At a panel discussion at Stanford University, I asked William Demmert, then Alaska's commissioner of education, for an interview. He said, "This is the kind of help we need. You must also interview my assistant, an Eskimo from Barrow, Alaska."

From the beginning, I knew I wanted a team to create this book. In particular, I wanted a Native American partner in shaping the content and conducting the interviews. Darryl Wilson, of the California Pit River people, brought the Native voice and viewpoint necessary to complete the circle. With his indispensable knowledge and many contacts, the project took a giant step forward.

We learned as we went along, starting in Santa Fe and on the Pine Ridge and Cheyenne River reservations. One name, one contact, led to others, an expanding web of connections that gradually brought the substance of the book into focus. Through numerous conferences, meetings, readings, and helpful referrals from 1991 to 1995, we met and interviewed many more Native people than we were able to include in this anthology.

We spoke to people from a wide range of tribal backgrounds—from Penobscot and Onondaga in the northeast, to Tlingit and Inupiaq in Alaska, to the Pueblo and California tribes of the west. We tried to strike a balance between men and women, youth and elders, traditional and contemporary. However, in making the final selections for this volume, we did not attempt to achieve a uniform geographical distribution. Rather, we sought out the leaders who seemed to have the greatest insight into the questions we posed.

In most interviews, we began by asking the participants to talk about their cultural background and spiritual beliefs. Then we asked them to discuss the historical uprooting of so many Native people from their way of life, resulting in estrangement from their beliefs and loss of self-determination and self-esteem. How can these be restored, and are they related to mistreatment of the earth, both for Indians and non-Indians? Finally, we asked what American Indians have to teach the larger American society about caring for the earth, and whether there is any hope that the gap between our worldviews can be bridged.

Just as we did not try to impose a geographic distribution, we did not try to elicit a uniformity of response to the questions. Our goal has been to hear what the leaders we interviewed had to say and present their words in as direct a fashion as we could.

Listening to those voices, we discovered a great capacity for the endurance and renewal of Native identity and self-determination. After centuries of Native Americans being treated as "savages" who must be "civilized," it is no wonder this is a long and arduous process.

We were also reminded that many of the "white ones" have lost touch with much of our own *inner* life and self-esteem, and this enables us to destroy the natural processes and resources of our planet. Native Americans recognize that when separated from their traditions and the wisdom of their elders, they too are capable of destroying their environment.

Our interviewees speak of the need for balance and harmony in life. When we asked, "What makes life out of balance?" we began to see the great difference between Native American and modern Euro-American cultures. Indian culture brings an emphasis on spirit and "soul" that so much of Western materialist culture has lost. Without a meeting of these two worlds there can, I believe, be little hope for wholeness, healing, and balance in our lives.

Frank Waters wrote that we and the Indians have projected onto each other from time immemorial our fears and prejudices, and thus our mutual failures.[2] If we remain ignorant of other cultures and unconscious of our differences, we project onto them our unconscious blame, negative feelings, and anything else we are not cognizant of *in ourselves*. We must cease projecting and act differently, so the Indian will no longer feel the white man is his enemy. There will be no peace until then.

A special quality of spirit runs like a golden thread among the expressions of those Indians who have remained close to their traditions, ceremonies, and ancient wisdom. This closeness keeps alive and nourishes a belief in an Invisible Power, a power that has many manifestations and names—Great Spirit, Great Wonder, Wakan Tanka, Creator. It engenders a sense of relatedness to all of life and the earth. It creates the sense of place that is so crucial to Indian well-being, and which explains why the loss of so much of their land has been devastating to them. It is also a source of the power that has given them the strength to survive.

We have come to cherish our contact with these First Americans in our own personal process of discovery. They are willing to offer their gifts and insights to help fight for the survival of the earth. We have felt our lives enriched and enlivened and hope our readers may be led to a similar experience.

Our unconsciousness and prejudices, our violence and cruelty to each other and *to our inner selves*, all reveal the need for a restoration of our own self-esteem and a change of values from our materialistic, aggressive ways. The healing way—finding a balance and harmony comparable to that of the traditional American Indian—is, I believe, essential to our own survival on the earth.

Will we listen?

—LOIS CROZIER-HOGLE

Notes

1. The words of Chief Seattle as related in Eli Gifford and R. Michael Cook, editors, *How Can One Sell the Air? Chief Seattle's Vision*. There is controversy about the only known written version of the speech reputed to have been given in the early 1850s by Chief Seathl (or Sea-ahth), as he was called. Dr. Henry Smith, a physician, apparently witnessed the speech and took extensive notes, but he did not write up and publish his notes as a translation of parts of the speech until 1887. Subsequent, more widely known versions of the speech have departed considerably from Smith's text. See Rudolf Kaiser, "Chief Seattle's Speech(es): American Origins and European Reception," in *Recovering the Word: Essays on Native American Literature*, edited by Brian Swann and Arnold Krupat.

2. Frank Waters, *Pumpkin Seed Point*, 13.

ACKNOWLEDGMENTS

My warm appreciation goes to all those American Indians who trusted us enough to let us into their lives. For the twenty-nine whose interviews we could not include here, we hope to see a second volume of this work!

Like a beautiful basket, a book is woven together from many strands. It has taken many hands to weave this book.

We first met Darryl Wilson when he read his poetry at a benefit in Berkeley for *News from Native California*. We value and appreciate his trust and friendship, no less than the honesty and beauty of his spirit and writing.

The eloquence of photographer Giuseppe Saitta's talent adds a unique and invaluable dimension to the book. His videotaped interviews of many of the participants did a great deal to enhance the text as well.

Ferne Jensen led us to Darryl and assisted with the early interviews. How could I have braved the Badlands of South Dakota on a freezing morning in October of 1990 alone? Before we tackled the back roads en route to the Pine Ridge reservation, frost had to be coaxed off every inch of glass on our car. Such tasks require a good friend!

Editor Jay Leibold has contributed with exceptional skill to the completion of this volume. He was sent to us (heaven sent) by Karen Nilsson of Tioga Press. We remember also Karen's many other gifts to us. Sadly, she has since died of cancer.

Elaine Dorfman of the Bancroft Oral History Library taught us enough about interviewing to summon the courage to begin.

Anne Medicine of the dean's staff at Stanford University connected us with Oren Lyons, Arvol Looking Horse, and others. Hers is one of the interviews we hope to see in a second volume.

The insights and experience of Alan Strain, a great friend of Native Americans, helped us all along the way and were enhanced by his patience and understanding.

Trudy Sherlock patiently drove us around the Santa Fe area and made valuable suggestions.

To Caleen Sisk, we extend our gratitude for helping to complete the interview with Florence Jones.

Barbara Green, her daughter Carolyn Green Westgaard, and Susan Stamm patiently transcribed our tapes.

Bill Broder and his sister-in-law, Esther Margolis of Newmarket Press, had early confidence in our project and helped in so many ways.

We were delighted to have the University of Texas Press discover our book through its able editor, Theresa May. It has been a privilege to work with her.

I discovered how difficult it is to raise money for a book. But the following generous people shared our vision and helped us: Madeleine Haas Russell and Susan Silk of the Columbia Foundation; Jim and Pat Compton of the Compton Foundation; James T. Rea of Brookside Capital; and Ruth Heller of Marin County. Theirs was a special kind of encouragement! The Green Foothills Foundation received and disbursed these funds, which were ably administered by Alice Forbes.

—LOIS CROZIER-HOGLE

EDITOR'S NOTE

These interviews have been edited from the question-and-answer format of the original transcript into a more essay-like form. Sometimes this entailed changing the order of paragraphs or adding a relevant paragraph from a follow-up session. But aside from editing for grammar and the hesitations normal to speech, the phrasing of the original transcripts has not been changed. When combining two separate interviews, we tried to keep material from each interview in separate sections of the final text. All interviewees were given the opportunity to review the final draft and make revisions and corrections.

—JAY LEIBOLD

PHOTOGRAPHER'S NOTE

Throughout my many years of working as photographer, filmmaker, and videographer, I have never had an assignment quite like this one. As I met and photographed the wonderful people you will meet in this anthology, I experienced a subtle process of transformation. Each contributor speaks about living in two worlds, yet all speak with a common voice.

I traveled most of the western United States to shoot these portraits, and in most cases I was allowed to interview my host on videotape. While I was photographing or interviewing, the people in this book became my teachers. They have a rich and generous amount of information to give about harmonious living in our small world.

These wise, powerful, and yet gracious people taught me what Native American people have really contributed to our nation and to the world. They will touch your heart and challenge your mind with their stories, their truth, their wisdom. I am immensely grateful for the gifts they have given to me.

—GIUSEPPE SAITTA

INTRODUCTION

Survival seems to be the focus of many of the thoughts presented here: survival of the earth, of nature, of the people. And survival of the Native cultures, customs, and languages particular to the northern hemisphere. The message that earth is a delicate and endangered body is clearly defined, and solutions to reviving earth's spirit and resources are offered.

As I read the penultimate draft of this volume provided by our editor, Jay Leibold, I could not help but be drawn taut between two thoughts, like rawhide drying in the sun between two stakes. In 1972, in San Francisco, I attended a powerful dance by Dennis Hastings (Omaha). Also in 1972, in Pit River country, I was given a legend concerning the moon by Craven Gibson, an elder of my people.

At the outset of the Dennis Hastings dance, the stage was dark. Light slowly filtered in, showing a pile of feathers and what appeared to be a dead eagle, twisted, feathers akimbo, silent. For a long moment there was only a hush. Then a feather moved. Then, a wing. The head, in agony, moved slightly. It seemed the movement would be the eagle's last.

But there was more movement. Eagle struggled to rise, but buckled back to earth. It was painful to watch. Eagle tried to rise again. As if in mortal combat, its spirit quickened. Eagle looked around uncertainly, shook its feathers back into their proper place, and began a slow circle dance. My heart danced with the tempo of eagle's feet upon the stage. Soon eagle was dancing in a wide circle, its wings fully extended, tail feathers catching the breeze and "taking flight" off the stage. I had just witnessed the revival and survival of our Native Nations.

Then, in the winter of 1972, Craven Gibson sent for me. Sitting by an oil lamp at the table in his little home in Big Valley, he greeted me as I entered his crooked door. We sipped coffee and he spoke of his concern about the way the earth was being damaged. He felt it was time to relate to the greater society a lesson he had learned from his grandmother.

Craven was born on Alcatraz Island in the 1860s, when it was used as a concentration camp for Indians and other dissidents. At the age of two, he (upon his mother's back) and other tribal members escaped confinement by swimming from Alcatraz to San Francisco in the night, fleeing their military pursuers to return home.

In a worried voice, he told me of how the moon was an earth at one time, but two "thinkings" clashed. One "thinking" was that the moon's resources belonged to whoever took them first. The other "thinking" was that they belonged to every generation, and they must not be abused but encouraged to grow in abundance.

The two "thinkings" clashed in war. The side wanting all the resources for themselves attacked those who honored future generations. It was a big war; soon each side was using the moon's resources at a rapid rate. It was not long before all the resources were exhausted. So, when the moon caught fire, there was not enough water left to put the flames out. The moon burned to death.

Between these two thoughts—the optimism of the dance by Dennis Hastings and the concern in the words of Craven Gibson—a succinct message from my aunt, Gladys O'Neal of Fall River Mills, came to me. This memory helped to bring the present volume into focus. In the summer of 1956, she said:

> Yes, we must speak the white man language to survive in this world, but we must speak our language to survive forever.

Within her words are many facets of wisdom. It was not only the language that she worried about, but the "word." We must use the correct word, always.

She knew the power of words, and that is precisely what *Surviving in Two Worlds* intends to present. Words from Native people with Native meaning. Pondered words. Words of pain. Words of injury. Words of healing.

It has always been a delight for me to meet and listen to Original Native elders—people of wisdom whose presence seems to be an "appointment" from a higher degree of universal power. People of spiritual purpose. Those who are familiar with the strengths of humanity as well as its weaknesses, and are willing to share this knowledge with us. Elders seem to be the ones who assume the duty of assessing and confronting threats to the earth that result from the insensitivity of humanity, and the elders seem also to be the ones working for a balanced solution.

Therefore, when wisdom speaks, I am inclined to listen carefully to the message, to nurture the growth of a vision, and to take some small part in all its vastness. (Nor do I mean to suggest that Native wisdom emits only from "elders," for it may blossom in our youth also.) This is the manner in which I approach the wisdom of my Native mountain people of California, and in this same manner I weighed the project of environmentalist Lois Crozier-Hogle when she came to me with her dream. She outlined a volume, complete with photographs, of Original Native people: the Native voice addressing world issues, world fears, world needs. Eloquent Native voices offering ideas of how we might help to arrest the destruction of earth's ecology, nurture Native values and traditions, and begin a healing process.

As Lois talked, I heard another voice, a cautious and ancient Native voice explaining how it might be possible to apply the *tini-ho-wi* (medicine) songs to a modern world and return a freshness that is always present, but of late unseen. Lois possessed the wisdom to see that the Native people given this "medicine" are themselves rare. She began a journey to locate some of these people and ask for their participation, and she asked if I would assist her.

Her "talk" was like listening to my grandmother long ago in a little shack in the mountains. Grams and I were sitting near a cast-iron heater, our bodies warmed by juniper wood, our spirits warmed by its glow. Grams spoke in a soft yet firm voice about our land, our culture, our language, our existence.

Lois talked about the whole of existence, and she knew that the "medicine language," the words with power to heal, could emit from the Original Natives of this hemisphere. I focused upon Lois's message, pondered, then accepted the invitation.

This "urge" to help could be likened to the knowledge in nature moving herds of animals and schools of salmon to migrate and return to their birthplace. It also depends upon *MisMisa*, that power dwelling within *Ako-Yet* (Mount Shasta), which balances all that we know and all we cannot know.

It is said by our people of ancient knowledge that when this world was made many seasons ago, *MisMisa* would make corrections for errors within Creation. *MisMisa* was appointed to dwell with *Ako-Yet*. Today, if Earth wanders from the sun and the Milky Way even a little, *MisMisa* makes a "correction," an "adjustment," bringing Earth back to its proper path and proper velocity. *MisMisa* is the reason we are in our present orbit. It is said that it is always singing, but you must listen carefully to hear it.

I was born in northeastern California. In the land of my mother, we call ourselves *Iss*, "the people," and are identified by academics as *A-juma-wi* (Achomawi). In the land of my father, we call ourselves *Awt'-e*, "the people," and are identified by academics as *Atsuge-wi*. Politically, we are known as the Pit River Tribe.

Through our narratives and legends, my people know that we were created in our homeland, and that the first "island" was made *exactly where my people live today*. Then Silver Grey Fox (the creator) spread earth in many directions until it was "finished." Earth was so huge that it took an entire lifetime to travel around it. It was pregnant with life. Silver Grey Fox made human beings from serviceberry branches, placed them on top of the *chema-ha* (ceremonial round house), and brought them to life by singing, "Tow-chinna, tow-chinna."

Around the little fires, when the stars are fluttering silver in the blue-black of the evening, it is whispered that a medicine child is dreamed of. That infant is "called" forward, a being with destiny, already prepared to fulfill an obligation. The child is like a reed growing to become a flute that will emit healing music.

The words of Native voices speaking in this volume are part of the melody of that composition. They not only must be listened to, they must be lived and breathed, allowed to pass through the spirit like sunlight through morning mist.

Surviving in Two Worlds is a gathering of information, wishes, and dreams from the northern hemisphere. It weaves together the traditional and the contemporary, the scholarly and the personal, practical politics and visions of the earth's future. It spans family histories from the People of the Dawn to the Trail of Tears to Alcatraz Island. It presents youth at the dawn of their careers and elders in the sunset of their lives.

I have had the opportunity to work, play, travel, and dream with many of those whose voices join together in this collection. A sterling memory is of my travels with Thomas Banyacya to Stockholm in 1972. Along with many other Natives, we were invited to the United Nations Conference on Human Environment. Working with Oren Lyons at United Nations head-quarters in New York was electrifying. I am intensely proud to have labored with Clifford Trafzer on *Dear Christopher* and with Greg Sarris on *The Sound of Rattles* and *Clappers*. At the grassroots level, toiling for a common goal with Dagmar Thorpe, Frank LaPena, Steven Crum, and Carlos Cordero has been most rewarding.

What the voices in this book all share is a dedication to keeping traditions alive and making ceremony an active and growing force in contemporary Native American society—whether by illuminating the customs and origins of his people, as does Lakota Pipe Holder Arvol Looking Horse; giving new expression to Native experience, as do writer Greg Sarris and artist Roxanne Swentzell; fighting for Native rights and sovereignty, as does John Echohawk of the Native American Rights Fund; or laboring in order that Native Alaskan languages may flourish, as do William Demmert and Edna Ahgeak MacLean.

The book is organized into five parts whose main purpose is to serve as reference points for the reader. The five parts reflect themes that are in fact woven into the fabric of each of the interviews: tradition, history and politics, healing, education, and culture—all with the daring to remain Original Native in the presence of immense opportunities to compromise.

Part 1, "Tradition Is Evidence for the Truth of Life," speaks directly to the spiritual aspects of Original Native people. We are fortunate to dwell in a world with people of such dedication. Each person in this volume has an *Ah'lo* (spiritual root, umbilical cord) that attaches him or her directly to a special place upon this hemisphere.

In Part II, "The World Torn in Two," we find words of our people explaining how our history was and continues to be manufactured for us, and how in this capacity we are continually "convinced" that we do not fit into the unfolding events of the world. The words in this section may hurt, and they may open old, improperly healed wounds, but they also manage to unfold new perspectives. Collectively, they can help to begin a new historical thought process for each of us.

Within Part III, "It Must Be Healed," we locate our medicine people, the "called for." They are extra special, whether their healing comes through the words of a song or, for the moment, from the pages of the *Journal of the American Medical Association*. In both instances these people follow the path as they are instructed by the Great Power that turns the earth around the sun and the sun around a greater wonder still.

Part IV, "The Children Are Our Future," presents Native people in education who must constantly struggle to maintain a standard of Native American presence. These scholars (our "scouts") must always be alert for changes in the education system. They know the Native child is our voice in approaching centuries. They also know that the meaning and purpose of our individual Native languages must be encouraged to come from our children like the melodies of a flute across a summer lake at dusk.

"We Can Have New Visions," the concluding section, shows that the Original Natives still live their culture and formulate that culture with artistic satisfaction. It shows too that most of our tribal communities still move upon their sacred course. The Native "way" is an acknowledgment of, and a balance within, nature. Native cultures emerged from nature and retain the original expression, an expression often "given" to a people through one or all of their dreamers, who then issued the "law" through a song, or a dance, or both.

Such is the power of expression. A message unfolding daily in a routine not yet met and acted out, but prepared for with meticulous ceremony. Our artists now create upon the pages of books instead of upon the stones of the valleys or within the caves of the mountains. The poets write in volumes instead of passing the messages from generation to generation through song and dance.

This anthology cannot boast to have answers to all the ecological and social problems of the world, but it does invite all people to begin, today, to take part in preserving nature and adjusting the way we live. This means not that we must "follow" a "leader," but that we must follow the emotional truth that is contained in our hearts and is a unifying spark that connects all of us, like lightning that fractures the night sky and charges earth with new spirit.

This volume was created from a dream of Lois Crozier-Hogle. It is a gift of many thoughts from the Native Nations, presented in English. In some instances the message may be a lecture on how the cycle of the spirit moves. At other times it is an invitation to become a part of the salvaging process of the earth. Sometimes it appears as a patient basket weaver:

> First thing I do is to know the design. Then I make the basket. I never try to make a basket unless I know the design. The design comes to me in a dream. Then I make the basket.
>
> (Lillian Snooks, Hat Creek, California, 1993.)

I discovered that Lillian is very worried that the young people do not want to learn how to make baskets, that they would rather not know. That, in their hesitation to know, the art will end one day. She fears that their longing to speak only English and their desire to be Americans may bring an end to what we know of as our tribe. This is why we must always have dreamers.

Dreamers are the spirit of the nations, the ones who caution us to touch our reality softly. They are the keepers of the secrets. A "keeper" could be born in each infant, "called" in a time that we have forgotten, but appearing now for our protection. Here we present the words of many "keepers."

It is said by the elders of my nation that the song that Silver Grey Fox sang as he created the world has been forgotten—that White Horse Bob was the last to know it. But it is also acknowledged that the song came from a "thought" that manifested itself into a "voice" that created that very "song." That it was a song that brought this universe into being. That we all can think, and we all can sing. And we must.

Surviving in Two Worlds is laced with lessons which, if lived by, may help many generations to thrive. But humanity must assist in its most potent manner—like the Ohlone (San Francisco) custom of holding hands just beyond the village circle and watching the sun rise, calling to its magical wonder.

We must hold hands. We must listen to those of wisdom among us who have issued us "laws" to live by in order to preserve and respect Earth. For this earth is not ours to damage as the moon was destroyed in the lesson of Craven Gibson. Instead, it is ours to cherish for the rest of time.

The strengths of the Native Nations must be revived and the positive spirit of the people must survive, like Dennis Hastings's eagle, who rose from near extinction to take flight. If we can listen to these voices, we may be able to move toward accomplishing some of these things for the children, for the future, for life.

—DARRYL BABE WILSON

TRADITION IS EVIDENCE
FOR THE TRUTH OF LIFE

Native spiritual traditions are the bedrock of cultural survival. This is articulated here in different ways by the carriers of four traditions: Chief Oren Lyons of the Haudenosaunee, Wintu medicine woman Florence Jones, Lakota Pipe Keeper Arvol Looking Horse, and Hopi spokesman Thomas Banyacya. Dagmar Thorpe and Frank LaPena provide a contemporary framework for understanding the role of tradition.

Dagmar Thorpe People of the Seventh Fire
Chief Oren Lyons It Is in Our Hands
Florence Jones Last of the Wintu Doctors
Arvol Looking Horse Mending the Sacred Hoop
Thomas Banyacya The Hopi Prophecy
Frank LaPena Tradition Is Evidence for the Truth of Life

Dagmar Thorpe

People of the Seventh Fire

Dagmar Thorpe is a citizen of the Sauk and Fox nation. She is the daughter of political activist Grace Thorpe and the granddaughter of legendary Olympic athlete Jim Thorpe. She is also the mother of a daughter, Tena Malotte.

The first years of her life were spent in mainstream America, including undergraduate education at Goddard College. The Native American occupation of Alcatraz Island in 1969 was a turning point for her. Since then, she has worked to preserve the belief systems and ways of life of Native people.

She helped to found the Seventh Generation Fund, the first national Native American foundation, and served as executive director. She has received awards from the National Committee for Responsive Philanthropy and from Native Americans in Philanthropy for her nationwide impact on increasing grants to Native Americans. She continues to serve as a philanthropic advisor and consultant to many foundations.

At the time of this interview, Dagmar Thorpe was executive director of the Ira Hiti Foundation (now the Foundation for Deep Ecology) in San Francisco. She has since returned home to her community in Oklahoma, where she is director of the Thakiwa Foundation, which was created by individual Sauk people to support their way of life.

The title of this interview is taken from her book, *People of the Seventh Fire*. The book documents projects by Native American nations, organizations, and individuals that are based upon traditional Native principles; the title refers to an Anishinabi prophecy that tells of a time when a new generation of Native people will work to recover their ways of life. The book was published by Akwe:Kon Press of Cornell University, in collaboration with *LifeWay*, an organization Thorpe founded in 1993 to advance Native thinking as a necessary element to revitalizing Native communities.

Dagmar Thorpe was interviewed by Darryl Wilson.

My life as it is now began with the Alcatraz Island occupation in 1969. That was a real turning point for me. Until then I had pretty much lived in white suburbia. Although my grandfather is well known as a Native person, I was not exposed to Native thinking or ways of life until I was in my late teens.

I am fair and light-complected and could have chosen to live my life either in mainstream America or the life which I have. I have chosen to align myself with and live the world view of Native people. The reason I made that choice is that Native thinking embraces spirituality. The foundation of Native thinking is based on spirituality—that dimension which connects us to each other as human beings and to life as a whole.

Although my philosophy and my understanding of things have evolved considerably, this has been within me all of my life. In the variety of things that I have done in my adult life, all my efforts have been to support the traditional spiritual beliefs and lifeways that Native people hold. This world view maintains a psychic balance within the universe. Native people play a role not only in terms of articulation to the world around us, but also in that this spiritual strength and balance helps to correct the confusion and the chaos that surrounds people living in a modern society.

For the past twenty-three years most of the work I have done has been to support Native people and our efforts to maintain our belief systems, spirituality, and way of life. I am convinced this effort will ensure a continuation of the lifeways of the Native people. It will assist the vision and the cosmology that Native people represent to enter the future.

Native people have been double-hit by the oppression of modern society: First, by the destruction of traditional values and belief systems within, and second, by the oppression that comes from the outside—economic oppression, theft of land and resources, and the destruction of a "way of life." This has created a sense of powerlessness about the future.

We are facing major problems, not only as Native people but as non-Native as well—issues around the environment, inequality, war and peace. All of these things have at their essence a value system or the lack thereof. People's energy is not directed toward creating things that support life, but things that may eventually destroy it. To me, a spiritual-based way of thinking—through *that* will evolve values, through *that* evolves belief, and as a consequence different decisions will be made.

The destruction of Native people and the destruction of the environment are essentially the same. It denies the spirit of Native people—and denies the spirit of the land, which can benefit American society as a whole. When I look at my own tribe, the Sauk and Fox, we were forcibly moved from the Great Lakes down to Oklahoma. The land and the character of the land is very different. If you look at most Oklahoma tribes, they have been removed from their traditional land base. To take Native land and take control of all the resources is to diminish the Native health and well-being by diminishing the spirit.

The programs that have been created by the federal government further deprive Native people of our own thinking and our ability to make decisions about our future. They diminish our concept of ourselves, pattern us in ways of modern technological society and a more mechanistic way of living.

In a film about Mother Theresa in New York City, the interviewer asked, "Why are you in one of the wealthiest cities in the country?" She said, "Because the people are so spiritually impoverished here."

To me, that is the absolute essence of what is happening in modern society today. It is directed toward the destruction of the human spirit. And until that can be regained, both within the Native and non-Native communities, the consciousness that is required to create broad social change will not happen.

It is critically important, in my mind, to protect and lend support to efforts of traditional Native people who are working in those ways—not only for the continuity and the survival of the Native people's thinking, but also for how those concepts can be shared with society as a whole.

The way to heal ourselves is through connecting with our own spirituality and way of life. Balancing the spiritual and the physical. This is accomplished through practicing ceremonies and prayer, through bringing them back into daily life. In a lot of places ceremonies are not being done any more, or they are being done by a handful of elders. That wisdom and knowledge and ability to emerge with that level of consciousness is lost.

Unless we work with the elders and renew those ceremonies, this wisdom and knowledge will continue to slip away. It is critically important. Otherwise we are lost. Those "ways" are a method and a process that have come through the evolution of our people into the present. Otherwise we end up a lost people, searching in scattered ways to re-create wholeness within ourselves.

I think the moment of weakness in which we lost some of these things is our own disbelief in ourselves and in our sovereignty. Also it is in lacking belief in our way of life—not acknowledging that it is equally valid, if not superior to a Western technological way of life. If you look at the way Western civilization has destroyed human beings and other civilizations, it cannot be a correct way of living.

The weakness comes from within ourselves. There has been horrible oppression and destruction of Native people. But among the traditionalists, that continuity and way of life is not gone. Some traditionalists discount what others have to say about their reality and their land. Although the government may say on their paper it is government land, in reality it is still Native land.

The continuity may be unrecognized for those of us who choose to follow the mainstream, but it is certainly there within the traditional people. I believe it is still there among all Native people, no matter who they are. It is a matter of refocusing that consciousness, shifting back into a balanced perspective again.

When you talk about healing, *that is not a moment in time*. Essentially, life is a process of continual healing. It is a process of expanding awareness and consciousness, so that you are continually gaining clarity about yourself and your relationship with the world.

The history of my family is that we are mixed bloods. We have been mixed bloods for quite a while now. But my grandfather was a fighter. He accomplished things that most people would not believe could be achieved. The belief that you can do what you set your mind to was passed on to my mother and it was passed on to me. I am hopeful it will also be passed on to my daughter.

I am hopeful that she will follow in the tradition, that her consciousness will evolve, that she will be healthy physically, spiritually, emotionally, and intellectually, that she will have a vision of herself and the earth that is healthy, and that she will be engaged in a continual process of healing.

When I look to the future, obviously things cannot continue along the same course. There needs to be a tremendous shift in the consciousness of people. Change has to occur. Because if things continue in the way they are, the life-giving forces of the planet and human beings will be diminished and eventually destroyed.

But if that change happens—if we can focus on what our basic needs are and not be driven by a consumer economy that propels us to buy things we don't need, that destroys resources and takes from the earth and does not examine appropriate technology—life may continue. Human beings must set guidelines to a more whole vision of what the earth is and what we can be as human beings.

The educational system as it is now is a rote process focused on creating consumer citizens—citizens who have the existing Western technological worldview, whose minds and thinking are narrow and particular. If education is to be a process of healing and change and transformation, it has to encourage people to *think*.

We must look at the whole process, the total dimension of what life is about, and educate our children to that process. "How do you think? How do you weigh decisions? What are your values?" They must take history as the experience from which we can learn, rather than accept it as a given.

A lot of us have had to overcome the education we've gone through in order to evolve into the human beings that we are. By sharing these things with our children, we'll be able to encourage them to evolve their awareness much earlier. A lot of people are lost by the time they become adults, and it is almost impossible to create that process of change within them.

If you start with the young, while their minds and spirits are evolving, then they will be healthier, stronger, fuller human beings. They will evolve without having to go through decades of trial and error, of having to define and find the ingredients they need. We can help put these together for our children.

But I want to be clear, in this interview, that I am not a spiritual leader. I am a child in the practice of my own Sauk and Fox way of life. I know some of my own things, I don't know a lot. I spent a lot of time in Western Shoshone country because that is where my daughter is enrolled, and that is the Native blood she carries. I want her to know her people and her way of life.

Most of what I have done has been in a supportive capacity. I think that the wisdom and knowledge that have been shown to me have helped me evolve considerably as a human being. For that I am extremely thankful to all those who have reached out to me. It has helped me in the understanding of my spirit and the formation of my character and humanity.

There are certain natural laws and powers that transcend whether or not I am a true traditional American Indian—or a traditional Buddhist, or wherever I happen to come from. Traditional spirituality shares a lot with Eastern tradition: our acknowledgment of the spirit within us, and that it is as real as the physical world. Since we cannot touch it, some question its existence. But we can't deny that there is a force within us.

There is an unseen force within all life. We are all interconnected, we are all co-equal. Those basic philosophies, I believe, are universal and natural laws that transcend and cut across our differences. It is there. It is a reality. A traditional way of thinking and way of life tends to facilitate that knowledge, because it is the "way" people have evolved to achieve spiritual balance through their own history.

That is what we have to tap into in order to create a healing process, a healing transformation for ourselves and the earth. In the way we were intended to—in a way that supports life.

There needs to be a level of consciousness that moves people to act. I look within myself. When I started out in my chosen life, I had a very small level of consciousness. It has continued to grow because I now have basic beliefs that I couldn't articulate when I was younger. But they have come to a fullness within me, an intensity, a depth, over time.

I think it is that consistency of having belief and having vision and maintaining faith that keeps a person conscious of a process that is continually evolving. And that is the precursor to change. It needs to happen so that we can change the way we relate to one another—and the way we relate to the earth.

Chief Oren Lyons

It Is in Our Hands

Oren Lyons serves as Faithkeeper of the Turtle Clan of the Onondaga Nation of the Haudenosaunee and sits in the Grand Council of Chiefs of the Haudenosaunee (People of the Longhouse, or Six Nations Iroquois). He is internationally recognized as a spokesman for the Iroquois and all indigenous peoples and is frequently consulted for presidential, congressional, and United Nations committees and forums.

He was born in 1930 on the Hederagus Reservation, in Seneca territory, and was given the name Jo-Ag-Quis-Ho (Bright Sun Makes a Path in the Snow). He is a scholar, a fine artist, and a prolific author. His paintings are in collections around the country, including the Smithsonian Institution. He co-authored *Exiled in the Land of the Free: Democracy, Indian Nations, and the U.S. Constitution* and has illustrated several books for children.

Chief Lyons has been Professor of American History at the State University of New York, Buffalo, since 1970, and is director of the doctoral program in Native American Studies there. He received a B.A. from Syracuse University in 1959, where he was an All-American lacrosse athlete, and an honorary law degree from City University of New York in 1987.

He was interviewed by Lois Crozier-Hogle, with a follow-up interview by Darryl Wilson.

My name is Jo-Ag-Quis-Ho, which is an old name. It comes from the Wolf Clan. My clan is the Wolf, but as I sit in council as a chief of the Onondaga Nation, I sit on behalf of the Turtle Clan. I'm what they called a "borrowed chief." The Turtles have borrowed me for twenty-four years. When I die, that name will be up for use again.

I was brought up in the Onondaga Nation territory my whole life, and I still live there. My grandmother lived there, my mother lives there, all my relations are there. I remember the Onondaga Indian school as a sort of an outpost of white people on Indian land. We all looked upon it as a battlefield of wills. I remember some of the principals attempted to change our direction forcibly, but we've always been independent and managed to survive.

We had one extraordinary woman who taught my father and our children after. But I also remember the hostility from other non-Indian teachers. Eventually I just dropped out of school. They didn't like me and I didn't like them. I'd rather hunt and fish. That was my school for the next seven years.

I grew up as a hunter, in the woods. They've been my best teacher throughout all of life. My father was a good hunter and I learned from him. He left the family when I was quite young, but he was a good influence on my life. I learned from myself, too, just being in the woods.

I grew up having to help feed a family. I had six brothers, one sister, and my mother. My mother was very, very strong. She held the family together. The entire family owes her everything.

I was the oldest. I spent many days and years in the woods with my shotgun. I learned to respect everything, how bountiful it is, a place where you can have true peace. It's a shame we're losing that. Some of our children may not have the privilege of knowing a real woods, a real forest, at the rate we're going.

I grew up in hardwood country. There's a lot of maple, oak, hickory, ironwood, poplar. I grew up in that area where you have real strong falls and real strong springs. Clear seasons. Cold winters and hot summers. Central New York is a beautiful place. It's the place we chose to stay and live from the beginning, and by good luck and good fortune we're still there. The hills still furnish us with what we need.

My mother was a Christian. My father was a longhouse chief. He was the Faithkeeper. They never had any problems. There were never any arguments. I remember him saying to my mother, "All I ask of you is that when we have the ceremonies, you are there with the children to make sure they behave." I learned to respect everyone's beliefs.

I always looked up to the chiefs. I remember as a young boy of six or seven, walking up to Chief George Thomas's house. He was the head of the Six Nation Confederacy. I remember knocking on his door. He was a big man and his wife was very kind. He looked at me and I said, "I want you to tell me about the nation. How does it work?"

He took me inside and gave me something to drink and we spent a little time. I don't remember much of the conversation. He said, "Keep coming to the longhouse. You'll learn."

I knew when there was smoke coming out of the longhouse, the chiefs were meeting. That always made me feel good. I wondered what they did there. The door was always open, so I'd peek in and see them sitting there. It was kind of scary so I usually wouldn't go in.

It seems like all of our people have very strong identity and strong vision. I don't think anybody trains us to it. Maybe the fact that we have the longhouse and our traditions and ceremonies helps.

I got my high school equivalency in the army, and I went to the University of Syracuse on an art and athletic scholarship. I was a bit rebellious as a child, but my art was pretty good. It seems to run in the family. If I had my preference, I'd be an artist. I never intended to be a teacher. I made the dean's list because I was a good artist, and I won several athletic awards, which surprised everybody, including myself.

When you become educated, it's important to be grounded in who you are. Once you are secure in your own identity, then you can learn anything anywhere in the world. But if you're not secure in your identity, when you go into a university you become whatever the university is. It is important to have pride in your own heritage. Know who you are first. Know your nation, your history, your clan and family. Even if you learn all you can in school, it's only half of what you already have.

When I came out of the army, Coach Roy Simmons at Syracuse University asked if I would consider playing lacrosse for them. He had a lot to do with my development outside of the territory. I learned patience from that man.

Patience is manifested in Indian life. I learned patience by hunting. I would sit still for hours. If you can sit still for hours, you learn something. But I learned patience from Coach Simmons, too. He had a lot of confidence in my abilities.

Lacrosse is a major tradition with the Iroquois. It's played around the world, but it originated with us. We call it "the Creator's game." There are two sides to it. We use it as a medicine game, and also for entertainment.

A whole community revolves around lacrosse. I love the game. It's one of the gifts we've given to the world. As a matter of fact, we made all the sticks, until plastics came in. All the universities came to the Six Nations. I still use a wood stick.

I played from 1945 to 1972. Last summer we took the Iroquois national team to Australia and competed as a nation against the United States, Canada, Australia, and England. It was the first time an indigenous nation participated. On the day of the games, our flag went up and everyone's hats went off to us. That was a great day for indigenous people.

When I was put up as a chief in 1967, it was a lifetime commitment. It says you will put the interests of your people ahead of your own interests. We must make our own living and do the work as well. The chiefs do not receive a salary. That makes for a quality leader.

I see spirituality simply as a service. Growing up, getting away from your own self and turning your concerns to other people. People who are out there doing service are about as spiritual as you can be.

The spiritual beliefs are in our ceremonies in the longhouse. I've been brought up with that all my life. When the people see the chief there, there's great attendance. That's how we carry on. We don't sit down and talk about spiritual beliefs. We just do what we're supposed to do. We sing the songs and carry on the ceremonies.

We are instructed to give thanks. We do our ceremonies and give thanks around the calendar. We have just completed our thanksgiving for the maple. The next thanksgiving will be for the first fruit, the strawberry, then the beans and squash, and then the green corn. After that will be the harvest, then the winter ceremony. The children see this and they gain the same respect. Eventually they understand it.

The earth is our mother. We believe that. I've met indigenous people from around the world and I've yet to find a difference of opinion on that. It's much more than a saying, it's much more than a word, it's a real compassion and a longevity.

There's never a time when we're not in some kind of communication with the earth. The ceremonies are the best way to be in close communion. It's a reminder in the community from the smallest child to the oldest person. You pay your respects for what life is all about.

It's imperative that we carry on the ceremonies. As long as we do, life will continue. But we are coming to times now when some of our people are starting to lose that. The world is in flux, and there's a danger of losing touch entirely.

Indians have been losing touch by attrition. It's not that the Indians wanted to do it, it's not as if we were just benignly standing by and watching it happen. It's been a policy of the federal government. They took our language away, they forced our children out, they moved people about, taking them away from the earth—I mean, what do you expect? It's amazing that we do have any connection at all at this point.

These past few years we've had some serious disruptions. Some of our young people took this idea of independence and coupled it with economics.

They picked up the idea of becoming powerful through commerce. They got into the idea of high-stakes gambling, casinos, smuggling. Mohawks have been fighting among themselves because of that influence. They've been victims of this commerce and it's very disruptive.

We're getting hooked in, just like the white man. They have gotten to our young people. We see them carrying automatic weapons and firing at their own people through the influence of organized crime. Are you going to blame Indian people for that when there's such outside pressure?

It's not so easy just to come back. It's not a simple thing. You have to deal with the communities. You have to stand there with your arms folded and say to them, "Whatever possessed you?"

The Indians are losing the high moral ground they used to hold. Some still hold that ground. The elders do, the traditional Circle of Elders. But we're losing those values. I know from my experience that I don't have near the knowledge of the elders. Although I'm getting older, I'm lacking in fundamental knowledge. If I don't have it, how will it go on to the next generation? If things don't turn around now, there won't be any teachers left.

The only power that's left to maintain the planet is the spiritual power. Spiritual power will outlast and outgrow the manifestations of economics, although it may be at severe penalty of human life. There isn't going to be a winner. You can't think in those terms.

The instruction for the Haudenosaunee chief is that we must make all of our decisions on behalf of the seventh generation that is coming. They must be able to enjoy life to the same degree that we have it here. We should not think only in terms of ourselves or our families or even our nation. We're talking about life itself on this earth. We're talking about animal life, the water, life as we see it in the world around us.

We don't question spiritual instructions. Someone might ask, "Why is it the seventh generation?" They will never get an answer. I don't know why the seventh. We just take it on faith.

We have an instruction and it's very clear. You'll find that in all the Indian territories. Everywhere I go, we are welcomed into ceremonies by the Lakota, Hopi, or any Indian nation. We don't have to have an explanation of how they live or what their principles are. That's a unity that we'd like to extend to the rest of the world.

Our prophecies say it's a very hard future we're looking at. We've been told that it's inevitable that man is going to destroy himself. It's similar to the vision Black Elk had. There were only the stumps of trees. The grass was no longer green and the color was brown. There were no leaves, no animals; there was devastation. One of our leaders, a man named Ganiodaio, "Handsome Lake," was shown these visions.[1] He said the same thing: "This will happen, inevitably. Just don't let it be your generation."

That means that as long as each generation strives, works, and does what it is supposed to do, there will be continuity. It puts it squarely in the hands of each generation. The generation that lets this happen will suffer beyond description. That's all there is to it.

There will never be peace until we stop making war on Mother Earth. We are bound to her from birth until death. When we lose the rhythm of the seasons and the moon, we are in trouble. It is up to the people to bring things back into balance. The next generation will make a difference as to whether life will continue on the earth.

If we can get the leaders of this nation to look seven generations ahead, we can have a change of direction. But the world is at dire risk at this moment. There has to be a new paradigm of life. As I sit here, I think of my people back home who still carry water in buckets. There is a great disparity in this land. Somewhere there has to be a sharing. We have to change this idea of supremacy of human beings as the ultimate authority. The human being is given a great deal of responsibility and he's not carrying that out at all.

I'm a champion of the continuation of the indigenous voice of sovereign Native nations. They have a lot to offer. The first basic principle of Native nations is peace. The second is equality and justice for the people. The third principle is discussion—the power of good minds. We hope to impart that.

We're publishing a book called *Exiled in the Land of the Free*. We decided to do this book when the United States was taking these big bows for the two-hundredth anniversary of the Constitution. We said, "Wait a minute, we'd better step in here and explain where democracy came from."

It certainly didn't come over on the boats of the Europeans, because they were fleeing kings and queens who were burning people at the stake. So where was the land of the free? Well, everybody here was free. Freedom was rampant here in the whole of North America. We didn't know anything else. We had true democracy and we had respect, personal respect and honor. We didn't write anything down because the spoken word would be honored. A spoken commitment was enough. More than enough.

So that process of having power with the people is an old one with us. The leaders do not really have any power. We don't have a police force, we don't have an army, so there's no way for us to enforce anything. We can only present and persuade the people, and a chief is servant of the people.

It's a lifelong work of serving the people. No, it's hard work. Nobody wants to be chief.

Note

1. Ganiodaio, or Handsome Lake, was a Seneca sachem, warrior, and religious leader who received a series of visions in 1799 that became known as the Code of Handsome Lake. The Code embraces both traditional Indian and Quaker values.

Florence Jones

Last of the Wintu Doctors

Florence Jones is the last healer in the medicine way of the Northern Wintu Nation in the Shasta, Redding, and Jones Valley areas of California.

She was born Florence Violet Curl in Baird, California, a town now under Lake Shasta. Her father had a mining claim and a ranch. Construction of the lake forced her family to move to Jones Valley in 1934, and she has lived there ever since.

Florence Jones was sent to the Indian school in Greenville as a child. After the school burned down she was sent to a public school in San Francisco. She returned home for good at the age of seventeen.

Of her eleven siblings, Florence says she was among the younger six who inherited portions of her father's land allotment. Her husband Andrew Jones sold some of the land before he passed away in 1980, but Florence still owns a small ranch on the river. Now in her eighties, she has been ailing lately. Her daughter, cousin, and grandson live on the ranch and help her. Only recently was she given an official permit by the federal government to conduct her traditional ceremonies on Mount Shasta, ceremonies that have been taking place in some form for over a thousand years.

She spoke to Darryl Wilson, who has known Florence and her family since childhood.

I was ten years old when I started training to be a Wintu doctor person. I had six older doctors to train me. I smoked my pipe and went into trance just like they did.

It is just like going to school and going to college and being a medical doctor or a lawyer. There's a lot of no-no's and a lot of things I had to go through. All the sacred places, sacred springs, and sacred mountains. They took me up to Mount Shasta to the bubbling spring, the sacred spring. That's where we start doctoring, right there. Then they took me up to Cold Spring Mountain. I had to go up there and stay for a few days.

To make a long story short, it took me thirty-eight years to become a full-fledged doctor. The two mountains I doctor is my power, which I doctor and get my power to help my people.

I am teaching the younger generation now, whoever wants to learn the Wintu. I have my classes every Sunday. A lot of them don't know my language, even if they are Wintu. The younger generation—they're not my children, but that's what I always call them—a lot of them want to be Indian doctors, but you have to learn your language first.

There are no elders now. I'm the only one who knows my language thoroughly. That is the reason I am teaching them—so they will understand their spiritual language and become whatever they want to be.

I lost twelve years of my training when I had to go to school. The government came along and took us away to a government school in Greenville. We were signed up for five years there. When that school burned down, I went to public school in San Francisco. But I never did forget my doctoring language. I prayed in the Indian way, all the time. I never forgot my prayers. I never forgot my doctoring dreams.

What happened to me, I came home when I was seventeen years old. I didn't feel good. I felt like I was in two worlds and something was pulling me from each side. I almost went insane. From my religion and the white religion, they were pulling me apart. My mother got scared and she told my dad to get four Indian doctors—that is the way the top-notchers do it, with four doctors.

Before they came, I passed out. I just dropped to the floor. They just leave me lay there. That's the way they do in our religion. They just lay you there until the doctors come, and then they put me on a blanket.

I didn't wake up until four days after that. When I came out of it, my mother was looking down—she was a doctor too—and she was talking to me in our language. She said, "You're all right now, we've got you back into your own religion power."

I looked up at my brothers and I said, "Gee, I just fainted a little while ago." They said, "You've been fainted for four days and you just woke up!"

My mother said, "These doctors have been watching over you and you were all right. You had to go through that change from the white religion into your own religion. These four doctors were doctoring you the whole time. They never came out of trance, they just kept on a-going."

After that, I was okay. I went back to training again. My aunt, Tildie Brock, was my teacher. She was blind then. She taught me until 1930, and then my uncle took over. When he was ninety-five years old, he said, "Well, you know more than I do about spiritual life. I can't teach you any more. You know it. You are following your great-great-grandmother's foot-steps. She was the top doctor in Northern California."

So I've been doctoring ever since.

When the medical doctors tell me someone is gone, I go into a trance. I ask my spiritual mountain, Doctor Mount Shasta, to ask the Great Creator. I say, "I don't know the medicines. You are the Creator. You made everything on the earth. We are asking you." And so they tell me to use this herb, that herb, and what to use for the poultice.

See, I don't just pick it up by itself. I get it from the Great Creator. That way I'm not picking just any kind of herbs.

Last week there was a lady down here, and the doctor said she was so weak they couldn't do nothing with her. So a doctor from Oklahoma came down. We doctored together at my spiritual ground. The old people, thousands of years back, doctored there.

We went under trance. He had his own way—he doesn't go into trance like I do. I go *into* trance. We did it to help this lady come out of the weakness. She wants to die, I told the daughter. We're going to pray for your mother, bring her back so she will not say she wants to die.

We doctored two nights up there. Yesterday we came down and she was talking and laughing. Right back to herself. She forgot all about it. I gave her some herbs to give her strength. Last night I went down there and she was just as happy as could be. She couldn't sleep all of this time, but the last two nights she slept like a baby.

So that's the way we doctor. In our way, you're not dead until the fourth day. That's the reason we can go into trance and bring these dead people back. We go out and pick up their heart-spirit and bring it in and put it in their chest. We tell the dead man's people they have to use these sticks to keep time with my song. You cannot miss a beat. If you do, the person will stay in a coma.

I had a cancer patient in Willow Creek, an Indian man named Ray who was married to a white woman. The medical doctor said, "Florence, will you please come over? All the doctors here have given up on him."

I said, "What do you think I do, make miracles?"

He said, "Please, Florence, will you come?"

Ray had cancer from his throat clear to his colon. See, when I go into a trance, I don't know what I am saying. I have to have an interpreter. And Emerson, my interpreter, said what I saw—the cancer was nothing but blisters, blisters, blisters clear down. I asked the two mountains I doctor, "What kind of herbs am I going to give this man? He is dead. What am I supposed to do for him?"

So, they translated to the Creator and named out all the herbs. There were three herbs to take and one poultice. I told the doctor, "In four days time there's going to be a hole in his stomach. Immediately put a tube in there to drain it."

In four days time the hole broke out. He almost died, but the Great Spirit was with him, I guess. Ray's wife said, "How am I going to make him drink that medicine?" I said, "Take a spoon, open his mouth, and put his head back. Even if it runs out of his mouth, some of it is going down."

She did that. Three days later, he woke up. On the fifth day he sat up. Inside of a week he was up and walking around the house. I told her to keep the medicine on him. I said, "This medicine is going to take one year to work."

In seven weeks time he went back to working in his shop and driving his car. After seven months, he pronounced himself well. I stopped in to see him. I said, "Are you taking your medicine?"

He looked over his shoulder at me and he said, "I'm going to let Jesus Christ take care of me."

I said, "Okay, let Jesus Christ take care of you. I'm off the hook now. I'm not your doctor any more. But Ray, you got only three more months and I can pronounce you a well man."

He was a rough talker. "Ah, hell," he said, "I'm well."

I said, "No, you're not. Right on the end of your heart, that cancer is still there. This medicine can erase that."

He said, "I'll let Jesus Christ take care of me."

So I went on up and doctored other people, then I flew down to Riverside to see my nieces. I was gone for three weeks. Emerson called and said, "You know what? Ray died for good this time. They were looking for you all over. They couldn't find you."

I said, "Well, I can't bring him back. He's already buried."

I baby sat him. I talked with him in every way I possibly could. He only had three months left. That's the way it goes. Lots of people don't want to understand. That's the biggest part of it. A lot of the young people are the same way.

If the Indian people don't believe in their own religion, truly believe in it, they are lost in this world. They've got to know their language. They've got to believe in a spiritual mountain.

I doctor Mount Shasta, the spirit. Then I have another mountain, Cold Spring Mountain. Some white men call it a haunted mountain. They go up there and make fun, and it puts them to sleep just like that.

Now, everybody can't go up there and get the Indian power to doctor. You've got to be spiritual. I was born spiritually. My mother was over sixty years old when I was born. When a child is born from a mother that old, they say the baby is going to be a spiritual doctor—or else evil.

They got six or maybe ten doctors to see whether I was a spiritual doctor or an evil child. If I was an evil child they'd have gotten rid of me a long time ago. But they said, "This child is born spiritually. She's going to be a top doctor someday when she grows up."

So that's the way I started my spiritual doctoring. They go into what we call a *thewt sōo*. It's like a roundhouse, but down in the ground. They doctored my mother and doctored me as a baby.

Being a doctor takes a lot of strength out of you. You have to be thoroughly steady, not scared of anything. I never was scared of anything when I was growing up. You have to be calm and understand everything on the face of the earth.

That's the reason I am here as long as I am. I understand people. I understand nature. I understand spiritual nature. Some people came from Washington, D.C., to see me. They said the world was going to come to an end. They went to all of the doctors. There were different scientists. Two of them came up to me and said, "Florence, some guy in New York predicted the world was going to end on this certain day. Do you see that?"

I said, "No, I don't see that. This world ain't going to end. Whoever is predicting that is wrong because the world is not ready to come to an end yet. But if people go like they're going today, in turmoil and not wanting to listen to nothing but themselves—the ones that predict these things only believe in their own selves, they don't know the true spiritual doctoring."

I ask the Great Spirit in myself to ask the Great Creator what's going to happen. That's where I get all of my information. Like they said there was going to be a big earthquake. "Do you see that?" they asked. I said, "There's going to be a lot of earthquakes but not a big one. Not now. When the world cycle goes around—maybe when it comes back to the old way, maybe then the earthquake will be so severe it will kill a lot of people. But I don't see that yet."

When I die, the Wintu doctoring will be over. There will be no more. I will take all of my doctoring spirit with me. The things that I use, they'll put in the sacred place with my permission. I don't want anybody to touch what I use. I want to put it in the place where the elders put all of their sacred things that they used when they were doctors.

I'm training the younger generation, if anything should happen to me, to take over the ceremony. I taught them everything they're supposed to know, and how to take care of it, and do all the praying.

But there's nobody capable of going through the training to be a doctor. You can't just hand it over. You've *got* to go through that training. It's a lifetime thing. That's the way with us. If you don't go through the training, you're just like anybody else.

I took two girls up to my sacred spring where I pray for everybody. I said to the Great Spirit on the mountain, "Ask the Great Creator, are these two girls going to be doctors or not be doctors?" And the answer was, "No, they can't be doctors. They can't smoke the pipe like I can."

Because I talk in my own language when I go into trance, and nobody knows my language. I've been teaching my relatives the language, but they just come maybe three or four times a month, and then they've got something else more important to do.

They all want to look like white people and do things like white people. My grandmother said, you can always have a television and all these electric things in your kitchen, that's okay, you can meet the white people halfway. But don't forget your religion, because the religion is the one thing that's going to keep you on the earth here longer than the white medical doctors. You have to believe in your own religion.

My advice to non-Native people is they've got to learn the spiritual world. Every human being is born with some spiritual in themselves that they don't take care of. That's the reason, today, that people are lost and all this turmoil is going on. They're so lost. That is the reason they start killing. They don't believe in anything.

The white people are just like they're floating in the air. They don't settle down. They just buy a home, then get up and sell it and go someplace else. There is nothing sacred on this earth for them. They're nervous and can't control anything in their bodies.

They are lost people in this world because they don't want to understand. The mothers and fathers drink and use dope. There is vulgar language all over. Children say the things they learn from the parents. The little ones look at them and say, "Well, if Mama and Daddy can do this, I can do it too." What kind of life is that?

When we were put down on earth, in the beginning, the human beings were supposed to take care of nature, take care of all the animals, down to the littlest animal. Which the Forest Service is supposed to do, but I don't agree with what they are doing. I've been fighting them for fifteen or twenty years now. I finally had to get a permit right from Washington, D.C., to open up my ceremony on Mount Shasta.

Where did the white people get their authority to rule everything in the United States? Who gave them that? I want to know. In the beginning we were all put down, spaced down, where we're supposed to live. In our background and roots. My people never did leave. We were put here to stay and up until my day of today, we're still here.

White people, I'd tell them to go back to their church. To the Indian people, I'd tell them to go back to their spiritual life. We have an open air church—the mountains and sacred rivers, sacred trees. All those trees are crying today from the loggers cutting them down. Those are sacred trees. They are supposed to stay and live like people live. Even now, they're cracking open rocks, the spiritual rocks that we go and pray on. Big huge rocks, they break them all up and destroy them.

I'm trying to get them to stop destroying. A lot of white people come to my ceremony and listen to me talk. And they come back for more. Every year more are coming. I tell them, "You can't understand Indian people, but you can understand what we're talking about, because I talk in plain English and you can understand me and go from there in your own religion."

Now there is development on Mount Shasta.[1] But it won't make the spirit leave. When that ski lift was put right on my spiritual mountain, I had a dream. The mountain said, "Look at me, snow all over me. What are these white people doing here, walking and tramping on my clothes? My beautiful white clothes. What are we going to do, what can I do?"

I said, "You are my spiritual power. You are my mountain that I doctor from. If you don't want that ski lift up there and those people tramping all over your beautiful white coat, just shake 'em up!"

Two days later it shook 'em up. Now what do you think about that?

That's the reason I am a doctor. I will speak to the mountains and they will listen to me. I speak in my own language. Being that I am a spiritual doctor, they give me their power. And I feel that I am just as equal to that spiritual mountain, in my way. They ask me what they can do. Then I tell them. So how are you going to explain that?

Note

1. Florence Jones is referring to a ski lift put in above Panther Meadows, near the site of her ceremonies. An avalanche took out the lift and ski lodge below it in the 1980s. Developers still have plans for a major resort on the mountain, but Indian leaders (including the Native American Heritage Commission of California) continue to warn against it. Mount Shasta is sacred not only to the Wintu, but to nearly all of the tribes in the area (see Darryl Wilson's Introduction). The U.S. Department of the Interior is wrangling over how much, if any, of the mountain to designate as a historic district. If a designation of any significance is approved, it would be a major recognition of the Native connection to sacred lands.

Arvol Looking Horse

Mending the Sacred Hoop

Arvol Looking Horse is Keeper of the Sacred Pipe for his people, the Minnecojou Lakota. At the time of this interview, he lived on the Cheyenne River Reservation in Green Grass, South Dakota.

Born in 1954, Mr. Looking Horse has been Pipe Keeper since the age of twelve. The pipe has been in his family for nineteen generations. The Keeper is often a medicine man or woman, and is the spiritual leader of the Minnecojou.

He was a rodeo rider until 1983, when a horse fell on him and crushed three of his vertebrae. The accident left him paralyzed from the waist down. He healed remarkably after a dream of the Sun Dance, in which he realized he was needed to be the Keeper of the Pipe.

Lois Crozier-Hogle and Ferne Jensen visited him in Green Grass, which is located in the hills alongside the Moreau River. The Sacred Pipe is kept in a seven-sided log building. It is opened only on religious occasions. The pipe was kept in hiding for seven years starting in 1980 due to fears of over-commercialization of Indian religion. It was brought back out in 1987.

After Lois and Ferne's visit to Green Grass, Darryl Wilson conducted a second interview with Arvol Looking Horse in which he related the origin of the pipe.

I can only talk about the things that I have gone through. I have had a responsibility for my people since I was twelve years old. I felt sick in high school. The teachers made me feel ashamed of who I was.

Growing up, everything was one-sided. The thing that really hurt me was the history that was taught. Every time I read something about Indian people, they called them "savages." Then they talked about Dick and Jane and Spot and the white picket fence. We couldn't see that because we have nothing to survive on, just the reservation that the government gave us.

I thought, "There's got to be a change from the negative to the positive."

I hope I am one of them to make that change. My brother, who was older than me, was everything. He was a good athlete. He won the state cross-country championship in South Dakota. He rodeo'd. He was a good wrestler and a good football player. He won plaques and trophies.

Whereas I was the opposite. I didn't speak English until I was six years old. I spoke my own language. I studied a lot. My brother really helped me a lot during my high school years. For some reason, I just felt sick. But in high school, everybody was helping my brother out, giving him this and that. He was great.

But what happened was, he killed himself. He hung himself at the Indian jail. He drank for about a month or two. I don't know what caused him to do this, but when they threw him in jail he hung himself. I was told by my grandparents. They were the ones who taught me, "Have respect for your mother and grandmother and Mother Earth."

Today we need to change. We've got to understand where our way of life is coming from. The sacred hoop was broken in 1890, if you look back at the Battle of Wounded Knee—but it wasn't a battle, it was a massacre.[1] Within a hundred years a lot of things have gone aside. A prophecy told us that 1990 would be a Mending of the Sacred Hoop.

At one time our people lived a life where we had respect for everything. But from 1890 to 1990, our way of life went underground. During this time, they killed off our medicine men like Sitting Bull and Big Foot. We could not practice our ways. The United States was supposed to be for freedom of religion, but we were denied the right to talk about our spirituality.

Our way of life was broken. During that time we couldn't practice our religion, but we still did, underground. We kept our tradition alive, and I am a product of that.

I am the nineteenth generation Keeper of the Sacred Pipe for the Lakota Sioux Nation. As keepers of the pipe, we must protect all of our sacred objects. We explain to our people our sacred traditions and identify our sacred places through ceremony. We teach the people to pray in sacred places: in the fields, on the mountains, and by the rivers.

I spoke my language first. All my life that is all I knew, our way of life. The stories that were told long time ago were handed down through the generations.

We've always been here on this Turtle Island. It was told that our people had a race—the two-legged and the four-legged had a race around the Black Hills. The two-legged won over the four-legged. From then on we use the four-legged. We use the buffalo for food, shelter, and clothing. They nourish us.

I was told after that our people were living in the Black Hills, in the big caves, and all the channels of the caves came to one spot. People we know today talk about that place, Wind Cave, near Hot Springs, South Dakota. I go back to the Black Hills and ask different people, "Do you think that cave goes to the center?" They say, "Yes. It always has."

Iktomi, the trickster, took the people out of the cave where they were living. Iktomi said, "Go on top, there's plenty of food." So our people went and they came on top. There was plenty of food, and plenty of other animals and creatures.

After that, we were told a flood took place. During the flood our people traveled farther and farther east. It rained for many days, and one woman left. She ran, and she fell down when she couldn't run any more. The water was starting to touch her feet when *Ka-kash-la Wam-bli*, Eagle, picked her up and took her on a high hill. When the flood was over, the eagle became a man.

The next story is that the people would always go back to the Black Hills to pray. Because this, to us, is like a big church. During that time we were told we could use the buffalo for food, shelter, and clothing.

The people sent out two scouts who traveled for many days. They tied a piece of rawhide string—for each day they traveled they tied a knot. They had many knots on their string. They couldn't find anything all that time. One day, away from the camp, they were sitting on the hill. They said the sun was shining *wichu-ka-a-hia* ("the sun in the middle"). It was a beautiful day in the rolling hills of South Dakota when they saw from the west a dust was coming.

When it came upon them it was the young, beautiful woman [White Buffalo Calf Woman]. She was holding something in her arms. She came upon them on this little hill. One scout had good thoughts, and one had bad thoughts. She pointed to the one with the bad thoughts and said, "Come to me. I know what your thoughts are."

When he came to her, a cloud enveloped them. There was the sound of rattlesnakes. When the cloud lifted the scout was all bones. She said to the other one, "Go back to your people. Tomorrow I will bring you a gift when the sun sets to right now."

Then she left. The scout went to his camp to tell the people. She told him how to prepare: "Put down some sage and plant some cherry trees." That's what they did. The next day they got the people together and they alternated sage, cherry tree, sage, cherry tree to the four directions.

Sure enough she was coming. She was coming and she was singing some prayer songs. She laid the bundle down and opened it. The pipe was in there. She said, "The red stone represents the blood of the people. We know it is good pipestone."[2]

She stayed for four days. After she gave the people the pipe and left, she changed into colors. The colors are for the four directions: the black, the yellow, the red, and the white.

We know that you use the pipe for health and happiness, and we pray for the balance of life. Our people make that journey when they reach the age of twelve to go purify themselves for four days. The first person died four times. When he went into the spirit world he became young again. From there on, everything has been in fours.

The pipe has stayed in my family for nineteen generations. In 1966 my grandmother died. Before she died, she dreamed I was the next Keeper. This comes through a dream or a vision. When I go into the spirit world I will do the same.

A lot of people call the pipe the Pipe of Peace. When you pray with the pipe you feel at peace. You smoke it to keep your nation together or to make a treaty or an agreement.

When we do that, we do it from the heart. We smoked the pipe of peace with the U.S. government in the 1851 treaty.[3] To us it was from the heart, but to them it was—they don't see where we come from, that is the way I see it.

Everything we do, we do from the heart. The abuse that is going on today, false medicine men charging fifty dollars for their ceremonies, they are not doing it from the heart. People are selling the Indian religious experience, such as the sweat lodge ceremony. This is disturbing to the spiritual leadership.

In our language, there are no foul words and there is no "good-bye." We say *tok-sa*, "I'll see you later." That is the way I was brought up in Green Grass with my grandparents. It was to hope people come and teach me.

When people first come to see you, you give them water or bread or whatever you have. You make them welcome. You shake their hand or hug them, and you share some of the food you are eating with the spirits, away from the house.

Our people say not to look at it as "religion." It's a *way of life*. From the time a child is born we have ceremonies throughout its life until the time it goes to the spirit world. Everything was in cycles. Mother Earth is in a cycle.

The year before I was born, the government said Indians could start drinking alcohol. My grandmother said, "That was the saddest day in my whole life, to see all the young men, the bars so packed." A year later I was born. I went to school and I got a negative feeling. What I want to do is correct the negative. The prophecy goes along with it. We have to share and re-educate our people. That is what the pipe is for.

There is good and bad in the prophecies. Like when the woman first brought out the pipe, the bad scout became skin and bones, and the good one did it right. That is the way the balance of life is, good and bad.

Part of the prophecy is that the buffalo will return. We used the buffalo for everything. They told us that the buffalo used to make the wind. Since 1890, when we started eating commodities, our people say, "We are not used to this canned stuff."

Everything you put into your system, you will have a reaction to it. Today we have a lot of diabetic people. We are not eating the right foods. We are eating cows. The cows put their rear against the wind, and the buffalo face the wind. People say we need to change and be like the buffalo: face the wind.

Some of the people say that we must bring the buffalo back. Get some acres of land. But right now, our reservation is like a checkerboard and they are fighting over the Black Hills. What we are doing is getting the people to understand about spirituality, about the Black Hills. It is not about money. It is not about gold.

The people I talk to really have a hard time. At night, it's really cold and the wind is blowing. In winter, the houses are cold. The snow and the rain comes in through windows. Some people have plastic over them. See how the people live—lots of obstacles are in the way. But we're here and we'll be here all the time.

Mother Earth has a beautiful spirit. Everything has a spirit—one blade of grass has a spirit. Mother Earth provides for everything. A person is born sacred. In our system, it all depends on the earth, how long we're going to live. I know that Mother Earth has a lot of strength, but the way things are going it is going to get worse if we do nothing. What we do to Mother Earth, we are doing to ourselves.

These are the things we have to understand. We ourselves have the knowledge our grandmothers brought down from generation to generation. Now I hear people say, "You've got to reach out and find yourself."

We put people up on the hill for four days in order to find themselves. This is because each person is unique. In time, they grow. Like a tree—the Tree of Life, the Sun Dance tree. We say, "You grow until you grow into the spirit world, learning every day."

So we are not the things that some people say. Just recently one of our Lakota, one of the people who helps the governor, made a statement saying the Indian people are "lawless, jobless, and godless." Today, back home, some people buy into that. Their minds are so closed they can't see anything else.

Be open and try to learn. Try to educate the people. This is the prophecy of 1990.

From our renewed spirituality our sacred hoop will be mended. This is when our young people will be coming back to their spirituality. Throughout the tradition they say more people will be talking about Mother Earth. Now we are involved in a lot of environmental issues. So that is what mending the sacred hoop is. Mending ourselves and the people and letting the people know that Mother Earth has a spirit.

Our people are coming back from the urban centers to the reservations. They're being called back to be among the people. There's a lot of hurt inside, with Wounded Knee and with the alcoholism within the families. That caused a lot of anger. We have to talk about it. It's called healing the hurt. Not only here, but all the people in this country should go through this process.

Our teaching is whole. When a person is born, a long time ago they called it *chik-sa* ["the belly button"]. They wrapped it up and took a small turtle and put it in there, and they carried that with them. That way, spiritually, they keep it home. When they go some place they know where home is and they can come back.

But when you sent people to the boarding schools they didn't keep track of *chik-sa*. So the elderly people say, "These people are looking for that. That is why their mind wanders. Their heart is in the right place but their mind wanders."

Today our spirits are looking for themselves all over. They are looking for security, they are looking to connect with Mother Earth. They say we have that within ourselves and we have to use it. First of all, they have to find themselves. And that's kind of a hard one.

We are trying to keep the language. On the reservation, the grassroots people speak the language. But the little ones, they don't understand and they are ashamed to be an Indian person. Probably from my age on down they are ashamed to be Indian. That's what we need to bring back. We've got to go to schools and tell them that we have our "ways" and that we should be proud of ourselves.

Some people say they look toward Indian people for spirituality. I really look at that as global. Each person can make a change as long as they know that they have that respect for each other and each other's beliefs. It doesn't matter how you pray, we know that there's one Creator. It doesn't matter who a person is, what position they have, we're all human.

The earth can really change a person. We know how simple life is, and we avoid the confusion of modern society. That's what I'm talking about. You've got to find that peace within yourself and you've got to work it out yourself.

A lot has happened in a hundred years. It is changing. That's why I try my best to get people going. There is a need to be more open. We say, "Kick the walls down that are built around ourselves." Like the Berlin wall that came down.

Knowledge, they told us, is like an eagle feather. The eagle feather is the highest honor to give to a person. You wear it on your head and that is respect. The knowledge should be kept in that eagle feather. We have to share and we have to re-educate our people. That is what the pipe is for.

Notes

1. In 1990 Arvol Looking Horse was a staff carrier for a procession that followed the trail of Big Foot on a ride to Wounded Knee to remember the events there one hundred years ago:

> On the 29th of December, 1890, at 9:00 a.m., the U.S. 7th Cavalry [Custer's regiment] launched an attack against Chief Big Foot's band camped at Wounded Knee, South Dakota. More than 300 unarmed Lakota men, women and children were killed, destroyed by artillery fired into the camp or hunted down in the creek beds where they had run to hide. Their bodies were thrown in a mass grave. This massacre has been referred to in U.S. history books as the last so called "battle" of the Indian wars. . . . The [1990] gathering included a traditional "wiping of tears" ceremony to bring the descendants out of their time of mourning in preparation for the survival of the next seven generations of their people. (Treaty Council News 2, no. 1, Spring, 1991.)

2. The stem of the pipe is made from the leg bone of a buffalo calf and is tied with eagle feathers and bird skins. It is wrapped in buffalo hair and red cloth. "In filling a pipe, all space (represented by the offerings to the powers of the six directions) and all things (represented by the grains of tobacco) are contracted within a single point (the bowl or heart of the pipe) so that the pipe contains, or really *is*, the universe." See *The Sacred Pipe*, Joseph Epes Brown, editor (p. 21).

3. The first major treaty between the U.S. government and the Sioux tribes was signed at Fort Laramie in 1851. Red Cloud signed the 1868 Fort Laramie treaty, which guaranteed the Indians "absolute and undisturbed use of the Great Sioux Reservation," which included the Black Hills, "in perpetuity." Eight years later the Black Hills were overrun with more than ten thousand whites searching for gold.

Thomas Banyacya

The Hopi Prophecy

Thomas Banyacya has been a prominent spokesman for the religious leaders of the Hopi people for many years. He was born a member of the Coyote clan in 1909.

In 1948 a group of Hopi elders, alarmed by the use of the atomic bomb and other dangers to their way of life, met in Shongopovi. Four young men who spoke English were invited to that meeting, in which the Hopi prophecies and the proper course of action was discussed. Their task was to interpret the message and take it to the English-speaking world.

At first Banyacya resisted, but the elders convinced him it was his duty. He is the only remaining interpreter from that original meeting, and he has become known throughout the world as the carrier of the Hopi prophecies and message.

The following text is an abridged version (about three-quarters of the original) of a talk on the Hopi prophecies given by Thomas Banyacya at the Stanford University Ecology Conference in 1989. (Omissions are indicated by ellipses.) He was introduced by Alan Strain, who recorded and transcribed the talk.

I want to thank all of you for coming here tonight and the people who made it possible for me to come here to bring the Hopi message, warnings that have been known to them for a long time.

Back in 1948 the Hopi Elders met for four days and they talked about many things. It really amazed me to hear those old people eighty, ninety, one hundred years old. So many things go way back in the history of all human life. They talked about a world before this one, and one before that, and how human life starts to cause the destruction of the worlds.

The last world was totally destroyed by flood. The first one, they said, was destroyed when everything froze and there was a great upheaval of land. Each time, a handful of appointed people came out to go to the next world. I guess it was supposed to last forever, but it seems like human beings always disturb the balance of nature, turn away from their own Great Spirit and try to do everything on their own. Then nature has to take over some other way.

It is amazing what the Hopi elders talked about, so many things that are actually going on here today. I was happy I listened to them in that 1948 meeting. We are supposed to carry this message wherever we can go—to meet many people, many nations, many languages.

The elders needed four young fellows to carry this message to the world. I know that I am not a member of a high religious society in Hopi, and in speaking English I cannot interpret or translate their message in the proper way.[1] But, after many attempts to get out of it, I made my commitment that I would help them all I can.

So I have gone to many Native people in this country first, because the old people told us to go around and see how many of our Native people are holding onto their culture, religion, ceremonies, and languages at this time. A great pressure is being brought by our white brothers and sisters trying to change our ways.

The Hopi elders never considered selling this Mother Earth. Mother

Earth is a living being, a powerful being. Everything comes from this Mother Earth. And we were not to cut it up or fence it or disturb it by taking the mineral resources out for destructive uses.

We consider the Four Corners area to be sacred. It is the spiritual center. A long time ago, upon the sacred mountains around there, they built shrines and they said, "This is the spiritual Center, to be held by prayer and ceremonies and making prayer feathers and other things." Something goes on there every month to keep this land in balance.

When they place their prayer feathers to the four mountains there, that means it goes to the end of this land in the four directions: the east coast, the west coast, south to the tip of South America, and north to Alaska. That was known to the elders a long time ago. They told us that in order to keep this land alive and in balance we had to perform our ceremonies in our own language, because language is very important.

We were placed in different areas by Great Spirit as different nations. Native people, who have the brown color of Mother Earth, were placed on this side of the world called America today. Most of the Native people were placed on this side to keep this land in balance with prayer, meditation, and ceremony. They said after the destruction of the last world by flood, a handful of people came out and were able to receive this knowledge from the Great Spirit. We met our ancestors. It is from them that we were able to learn this type of instruction to keep this land beautiful.

Everything was in order, clean, beautiful. When it rained you could drink right out of wherever the rain water was.

In the very beginning, before we separated from our white brother—we have the same mother, but the color was different—we each received two sets of stone tablets in which all of Great Spirit's knowledge, prophecies, and warnings were set. They said Great Spirit breathed into those sacred stone tablets. They were given to two brothers who were to carry this knowledge wherever they go. The younger brother stayed here. We have that stone tablet set in Hopi today.

The other was given to the white brother. He was given a special message to record things, to invent things, and to make life very beautiful and clean on the other side of the world. So he took some people with him and went around the world. The Native people here were to cover this continent, so we migrated to different areas. We were told that when we see a great star up here in the sky, that means our white brother went around the world someplace and has reached his destination.

He was going to come back again, so we stopped. We were not to wander anymore, but to stop where we were and wait for our white brothers to come. He was going to come and help us with his inventions to make life much better and easier, and find ways to keep this land alive and beautiful for the Great Spirit.

But these old people said that when the white brother came, he had turned away from his spiritual teachings and instructions. Instead, he came with a cross.

One old man from Oraibi told me about the picturegraph on the hillside. It was drawn in the rock and covered with sand and dust. So I rubbed the rock and finally found it and made a copy of it, and that is what is on the board.[2]

So now I understand what the old people were talking about in 1948. The rock contains all the prophet's warnings of destruction and the problems we face and how we can correct things in later times. We call him Masaw. He met us the first time when the handful of people came out from the other world that was destroyed by flood. Today all people are descended from those who escaped that destruction. He gave us instructions for everything. That is the way the circle was given to us. As long as we listen to his instructions on how to take care of this land and life, there is no end to this circle.

Everything you can see that forms a circle always has a center. There is quite a lot of meaning to that. That is why when we perform a ceremony we always form a circle. Because we still listen and follow the lower path [in the drawing], there is no end to this land and life as long as we follow the law of the Great Spirit.

There is a little rectangular shape. Here, they said, is where we separate from our white brothers. Two brothers were given the same instructions. Our white brother was given special medicine to make and invent things and come back and look for us at a later time. The younger brother was to follow the lower path. So for a while we did that.

Then our white brother came back. Instead of bringing the spiritual circle, he brought a cross.

And we knew he might do that. He brought a cross, and that means there is going to be a lot of changes here in this world. He is going to do many things his own way. He is going to invent many things, he is going to misuse power again. So we must not fall for these inventions.

There are certain things that the Hopi could use, as long as he paid for them and did not accept any handouts. If we get to the point where we can't pay for them, all we have to do is just turn them off. Or not sign a written document, because there is a danger that the government would eventually use that as a basis to get some kind of return, either money or land. If we sign it without reading it, we are going to get caught and will not be able to get out for a long time, they said.

When the white brother came back, he brought a few things that people wanted to have. They thought, "Go up there" [to the upper path]. We're supposed to have some things, but to stay on the spiritual path. But some of the Native people went up there and wanted more and more things.

The second circle represents more advancement, scientific things and inventions. The summer I was up to the four-day meeting, an old man who was eighty-six years old said, "Pretty soon that carriage being pulled by animals will run by itself." And that is the automobile.

Then he told me another prophecy that I didn't understand: "He's going to invent something so that we're going to talk to each other long distance places through spider webs." I did not know what he meant, but when you look up in the sky the telephone lines look like cobwebs running in every direction.

Then he said, "They're going to build a road up in the sky someday. White people will be traveling it. I don't see how it's going to be built— what's going to hold that road up?" Then we realized that there will be airplanes carrying people. A lot of people travel on that road up in the sky.

When they get to that point, then they are going to invent many things, he told me. One of them would be something we knew in our ceremonies, the gourd rattle. "It is a gourd full of ashes that our white brothers may invent someday, and if he ever allows that to fall on earth it will just burn everything to ashes. We won't be able to go there for many years. Many living things will die from heat. Many sicknesses will come out of it. Our medicine will not be able to cure them. There will be a long, long period of sickness coming into that area."

This is the atom bomb. They described it exactly the way it happened. They said this message is really important. "Many things go to make that atom bomb, many resources." In the Hopi language, I was amazed to hear that. I was writing notes while he was talking, but I just listened and wondered where he received all this information.

He said, "That's what happened, that second circle." That's where they threw the atom bomb. So we refer to those circles as the First World War and then the Second World War.[3]

Three is a sacred number to the Hopi. The three represent the advance of scientific things. The fourth is the final one in all our ceremonies. From there on, we started going toward the other end of that upper line. That fourth circle represents one of our Native people who joined our white brothers in the invention of many things, and also went after power, telling his own people, "Forget your culture and your ceremonies."

The elder said, "They are going to try this and try that and they are going to succeed in many things all right, but at the end they are going to blow this world up with the power they built."

So [in the drawing] there is a line coming back down at the end to the lower road, where Native people are still holding onto the path laid down by the Great Spirit, desperately holding on.

It is amazing that the white brother did get a recording of this thing, too. I read the Bible, and it teaches many things similar to the Hopi knowledge. But our white brothers have not followed the instruction, when you consider what has happened to the Original Native people in this land today. Original Native people knew he was coming, so they went and met him and gave him food and lodging, everything that you would do for anyone that has been gone for a long time. Of course, he brought the cross and he almost destroyed them. They were so shocked at the white man. Why was he cutting their hands off? Why sometimes cutting their ears off?

Why just tearing them apart? Why did the white man do that to the Native person? So a lot of them ran off to hide in mountains and jungles.

The eastern nations welcomed our brothers over there, too. We gave them food and lodging to take care of them in winter months. We gave them turkey, gave them potatoes. We gave them corn, beans, pumpkins. We gave them everything. We even gave them our land. But they brought the cross and started pushing our people. They are still doing it to the western part, passing laws and regulations. Many of the Native people are landless today. . . .

When the white brother begins to see the wrongness of this, he may realize the danger and shame of it. He may look at what he is doing. Now he may start to get together many people and start to change and stop this wrong.

We may be able to get together and clean up our own mess today. Because now we're going to see natural disasters. Mother Earth is going to shake us up. She is in pain. We're taking all these natural mineral resources out for destructive uses.

An old man summed this up. He said, "You know what happens if you throw this rock up in the sky and it sticks way up there? It always comes back down. If you make this atom bomb and throw it all around the world, people are going to suffer. Pretty soon they're going to get sick and tired of it and pretty soon they're going to tell the people who are selling it to stop it. What you throw around the world, it's going to come back."

This is why I am very concerned for this country. So I am willing to tell you that we are facing this terrible thing if we don't start correction.

You give orders, you taxpayers put men in Congress. Surely there must be some way that you voters can get to them and put a stop to it before this whole world faces a terrible thing on the other end. This is what I felt as I came from my elders to bring you this message. They told me, "It's going to be hard. People are going to laugh at you. Going to call you crazy. And they will try to stop you from carrying this message."

Well, I found it's very important to do. One of the elders told me, "Sooner or later many people are going to realize the danger. They're going to join themselves to their leaders with their heart. And they are going to change their ways and stop it with truth, with facts, with kindness, with true happiness, with real true love. We are going to start to correct this thing."

If we don't, that will be the final cleansing by the Creator. If we, the people who messed this up, cannot correct or change the wrongdoing and clean up the mess, then it will be done by three purifiers. Those who took us up two times first almost destroyed themselves. Many more powerful things are going to come, and we will know their real mission is to end the world. That is, to save this world from being totally destroyed by human beings, they will have to use their power to purify the earth.

So we've got to go to the last stages. It's up to us human beings to do something. You have religious groups, you know how to pray, you know how to sing. Let us get together. Let's stop saying, "If you don't belong to *this* church, you can't be saved." Let's put that aside. We are all living together on this planet Earth that is in trouble right now because we are disturbing this land and life with this power we developed.

I have been representing elders, spiritual leaders, who talk about this in Hopi, who still hold on to the original form of self-government existing there. The Hopi still have that and they have no treaty with the U.S. government. We hold on to our sovereign powers, being first people here. . . .

Many Natives know about this thing. The Six Nations people know, the Lakota know. The white people have pushed our people across the land, to the western edge. The elders said, "Some day you're going to see a lot of our young people gathered on the western edge, and they're going to start speaking the white man's language. They are going to start asking questions: You ruined all these things, but why? Why aren't you following the instructions of these writings?"

I look to that lower road [on the drawing] as a narrow road going to eternal life. It is the road of the Great Spirit. The upper road is the materialistic path, having all types of material things and scientific advancement. But the two roads connect, so there is a chance for us to come together. . . .[4]

We're going to clean up our mess. If we don't, then these purifiers are going to have to rise. But if we start to clean up our mess, when they come they will punish hardly anyone. That's what I would like to see happen.

That's why I made up my mind to go as far as I can. Because I know there are a lot of young people here who are facing the future—but what kind of future is it?

You know that a mother sometimes stays up late with the baby. Maybe the baby is sick or doesn't want to go to sleep. And she has to stay up late, tell a story or something, and then get up early in the morning and start cooking and cleaning up. She asks her family to come over and eat. They all come and eat and then go away. Nobody cleans up their mess. The mother waits for somebody to come and clean it up, but nobody comes.

It used to be, with most Native people and white people, man walked up front and women and children followed. Sometime they are going to start walking side by side, man and woman. And later, woman is going to be up front. It is up to womanfolks, because man created this mess and he doesn't want to clean it up. It is up to woman to start cleaning up this mess. Because what kind of a life are you going to leave for the next generation?

We may be able to remember some of the things old people used to talk about, but we have forgotten them. When you mention those things, then you remember. The spark within you comes when you pray and meditate. You can heal somebody with that. Every individual person has that power within you. But it seems like we expect somebody else to do it for us.

We can pray, we can meditate, we can use some simple things with faith and courage. Everyone can do something to correct the change so that this will not come up. Because once we clean up this mess together, then the Great Spirit will come. He is watching us. If we clean up our mess, he will come and whoever survived, he will welcome all of them, and he will lead them again. It will be a new life from there. Clean, beautiful, we will be one people. We will just live out there, use the land, grow things, share it.

So I hope that will bring us all together. I hope there won't be any earthquake while I'm standing here [laughter]. Thank you very much.

Notes

1. Introducing Banyacya to the audience, Alan Strain touched on some of the difficulties of translating from Hopi into English. On a visit to the Hopi reservation in the 1950s, Banyacya took Strain and some of his students to meet Dan Katchongva, an elder and major spokesman for Hopi traditionals. Strain described the meeting:

> Dan would speak for some time, maybe five or ten minutes. Thomas listened intently. Finally Dan would stop and turn to Thomas. But he sat quietly, his eyes closed, often for as long as Dan had spoken. Finally he would begin, softly and simply, explaining in English what Dan had said. Occasionally he would shrug or put up his hands, saying that he could not find the right words in English.
>
> On the way back to Thomas's house I asked about the Hopi for which he could not find the right English words. Thomas laughed and said, "Sometimes you can't say Hopi in English." I asked, "Would it help if you translated after each sentence, not after long speeches?" Again, the laugh. "Like I told you, sometimes you can't say Hopi in English." I persisted: "Well, can you describe what you are doing as you translate?"
>
> Thomas said, "First I listen very carefully in Hopi. No English! Then I sit until the same spirit and meaning comes to me in English. But sometimes there is no English that has the same meaning."
>
> When I returned to the Bay Area, I read for the first time Benjamin Lee Whorf's discussion of the Hopi language in his book Language, Thought, and Reality. Whorf makes clear how fundamentally different are the grammar and syntax of English and Hopi. English is a "subject-predicate" language. Hopi is not. It does not reify or divide the continuums we experience into separate "things."

2. The drawing referred to here was found on what is known as Prophecy Rock. Many Hopi prefer that the drawing not be reproduced. It should be noted that the drawing has different interpretations and that the prophecy itself predates the drawing.

In the drawing a large figure stands beside a vertical line. This is said to be Masaw guiding the people up to this, the Fourth World, teaching them their way of life and giving them instructions. Next to the vertical line is a circle (the physical world, Creation). The vertical line becomes a kind of rectangle, from which two lines extend horizontally. The upper line is considered the materialist path of the white people, the lower line the true path of the Hopi. There are three circles on the lower line and three or four figures (originally headless) atop the upper line. The upper line becomes jagged and discontinuous, while the lower line continues straight, with a figure (possibly Masaw returning) holding what may be a corn plant or a cane (symbolizing long life and bounty) farther along it. Two vertical lines connect the upper and lower lines, showing that it is possible for those who have changed paths to return to the Hopi way.

Although Banyacya does not use the term in this talk, the Elder Brother is often called Pahaana.

3. There are said to be three phases to the purification. The First and Second World Wars are often interpreted as the first two "shakings up." The next one is frequently associated with a powerful nation or person in a red cap or cloak. However, if the next one fails, there may be a fourth and even more powerful purifier that comes from the west and wreaks great destruction. It would swarm over the land like ants and cause all machinery to stop working. The two circles in the drawing are associated with Western scientific inventions, particularly the two atomic bombs dropped on Japan.

4. In the portion of the talk following this paragraph, Banyacya describes his travels throughout the United States and across the globe, including a 1972 trip to Stockholm where he spoke on the Hopi prophecy for a United Nations environmental conference. He traveled on his buckskin Hopi passport and met Oren Lyons, who was traveling on an Onondaga passport, in London.

Banyacya goes on to say that an elder once showed him a swastika and a sun symbol that are part of the prophecy, indicating that the first two phases of war are linked with the German and Japanese people. He mentions again that the third purifier will have a red hat or cloak.

He also mentions an earthquake that took place in Southern California after a recent talk he gave there. This helps to explain why the last line of the talk draws a laugh from the audience.

Frank LaPena

Tradition Is Evidence for the Truth of Life

Frank LaPena (Wintu-Nomtipom) is Professor of Art and Director of Native American Studies at California State University, Sacramento. He is a widely recognized artist, writer, and ethnographic consultant. He is also a traditional dancer and singer in the Indian community and speaks the Wintu language. He has helped raise seven children: two biological children and five step-children.

Frank LaPena was born in San Francisco. At the age of five he was put into the Indian boarding school system, attending two different schools. He studied at California State, Chico, and at San Francisco State, and earned a master's in anthropology from California State, Sacramento, in 1978.

The first exhibition of his art came in 1960. Since then his work has been shown in galleries and museums all over California and the country. It is in the collections of the Museum of Modern Art in New York, the Heard Museum in Phoenix, the Turtle Foundation Center for Living Arts in Buffalo, the Crocker Art Museum in Sacramento, and many others. His art and writings have also appeared in numerous books, including *The Sound of Rattles and Clappers* (1994) and *Earth Song, Sky Spirit* (1993). In addition, Professor LaPena has served as consultant to the Smithsonian Institution, the Heye Center, and the Wheelwright Museum, among others.

He spoke with Darryl Wilson.

I think the easiest way for me to talk about the spirit is through my participation in the Hesi ceremony. All of my work has a connection to this dance or other ceremonies.

In the old days, the Hesi ceremony, also known as the Big Head ceremony, was done by many tribes in north-central California, including my own relatives in the Wintu area. It addressed the continuation of life, the maintenance of harmony and balance, and respect for life and all living things on earth.

This is the main focus of the ceremony. At the same time, because earth moves, and so do people, there are certain times it needs to be done to let the earth rest, or to bring it awake again. So you have a cycle and a pattern. It can also be done for healing, for direction, or for special kinds of bringing balance to the tribe and individuals.

The ceremony is a very specific thing in expression, in being and showing. It is a personification of the spirit on earth. But it is not my place to give more than this philosophical statement about it.

There is also a more fundamental way of thinking about life. In tradition we acknowledge our connection to the spirit as all-pervasive and all-being at all times. It is consistency itself. That is a reflection of the spirit.

So there is that larger, more universal sense, which is directed from a tribal consciousness.

Those two ways are reflected in how I think and feel while doing my art. I believe it is possible to do one's work with a sense of the spirit that will become evident to the viewer and listener. I believe that. It is not a simplistic thing. Not only are the sacred and spiritual important, but in fact to work in the universal mind is to see it reflected in one's work.

So I see my life in several ways. There is nothing more moving than being in a ceremony. As you go through the three or four days of it, you see the people and understand how the spirit is coming across. You see it in the joy, the smiles, the kind of sharing that happens. The same thing happens in a ceremony of lesser days, such as the Bear Dance.

When I am thinking about the spirit, I am really thinking about the connection to some of the people who help maintain the spirit for me and my family. You cannot be involved with tradition in the way I am without getting the children involved. I married a non-Indian, and I brought her kids to the ceremony. And in the traditional way, the elders accepted them. They allowed them to be there and listen.

I also took my other kids to the ceremony so they would receive a greater understanding of what it meant to be part of a larger community. This was important because I was put in a federal Indian boarding school at five years old, and later a foster home. So I took my boy when he was two years old. I had him participate in the ceremony and talked to him just as if he was an adult. He learned from the very beginning.

When someone learns to dance for the first time, and we are going to dance in public, if they haven't put their ego aside, they are bashful or ashamed. But if a person has learned the *truth* of it, being bashful or ashamed doesn't count. You can go out there and become one who is a practitioner—because of what you are doing rather than what people are thinking as they look at you. You learn another level of humility. You also learn another level of who you are as a living being. You learn that you have something to offer, just as someone who is older does.

It is all part of being one and the same. Being a part of life, expressing life. This awareness and connection sensitizes not only your consciousness but your spirit to the meaning of life. The meaning of life is respect for all life forms, respect for individuals, and respect for the inanimate world as well. The living, spiritual part is an ingredient in all things, including natural things like rocks.

Today we have a disconnection in how we get food on our table, between life and the taking of life. We go to a market and put down our money. That skewed sense of money is causing a lot of our problems. In the old days the people would pray because they needed food. When they killed a living form, they would pray and thank it for giving its life—which in turn sustained their lives. They had to butcher and prepare their food from this once-living being.

If we were more conscious of our connection, if we were closer to the process of life and death, we would have a greater understanding of the sacrifice and what it really means. Our heightened awareness and appreciation for life would undoubtedly affect our use or mutilation of natural resources.

The missionization of California from about 1769 to 1833 not only destroyed the people, but took away the land and enslaved the people to build the mission system. By the time we see the epidemics of the 1830s, the annexation to America through the Bear Flag Republic, and the Gold Rush, we have witnessed three or four major events of peoples who are not accustomed to force being pushed from their land, along with the introduction of foreign ideology and the introduction of diseases.

So you have a major destruction of the people. That cannot help but affect the continuation of one's philosophy, religion, language, or style of life. When we look at history and contemporary Indians, we see the result of that genocide. It is very specific. If a person does not have access to tradition, they will lose a holistic understanding of life. Fortunately there have been elders who survived with knowledge of the culture and traditions.

And, as medicine people and doctor people tell me, you can always learn from the spirit. To be an earth-taught person and a spirit-taught person are two different things. One is formal and material and of this earth. The other is chosen by the spirit and is of greater consequence. Both require a specific amount of time and obligation, which most people have a hard time finding.

I look on the tradition carriers and I respect them. I acknowledge them. I consider them to be highly important and motivated because they have had to overcome a great many adversities—including their own people, who might have been brainwashed and forced to become a part of the new system.

I know that some of the younger people—my generation and just after me—asked why their parents and grandparents didn't teach them tradition. The fact is, many were taken away to federal Indian boarding schools. They were whipped and punished, put into dark rooms, and kept awake and isolated whenever they attempted to practice their traditions.

So we learned we needed to take a more elevated view of what happened to people of our own community and tribe. In spite of all of the hazards, tradition is still carried on. It is carried on because the Indian people realized that life without religion and tradition is not truthful, correct, or meaningful.

The idea of the truth of life is something that we are not told enough about. Yet tradition reflects that, it operates from that. That is what it is. It is the evidence for the truth of life: the actual healings, connections, ceremonies, songs. It is the function of all of that truth.

Its absence is the destruction of water, air, and fertile ground, as well as a lack of tolerance for cultures different than our own. I was recently reading a mission document that said, "These Indians have no music, but they learn how to sing and read music very well." In fact, we had and still have music that respects the earth and the spirits of the earth and all living things. Yet non-Indian institutions mislead the white people, as well as some Indian people.

Tradition says, "There is another story and we need to have that story heard." There are some fundamental truths that have to be known. When we look at the education of our children from elementary school through college, most people are ignorant of how indigenous peoples lived here prior to white contact. The truth contradicts the story that the dominant society has provided up to this point. This is easily understood: anywhere in the world that colonial powers have come in and taken over, they rewrite history, establishing new criteria and suppressing the actual culture that is there.

People of knowledge have to change that. They have to challenge the system and talk to the youth and elders to find the truths to pass on. This search can reveal the life-force that oral tradition has always lived by: the telling and retelling of truth.

Unless we can understand how the dominant society works, it will be difficult. But if you understand that, you can work it to your advantage. This is one thing I see happening. Education is being defined from an Indian perspective.

Look at the question of burial remains and whether they should be returned. The question is a moral and ethical one. Do *we* want to promote the stealing of burial goods to satisfy some level of curiosity? We understand innately that the graves being robbed are human beings and that they had a standard and a quality of living you don't have to rob graves to learn about. What you really need to do is to understand their philosophy of life.

In our ceremonies I talk and sing about sacred mountains, sacred springs, sacred caves and rocks. The story of their being is the story of the truth of the sacred. The expression of it, the variety of it, the way it works. So you don't need to go back and rob graves. Graves and bones are not something that you should go out and search for in order to satisfy your curiosity.

When you do come across them, take care of them. Rebury them with respect. Don't stick them in a box for twenty-five years and claim you are going to make a study. You have to act on it. The lack of action tells me what you are *really* about.

Some people are not concerned about the spirit. They are only concerned about controlling and maintaining the status quo. That is probably the biggest gap between Native Americans and white society. It is only in recent times, after violation of and destruction to the ecosystem—even as we talk now—that the white culture is beginning to realize that to be spiritual is to respect and appreciate. If they had done that from the start we would not have the problems we have today.

I would like to think the gap can be bridged. That is what I try to do.

But there is another thing when we talk about academia, which I am part of. What sometimes happens is that academia talks about Indian people as fatalistic, as not taking advantage of opportunities because of a belief system that is not rational or scientific.

I think there is an even more fundamental problem. If there is in fact a spirit that lives and exists and we have it, then there is a possibility that the spirit is a part of these academics as well. By not acknowledging the larger view, they violate their own spirit.

We like to think it is not too late. But how fast are we human beings going to change? How soon are we going to understand that it is a problem right *now*, not ten years from now?

I am part of academia, but my soul is not a part of it. I believe that the world and the life-force of spirit is more important than some of the systems that I see. If you know yourself, you will not be in conflict with the way you have to live. But if you are and you know yourself well enough, you will change. One needs to make change if for no other reason than we are not static.

Art has an important function today. What it's about is challenging the norm, challenging complacency. It deals with issues that are heartfelt and that have some sense of social commentary. That's one tie, but there's also the art of joy, the art of using certain kinds of colors, dealing with certain things that are meaningful because we live today, we're part of the twentieth century going into the twenty-first century.

Art is something that I did very early. It was a way to capture some magic, I guess you could say. I remember when my mother colored a picture of a marine in a coloring book during the Second World War. When she colored it, it became real, it came alive with color. I was impressed by that. I remember it specifically because I took that piece of art and packed it around for a good long time. It was something precious.

To say that Indian art is only of one kind, or that there's only a certain number of expressions, is really to limit it. Art exists as part of the life-force and its diversity. Indian art is unlimited: it's conceptual art, it's video, it's singing, it's dancing, it's painting and sculpture—it covers all the arts, and anyone who begins to look at Native American art will sense that.

I always look at 1978, when freedom of religion finally came for Indian people in a land that talks of being "under God." That's a very late time to talk about freedom of religion for Indian people here. What really puts that date into perspective is the denial of the Freedom of Religion Act by the Supreme Court in 1988.[1] As long as people are not allowed to use the land as tradition defines, as long as we are controlled, not only by corporations but by systems that do not allow an autonomous existence, then there is always going to be a problem of people being caught up in the system.

On the other hand, the idea of tradition, and the idea that it holds answers, means that people are going to have to make a great many sacrifices to go back and get that information.

It is not easy to carry on the traditions today. We need to do ceremony and to practice with certain kinds of traditional materials. American laws say you cannot use these materials. There are fences up and people who talk about land ownership. In fact, tradition doesn't talk about ownership. It talks about everyone being a part of everything else.

If freedom of religion is a fact, then Indians ought to have freedom of religion. That is the key to all levels of existence. That recognition must be given to Indian people. This needs to be a pluralistic society where many cultures can function as they are given to live by the spirit. A greater latitude and variety of human expression in the United States needs to be recognized. And right now, it is not.

As I look at the system today, I think of the Wintu prophecy, which says that time will change "our" world. It talks about an earth change, disenfranchisement in religion, language, and land use. It even identifies specific places on the land.

That prophecy is coming forth. At the same time, it talks about the hope tradition holds for maintaining some sort of understanding of the preservation of life. It says that if you know tradition, you can go back to the earth, you can find answers. The people who take the time to address the earth can be told by the earth what some of the answers are to maintain it.

Note

1. See the interview with John Echohawk, Note 1, in the next section.

THE WORLD TORN IN TWO

The arrival of Columbus five hundred years ago began a process that forced Native people to make difficult and often devastating decisions. Dispossession of land was inextricably linked to the attempted destruction of Indian cultures. John Echohawk, Steven Crum, and Carlos Cordero outline legal, historical, and political consequences of five hundred years of Indian-European contact. The story of Rose Johnson/Tsosie shows the effects on one woman's life. Janine Pease Pretty on Top articulates the challenges of present-day contact in Montana and suggests ways to strengthen and rebuild communities for the next five hundred years.

John Echohawk

We Are Sovereign Peoples

John Echohawk (Pawnee) is executive director of the Native American Rights Fund in Boulder, Colorado. He was born in Albuquerque and grew up in the Four Corners area. He was the first American Indian graduate of the law school at the University of New Mexico, receiving his J.D. degree in 1970.

A cofounder of the nonprofit Native American Rights Fund in 1970, he quickly became a leader in the battle for Indian sovereignty and the protection of natural resources. Among his achievements, he has succeeded in compelling the return of Pawnee burial remains from the Nebraska Historical Society; won land claims and compensation for the Catawba tribe of South Carolina; and helped to bring about a water-rights settlement between the state of Montana and the Northern Cheyenne. Currently he is focusing on the legislative campaign for Native American religious freedom.[1]

Mr. Echohawk was named "one of the 100 most influential lawyers" by the *National Law Journal* in 1994. He has received awards from the Americans for Indian Opportunity, the National Congress of American Indians, and the White Buffalo Council, among others. He serves on the boards of several Native American and environmental organizations and also worked on President Clinton's transition team. The Native American Rights

Fund, which he has served as executive director since 1977, was co-recipient of the Carter-Menil Human Rights Foundation prize in 1992. He was interviewed by Lois Crozier-Hogle.

Let me begin by saying that I'm an attorney and my legal involvements are the perspective I come with. I think that spiritually, the religions of Native American tribes have universally respected the relationship between human beings and the rest of the earth.

That relationship is basically that human beings are a part of the earth and have no special rights over any other living or nonliving creature. They're just part of the universe. This is something I've learned as part of my upbringing.

What I've also learned as I've studied throughout the years and traveled and worked as a lawyer with many Native people all across the country is that this unique part of Native American spirituality is missing from non-Indian society. I think that realization is finally starting to dawn on a lot of people through the environmental movement. A relationship exists that's natural and unchangeable. People don't control everything. They're a part of everything. It's really gratifying to me that people are starting to realize this, because it's something I've always known. Hopefully books like this one can help that process.

Much of it has to do with religion and the failure of organized religions to understand, comprehend, and include within their doctrine this understanding of the basic relationship between human beings and the universe—that they are part of it and not in control of it. Control is not preordained or anything; the universe is just here and we're part of it.

In my view, most organized religions have not incorporated that as part of their doctrine. A majority of people subscribe to those religions, and that's why we're in the mess that we are in. There's no understanding from the spiritual leaders of the dominant society about this basic relationship.

That explains my feelings in terms of our connection with the earth. We're one of the creatures on the earth, and that's the reality. That's the basis for spirituality, understanding our surroundings, and living within it.

I became interested in Native American issues in law school. These issues had not been taught to me in my previous schooling. I didn't get exposed to them until I started studying legal issues relating to Native American people.

I found that the estrangement that had happened to me and other Native Americans was basically the result of a political and legal process that we didn't understand very well and weren't able to participate in. Things can be done about that. Legally binding promises have been made to our people in treaties. But these rights were not the reality at home on the reservations.

Then we learned something about the legal process, which is that it doesn't matter what's written down on paper. If you don't have the lawyers to enforce that piece of paper in the courts, then it's not worth the paper it's written on.

We started to understand why our people are in the situation they're in. For the most part they cannot afford lawyers and don't know the legal process. We had legal rights, but they were going unenforced.

That's why we founded the Native American Rights Fund. We hire lawyers who are expert in Indian law and make these lawyers available to represent those Indian tribes and individuals in major cases across the country involving Indian rights. We were using the same strategy that had already been identified by the civil rights movement: to try to put meaning into this country's principle of "equal justice for all." It is written in stone on the U.S. Supreme Court building, but it's basically not true. It's equal justice if you're rich. If you're poor you don't get any. That's America.

We had to find out how to raise money and get lawyers to participate in the legal process so we could get this equal justice. This strategy was originally started by the civil rights movement, using lobbying and litigation.

In the 1960s we were dealing with a federal Indian policy that called for termination of Indian tribes on the basis that the way Indian people were was no good and they had to change. And the only way to force them to change was by terminating their rights as Indians, selling their lands, and sending them off to the big city.

The civil rights movement changed that. White Americans had no monopoly on who was right and wrong, who was good and bad. The Indian people started pushing for a new policy, one of self-determination. Beginning in the sixties, there were enough enlightened leaders in Washington, starting with President Kennedy, to where the termination policy was finally ended by the federal government. A new policy, Indian self-determination, was implemented.[2]

These discussions were started during the Kennedy and then the Johnson administrations. President Nixon, in 1970, was the first president to enunciate the Indian self-determination policy and discredit the old policy. Part of that self-determination policy is recognizing what's in the law books and what we've litigated for our tribal clients, and encouraging other tribes who have lawyers.

It's a sovereignty issue: tribes are sovereign nations. Treaties are made between sovereigns, and tribes have treaties. The legal force and significance of those treaties has not changed to any great degree. It's been the politics. The politics suppressed the legal right to sovereignty.

That's where the power of the courts comes into play. The politics isn't in the courts. The judges have to enforce the law. The law is that tribes are sovereign. So we just forgot about the political process and pressed ahead in the courts. Decision after decision said that tribes are sovereign governments and have treaty rights.

This in turn drove the political process. They had to recognize what their own courts were saying. That has formed the basis for the self-determination policy. Tribes can be self-determining because they're sovereign governments with the power to make their own decisions about their own lives and their own resources. That goes against the old termination policy, which was to dismantle everything Indian, including the tribal governments.[3]

It's remarkable we survived the termination period and everything before that. It's a terrible history of broken promises and forced assimilation. The situation really resulted in the generation before mine being very suppressed and coming out of an era of American history where it wasn't good to be an Indian person. It wasn't good to be a minority person of any kind. The prejudice and discrimination were terrible. Now we're trying to get out of the mentality of the bad policies that were forced on us.

Things are gradually changing in Indian country. Now we are free to be ourselves. We have power over our own lives and power to make our own decisions based on our own beliefs and our own ways, not what somebody else says.

I've seen tremendous changes in the twenty years I've been in the law business in Indian country. Part of this is that the tribes have control over their own lands and can do with their lands as they choose to, not as somebody makes them do without consulting them. That's true self-determination and sovereignty.

This leads us to an issue that some of the environmentalists have not fully understood. They are just now starting to understand in a better way. That is that tribes are governments. There are over three hundred different tribes in the Lower 48. Not all tribes are going to take a totally anti-development stance in regard to their lands. Some tribes are going to choose for social and economic reasons to do some development that certain environmentalists are not going to like.

This puts some environmentalists in a difficult spot. They may be against any development, yet they see a tribe finally getting control of their own lands and making a decision the environmentalists don't necessarily support. It's the tribes' right to do that.

Tribes, just like states, are bound by the federal environmental laws in meeting the minimum standards required by law. This is a sovereign power they have now—to regulate their own environment, to increase those standards if they choose to do that. To me, that's only right.

I think what you will see is that tribal governments will be a different kind of government than most environmentalists are used to. Tribes, because of who they are, are going to have a different perspective. They understand that they don't really control the land they have, or the earth in general. They have a relationship, they are a part of that land. They're the same as the creatures who live on that land. Tribes have been living on the land since time immemorial. As a tribe, they're looking to the future in a way that sees their future generations always living on that land. It's home to them. They are not going to pollute and destroy their home, the place that belongs to their future generations.

Native people who have that kind of attitude are very different from other government officials who have dealt with these issues. Environmentalists haven't had the perspective of tribal government leaders. They are going to see a different kind of government official. That's not to say tribes will always decide against development. Those decisions are going to be based on a thorough assessment of the long-term consequences for that tribe and their future generations.

Tribes see themselves as guardians for the future generations of tribal members. They're not planning to move out of there at the end of their lifetime and run off to find another place to tear up and pollute. That's not the nature of tribal governments.

We need other government leaders to understand these issues based on the long term. Is development going to ruin the land and make it unavailable for future generations? Such development is shortsighted. The attitude non-Indians have had as a result of their history and their culture hasn't included this basic relationship between human beings and the earth. They haven't made that connection because they have always felt like they're in control and can always manage to sustain no matter what. They're starting to see now that they're wrong. The earth is not a commodity to be bought and sold.

These are lands that people have lived on from the beginning of time. As tribal members, they want to hold on to that land and use it to sustain themselves and their families and keep it for future generations. That's only natural. That's part of Native American philosophy and religion. It's just deeply ingrained. The land has to be used in a rational, intelligent manner.

The modern Indian rights movement is a quarter of a century old. We've made some progress. People are starting to understand the terms of Indian nationhood and sovereignty. Tribes are not going to disappear. We're not the vanishing Americans.

We've been suppressed Native Americans and we've survived because we've learned how this system works. We've become educated. We're going to resume our rightful place on this continent as the original inhabitants. Hopefully the great American myth about Columbus discovering America, which every school kid learns, will be buried. Native Americans discovered it a long time before that. The myth assumes no one existed on this land, and that's totally wrong.

We were here since time immemorial. People will come to understand that we're still here and we're growing and getting stronger. There are three sovereigns within the continental United States: the federal government, the state governments, and the tribal governments. We can take our place among the family of nations, the family of governments, and participate.

People have a lot to learn from Native Americans. The most critical thing is to understand the relationship between human beings and the earth and its creatures. We're a mere part of it. If we don't watch ourselves, we're going to end up destroying it all. It's within our power to do that.

It's our choice. We can't continue to go the way this country and the world have gone so far, which is to develop and exploit at all costs. We have to understand that there are environmental consequences to everything that's done. We need to assess the relationship between human beings and the earth and its creatures.

It's a natural law. There's no getting around it. Man has got no control over that. It controls man.

Notes

1. Frank LaPena, Steven Crum, and others in this volume comment on the ineffectuality of the American Indian Religious Freedom Act of 1978. Since this interview was completed, John Echohawk has written, "Recent Supreme Court decisions have denied protection for Native religious practices. In *Lyng* v. *Northwest Indian Cemetery Association*, a 1988 Supreme Court decision, the court ruled that the federal government may bulldoze an irreplaceable tribal religious site without violating the First Amendment. In *Employment Division of Oregon* v. *Smith*, a 1990 decision, the court ruled that the First Amendment does not include protection for the sacramental use of peyote in Indian religious ceremonies. As disclosed in nine congressional oversight hearings held in 1992 and 1993, the Supreme Court decisions have produced a loophole in the First Amendment and a frightening human rights crisis for Native Americans. U.S. Forest Service bulldozers accomplish today what U.S. troops did in the 1890s" (*Buzzworm 6*, no. 2 (Jan.–Feb. 1994).

Congress passed a law in 1994 essentially overturning the effect of the 1990 *Smith* decision by giving protection to the religious use of peyote by Native Americans. So far, attempts to overturn the effects of the 1988 *Lyng* decision have not been successful in Congress. Thus, Native American religious sites on former tribal lands now owned by the federal government go unprotected.

2. The Self-Determination Act and Education Act was signed into law in 1975. Legislation for the "termination" policy was originally passed in the 1930s, but the policy was not put into effect until the 1950s. Its proclaimed goal was to "Americanize" Indians through "relocation" and by cutting off federal benefits and protections. "By 1960," Peter Nabokov writes, "the process had rearranged the map of Indian America, as the U.S. Census counted nearly a third of the country's 525,000 Native Americans as 'urban Indians'" (*Native American Testimony*, 336).

3. The Indian Reorganization Act of 1934 undertook a major reform of federal policy toward American Indians. It created the framework for current forms of tribal government for many tribes. In spite of the good intentions of its architect, John Collier, there has been controversy over the nature of these governments. This was an issue in the 1973 occupation of Wounded Knee:

> *Supporters of the tribal government argued that only through the Indian Reorganization Act did the Indians have self-government and that attacking the existing tribal government was in essence advocating anarchy, a condition that the United States could not allow under any circumstances. The response of those people who supported the traditionals and militants was that self-government was a delusion, because the existing tribal government had been created by the United States simply to serve its own purposes, supplanting the traditional government and customs with an alien institution and its rules and regulations. (Vine Deloria, Jr., and Clifford Lytle,* The Nations Within, *13.)*

Deloria and Lytle conclude, "In setting the theoretical framework for reconstituting an ancient feeling of sovereignty, [John Collier] prepared the ground for an entirely new expression of Indian communal and corporate existence. We are just beginning to recognize the nature of this expression" (ibid., 264).

Steven Crum

How Beautiful Is Our Land

Steven Crum is a member of the Tosa Wihi, or White Knife Band, of the Western Shoshone Nation of the Great Basin. He is Associate Professor of Native American Studies at the University of California, Davis.

He was born in Phoenix and received his B.A. from Arizona State University. In 1983 he earned his Ph.D. in history from the University of Utah.

Dr. Crum has published numerous articles on the Indians of the Great Basin and on the history of American Indian higher education, and is the author of *The Road on Which We Came: A History of the Western Shoshone* (1994). He was named Distinguished Indian Educator of the Year by the California Indian Education Conference in 1995.

He was interviewed by Darryl Wilson.

I'm from the Western Shoshone tribe of Nevada. There are 3,500 of us. The Northern Shoshone live in Idaho, and the Eastern Shoshone live in Wyoming. Those of us living in Nevada and Death Valley, California, are the Western Shoshone. We received these designations in a series of treaties negotiated with the federal government in 1863. Hence we got stuck with the label "Western Shoshone."

Traditionally we called ourselves *Newe*, which means "The People." Other tribes also called themselves "The People." I am from a small Shoshone group in northeastern Nevada called the *Tosa Wihi*, or White Knife. We got this name because our ancestors used a quarry in Nevada to make white arrowheads and white knives. The other Shoshone groups in the Great Basin also called us "White Knives." When the Duck Valley Reservation was created in 1877, most "White Knives" moved there because they considered it part of our hunting territory—they considered it to be home.

The rest stayed elsewhere in Nevada. Duck Valley was created by the U.S. government in an effort to force all the Western Shoshone to move there. But this concentration policy failed. In the years after 1877, only one-third of the Great Basin Shoshones moved to Duck Valley. Traditionally, the Shoshone are deeply attached to the land—the Reese River Valley, Ruby Valley, Death Valley, and other regions. So when the government told them to move to Duck Valley, they said, "No, we are not going to move. This is home. Our roots are in this valley or on that mountain range."

This is why we make reference to Mother Earth, *Pia Sokopia*. There is the special relationship between us and the earth that we live on. It has to do with living in unison with nature and the land and preserving it for ourselves and for future generations.

Indian families traveled to the mountains to dig roots. I've watched

Indian people dig *tosa*, a big, long root like a sweet potato. When they dug the root out there was a hole in the ground. The older people covered up that hole and said a prayer. They prayed when using the root for medicine.

Here is an example of deep respect for something coming from the earth. When we take something from the earth, we pray to acknowledge thankfulness to the earth for providing for us.

If you went to the Great Basin in 1490, before the arrival of Columbus, you would find a group of people living in harmony with nature. You would learn that we did not exploit the earth, that we were not thinking about materialism or dominating the land. We lived with it.

In October you would find the people harvesting pine nuts. We didn't just go out there and pick nuts. There are certain religious ceremonies associated with the harvest. The Shoshones would go out there and conduct round dances and give prayers to the Creator.

We gathered, but we took only what we needed. We conducted rabbit drives. A strong work ethic existed, and still exists. But we were not thinking in terms of profit-making schemes.

Marriages between Shoshones in the nineteenth and twentieth centuries depended upon the quality of the human being. We were judged on our productivity. This is still a strong virtue in our tribe. We frown upon laziness. That is one thing that I like about being a scholar. I am working, researching and writing, and that is cherished in my tribe.

Back in 1490 in the Great Basin, you would find no warfare. We had family squabbles and differences before the coming of the white man, but there was no such thing as mass-scale war between the tribes in the Great Basin. Warfare emerged at a later date for some tribes when we were being confined to smaller and smaller geographic areas.

In the years after 1492 the whole situation changed. The Spanish and other Europeans came to this world. They brought with them the notion of superiority. They considered themselves a superior form of human being and the Natives as inferior. This type of thinking goes way back into European history. If you take a look at the writings of Aristotle and others, they were advancing the notion that some people were born into this world to be the *rulers* and others to be the *ruled*.

During 1512–1513 the Spaniards passed the Laws of Burgos to enforce this type of thinking. One of the laws created the *encomienda*. This granted villages of Indians to a Spanish master.[1] The Natives had to provide the Spanish master with labor. They had to grow crops for the conquistador. He was to feed and clothe them and make sure they were Christianized. This paternalism is directly linked to the European notion of the superior person over the inferior.

Paternalism exists in this nation. In the Supreme Court decision of 1831, *Cherokee Nations* vs. *Georgia*, all tribal people living in the United States were classified as "domestic dependent nations," not foreign nations.

Furthermore, the court ruled that tribal people are "wards" of the government and the federal government is the "guardian" of the tribal people. We are still "wards." We have had to live with paternalism and interference for hundreds of years.

One would think that a country believing in freedom and democracy would give a little bit of freedom to the Native people.

So this has not been the most suitable situation for us. If you go to Nevada today, you will find that the Shoshone people cannot do what they used to. We are subject to hunting laws. We have to secure a hunting license from the state of Nevada. We have to live by their hunting seasons.

Our religion is restricted, too. We were given religious freedom in relatively recent history, with the civil rights movement. We were given freedom of speech, press, assembly, and religion. This is strange, considering that the U.S. Constitution gave other Americans these basic freedoms in the eighteenth century.

What happened to freedom? What happened to democracy? It was not until 1978 that Congress passed the American Indian Religious Freedom Act, which applied the principle of religious freedom to all Indians, not just those on the reservations. Unfortunately, the Supreme Court has not totally endorsed this 1978 Congressional act.[2]

Generally speaking, for much of its history the United States did not want us to identify as Natives. It has always thought in terms of assimilating and blending Indians into the larger population. The melting pot theory blends everybody together and comes up with human beings lacking particular ethnic identities. America doesn't want people to be different. It doesn't want cultural pluralism. Certainly, over the years, many people have favored an English-only policy.

Richard Pratt was an army captain who created the reservation boarding-school system in the late nineteenth century. The whole policy was to remove Native children as far away from their home environment as possible. Pratt coined the popular phrase, "Kill the Indian and save the man!"[3] What does this tell us about U.S. history?

The Native people were not the only ones subject to assimilation in America. Other ethnic minorities were as well. In the eighteenth century, German communities existed within the thirteen English colonies. That really bothered the English. Benjamin Franklin was among those who came up with the idea of dissolving the "German" identity. He argued there should be no German enclaves or communities in the English colonies.

Native Americans really have to be proud of holding onto our own identity. We are not rootless. A lot of Native people could produce their own tribal version of *Roots*, because we know our tribal identities. We need to be proud of that. Here it is five hundred years later and we still know who we are. Too bad for the assimilationists!

Congress needs to produce a major publication depicting the truth about Native American history and culture. This study needs to focus on positive Native values and practices.

Look at the Native work schedule. Before white contact you might see Native people taking an extended break. At various times of the year they worked very hard and they were very productive. During the salmon runs and during the acorn harvests they were very productive. Then they took time off to recuperate; they would make baskets or whatever. This is just the opposite of the puritanical work ethic in which you have to feel guilty if you are not continuously working. Taking time off from work is something that is healthy.

Taking time off from hard work was one reason why whites labeled us as lazy years ago. Suppose this was the year 1841 and John Bidwell went along the rivers of California and observed the Maidu Indians during a period when they were taking their vacation. What would he have concluded? He would have concluded that here was a bunch of lazy Indians.[4] But in reality, it was one of those times when the Indians took time off from productive work. It was not during the acorn harvest, so they had a little bit of time off for themselves.

The modern world is caught up in the mentality of taking everything now. We must wake up to the fact that we are destroying the environment. Euro-Americans think mainly in terms of exploitation: "Take now because the world is coming to an end anyway." They're dominating the land, not living with it.

It is happening in this part of the country with the redwoods, and it has to stop. I went to Sequoia National Park. Among the big trees, I was completely overwhelmed by the sense of "awesomeness." I felt like a tiny speck. I like to think that these massive trees are going to be here indefinitely, but there are business people who would love to get their hands on them.

Those who believe in conserving the earth need to convert those who do not think like us. It is going to take a lot of work. Whether we can do this remains to be seen.

The Shoshone people have a song that talks about the land. It has beautiful lyrics. It is a round dance song that was sung at pine-nut harvest-time some years back. I can't sing it by myself. If there were other Shoshones here I could sing along with them:

> *How beautiful is our land*
> *How beautiful is our land*
> *Forever beside the water, the water*
> *How beautiful is our land*
>
> *How beautiful is our land*
> *How beautiful is our land*
> *The earth with flowers on it, next to the water*
> *How beautiful is our land.*

Some people would want to modify this song. They would say it's too repetitive. Who wants to hear it over and over again? But when it is repeated over and over again, we don't forget.

I am somewhat disappointed with America's academic community, which largely fails to acknowledge the Native presence and Native contributions. Some of the teaching and research in the universities perpetuates notions of dominating the earth and having control over other beings. Their terms perpetuate narrow types of thinking. If you take courses in philosophy, what are you required to read? Aristotle, Freud. You are not going to find philosophy courses using books such as *Black Elk Speaks* or *My People, The Sioux* by Luther Standing Bear.

A lot of changes need to take place in academia. I am going to stay and battle it out. Some within the white academic community still present us in a negative light. We are "treacherous Modocs," the "lowest cricket eaters of the Great Basin." Julian Steward, one of the best-known anthropologists in the nation, said of the Shoshone, "Their arts and crafts were among the poorest of America."[5]

Who is he to make this judgment? When he came to study us in the 1930s, he did not look at all of our culture. He looked at only those things that were visible to his narrow vision, like the hunting and gathering economy. It never occurred to him to examine our music, songs, dance, or religion. For some reason he blocked this out of his mind. He called our culture "gastric."

This is why I am staying in here and battling it out!

Notes

1. "The largest holding was awarded by Charles V to Cortes, who, as the newly titled Marques del Valle, acquired an *encomienda* encompassing the fertile valley of Oaxaca and villages in Morelos, Puebla, and Veracruz—a total of 23 towns and over 200,000 Indians." Mary Helms, *Middle America: A Cultural History of Heartland and Frontiers*, 149.

2. See John Echohawk's interview, Note 1.

3. See Hazel W. Hertzberg, *The Search for an American Indian Identity*, 16. Pratt founded the Carlisle Indian School in 1879. He said, "I believe ... [in] immersing the Indians in our civilization and when we get them there under, holding them there until they are thoroughly soaked." He believed he was promoting their best interest. In 1916 he wrote, "If I had a superintendent of schools who could not see in every little Indian boy a possible President of the United States, I would dismiss him."

4. John Bidwell was a pioneer who settled northern California in the 1840s and used Maidu Indians as a labor force. See Dorothy Hill, *The Indians of Chico Rancheria*.

5. Julian H. Steward, "Shoshonean Tribes: Utah, Idaho, Nevada, Eastern California," 1936, unpublished manuscript, Steward papers, Box 10, University of Illinois at Urbana-Champaign archives.

Carlos Cordero

Reviving Native Technologies

Carlos Cordero (Maya) was born in Mexico City. He studied economics and political science at the University of the Americas there. He also has studied at the University of California, Los Angeles, and at a number of other California institutions. He earned his M.A. in psychology from California State University, Sonoma.

In the 1960s he came to the United States and became a leader in developing the idea of an ethnic studies curriculum. He helped to create models for alternative schools and to implement at the elementary level a system called Escuela Calmecac.

He joined the Board of Trustees of D.Q. University in 1973. D.Q. is an institution in Davis, California, run by and for Native American scholars. Carlos Cordero served as its president from 1983 to 1994. He describes his association with the institution as follows: "When D.Q. University was created in 1971, I was attracted to the notion of an institution whose goal was the validation of the Indian knowledge base. To me, this meant supporting a locus of control that was not distorted by the presence of European scholars and students, and allowed Native scholars and students to engage in exploration and inquiry."

He continues to be engaged in research to document and advance the knowledge base of indigenous peoples.

He was interviewed by Darryl Wilson, with a follow-up interview by Giuseppe Saitta.

I have always had a sense of wonder about the nexus between this continent and Europe. When the potato—an underground crop that in its original form was not subject to diseases such as blight—was introduced into Europe from "America" in the seventeenth century, the European population doubled in size. Prior to the introduction of Native foods from this continent, Europe went through famines that maintained a check on the population.

And you wonder, again, at this strange event. The wealth of this continent allowed the European populations to explode, which ensured both the rate and the magnitude of European intervention. The wealth from this hemisphere hastened the almost total destruction of many Original Native cultures.

Think about that strange phenomenon. For almost a thousand years, Europe suffered a peculiar mental state of denying the world. By that I mean denial of the natural world in the Middle Ages, the adoption of an idiosyncratic religion from the Middle East that underscores the idea of human beings being kicked out of paradise and separated from a state of grace by their Creator.

The Judeo-Christian-Islam tradition established a hierarchical relationship between the Creator and humans. The Creator is above and the humans are below. This paradigm allowed the European to subjugate non-European peoples and nature, because it is an exact replica of the relationship between the European and his concept of God.

There is a fundamental difference between the European concept of humanity in the world and the Native concept of spirituality. They are not only incompatible, but antagonistic. Indians, and certainly my mother's people the Maya, never defined humanity as being out of a state of grace with the universe. We weren't kicked out of paradise or any of those strange things.

The Maya strongly believed in a reciprocal relationship between humans and the Creator or creators. Along with other Native peoples of this continent, they talked about a rootedness, a sense of belonging on this planet and in this universe. The creative force was expressed in a manner that "humanized" the existence of people.

To be human among the Indians is to be spiritual. To be spiritual among the Europeans is to transcend the human world. They have said that they are separate from the Creator. So that which is spiritual cannot be human. From an Indian perspective, that is bizarre!

The behavior of contemporary European-based populations reflects that their inner consciousness has been distorted and impaired. The conquerors have done psychic harm to themselves. They cannot handle space, for example. European and Anglo populations complain about their loneliness, alienation, and feeling of powerlessness. This tells you of a rigid mental state and a cultural expression that tends to be compulsive, resulting in the inability to stop the damage to the environment.

The dynamic of the European cultures is one of obsession with control. Control not only of the environment and other populations, but among themselves. The pre-Columbian Indian concept was that control was the communion between humans and the Creator, humans and their environment, humans and humans.

So the change that needs to happen to heal the earth can't come from the European cultural base, but must come from the Original Native bases that re-establish an inner psychic equilibrium with each other and the environment.

This harmony is needed by a highly technological society that has produced weapons of horrific power it cannot control. With all of his exo-technology—the extension of the senses through outer technology—the European has atrophied his internal technology, his natural human capacities to be in balance and in harmony with nature.

The Indian knowledge-base—culture, science, and philosophy—has technologies of ritual and ceremony. I am using the word technology in a modern sense, which is unfortunate. We should be having this conversation in the Indian languages. Realities are so complex that modern European languages are not useful instruments to convey the experience we are discussing here. One of the things that we must do is to make a concerted effort to accomplish the revival of Indian languages. They have that inner technology.

If we allow the Indian model to revive and be useful, the disparity between humans and technology will begin to diminish. Then the ability to conceptualize contemporary problems—the environment, the ozone layer, ecology, science itself—can emerge. You would have scientists who come from a more harmonious and balanced sense of who they are as a people.

Scientists of the world are a minority. Why is that? We should start to think about why science is so rarified and scientists are so rare. Indian cultures encourage the development of science. But when the invasion took place five hundred years ago, there was no moment for Indian scientists to develop responses to the infections.

The time has come, five hundred years later, to engage in science based on the Indian culture and re-establish natural solutions to the problems created by civilization in the past five hundred years.

It's interesting that Chiapas is once again bringing to the attention of the world a peculiar reality about being Indian in Latin America. We tend to think that the moment of conquest and colonization took place five hundred years ago and that it's over. The reality is that there has been an ebb and flow, a dynamic reality between efforts to suppress and oppress and efforts to resist.

The reality is that the Native people have always been engaged in the process of resisting. They've been called bandits when they do this, or ingrates, infidels, revolutionaries—a number of names. What they've been doing, though, is nothing more than reacting to contact with humans who believe they have a divine right to engage in group oppression in order to justify conquest and colonization.

The resistance to that is what's going on in Chiapas. But it is not new. It's not something that belongs to any cause other than the fact that there have always been Native people who have maintained a relative degree of cultural continuity, who have insisted on defining their humanity from their own cultural perspective, and who have refused to be conquered and colonized.

We act surprised that these things happen again in Chiapas. Yet with gang violence in the barrios of Los Angeles, for example, we are witnessing a process of homicide—which in fact is a process of suicide. Descendants of oppressed communities will always give vent to that force of death by turning it inward. When gangs fight each other, it is an inward process. It is the killing of one who looks like one's self.

This process of entropy is part of the pain that is experienced by these communities. Sometimes it is directed outwardly. In Mexico, the federal government is being targeted as being responsible for allowing entities like the cattle industry to come in and force people from lands that they have been living on for generations. They're trying to convey a message, a cry saying, Pay attention to what you're doing to us in the name of civilization and Christianity, in the name of business and economics, modernity and progress.

I do not see it being resolved, because for the government to resolve something in Chiapas would demand that they resolve the same thing in the rest of the country. And as happened in China with Tianamen Square, as well as in Mexico in 1968, the reason governments don't do this is that they know at some level that if they do for one, they have to do for others.

On the other hand, it is clear to the indigenous people of Chiapas that they have no choice but to demonstrate that they have been pushed beyond a certain point. This is where the ideology of Zapata comes in, an intellectual who suggested that you had a choice in life to live on your knees or to die standing up. Recall that Zapata was an Indian. Zapata's ideology comes from an Indian frame of reference, and the Mexican Revolution had a lot to do with Indian ideas of relationship to the land. The *ejido* is a particularly Mexican communal and tribal relationship between the people and the land.[1]

As to what I see for the future, I suggest the following. Given that the dominant government is committed to transnational systems of economics and agribusiness, they are unable to see appropriate decentralized approaches to sustainable agriculture. It seems to me that to the degree that

Native populations can acquire scientific and technical knowledge to become self-sufficient in a hostile context, they will then be able to prevail ideologically. But I do not see this happening without the necessary infrastructure of training and education.

This is what brings me into the field of education. I am convinced that peaceful social and historic change can be accomplished for Native populations if we focus our energies and resources on developing technologies that accelerate the cognitive development of individuals. You can become informed and educated in shorter periods of time without doing away with the high standards of excellence. In order to go back to the ways of being Native before Columbus, the Native people have to enable themselves not only to provide for their own communities but also to deal with the dominant society, because that society is not going to go away.

The main problem facing both Native communities and the governments that control them is the growth of population. That is the main issue. Unless those two groups begin to address that common problem, the process of polarization will continue and the resolution won't happen. It will be a typical Mexican standoff, a stalemate. The dynamic of tension will continue. The resistance will surface and it will be suppressed, and it will surface and it will be suppressed. It will just be that same historical ebb and flow that has been happening in Latin America for the last five hundred years.

It is true that recently there has been a change in the portrayal of Native people in the media. It's been more positive. The problem with that, though, is even if it moves from negative stereotypes to positive stereotypes, it's still stereotypes.

I think we need to be very critical and skeptical about the representation of Native people and their beliefs and ideas. A lot of what's being voiced by Native individuals or leaders may actually be in origin a European version of what an Indian was or ought to be. We have to be very careful of the transfiguration of the idea of the "noble savage." Over the last four hundred years of contact, the stereotype went from the noble savage to the murderous savage to, now, the enlightened and wise savage.

What we need to do is truly go back to information that shows how pre-Columbian Indians really saw themselves vis à vis other humans and the environment. We know that they had a kind of grounding in reality that defined humanity as relative to other humans and the environment. But we also know there is evidence that pre-Columbian populations engaged in behaviors that were anti-human and that were harmful to the environment. So I'm very leery of the portrayal of the Native as an ecological guru, when in fact some of those ideas, if you really look hard at them, may or may not come from Native origins.

I think Native people have a profound wisdom. The reality, though, is that since Columbus we have had a holocaust, a massive loss of humanity and culture, along with the introduction of the culture of poverty and the experience of conquest and colonization. This has distorted Native populations. It is problematic to say that we have not also become people who have engaged in a lot of violence—domestic violence, drug and alcohol abuse, and political abuse of one another.

If we take a hard look throughout the Americas, a lot of that behavior is being acted out by Natives while at the same time they engage in rhetoric about how Native people are the keepers of the earth who live only harmoniously. The clash between those two versions of reality creates a problem for me to the point of saying that we should admit that at present we really are, in relative terms, at times schizocultural.

Nevertheless, Indian philosophies can be useful to environmentalists in their search for awareness. I see a return to activities humans were engaged in five hundred years ago, a freedom that will allow us to explore not only the pre-Columbian paradigm but to amplify new paradigms the Europeans can benefit from.

I believe the ego-strength of Indian individuals and communities will return. It has never really gone away. We know that in each Indian community people with great ego-strength have always existed. In the next thirty years we will see larger numbers of these individuals coming back and flourishing, to the benefit of their community and the whole world. I am very optimistic that the Indian will play a significant role in the life of our planet.

The first step is the declaration of the right to education for all people. We must believe that to be human is to be educated. We must say that we cannot tolerate one human who is not educated. Nothing can change unless we accomplish this. Right now there are artificial barriers between us and our access to education at all levels. The Indian knowledge-base is tolerated in the colleges and universities of the dominant society only as an exotic curiosity.

We need to give Native people a place in the sun—literally and figuratively. Native people must have a land base. There is a difference in psychology. A psychoanalyst says that you must have a couch to find your ego boundaries and ego strength; Native individuals and populations must have land. Not land in the European definition of ownership, but an unbroken ability to connect with the essence of their humanity, based on a natural connection with the earth, the planet, and the universe.

To the degree that America denies Native people contact with the land, it will succeed in the destruction of the American Indian. Allowing the Native people to have the direct sensory contact with nature will guarantee survival of the Indian people. Having an actual place where you can *be where you want to be* is without question one of the things that we can do to revive the present human state of lost self-esteem.

I ask the readers of this anthology to critically examine their own behavior. They must connect who they are with who they claim to be. It seems to me that if we are to practice what we preach, we cannot simply be different from the models the Europeans have given us, but we somehow must be better.

It is important to remember the endurance and vitality of Native people. And yet we are still fragmented, full of personal and social and political dysfunctions. We spend too much time and energy fighting one another, and not enough coming together to engage in serious work, such as documenting a pre-Columbian frame of reference.

We come from great people, and so we must act like great people. Because we *are* great people.

Note

1. In the traditional *ejido*, land is held in common by the community, with some parcels being portioned out to individual farmers. *Ejidos* were expropriated to form haciendas during the nineteenth century, particularly under the rule of Porfirio Díaz. Agrarian reform following the Mexican constitution of 1917 reinstituted the *ejido* system to some degree. In 1991, 28,000 cooperatives accounted for half of Mexico's arable land. Distribution of land back to communities ended in early 1992, and farmers may now sell their land to private holders.

Rose Johnson/Tsosie

Our Testimonies Will Carry Us Through

Rose Wyvette Johnson/Tsosie, a full-blood Navajo, was born on the reservation in Arizona. She and her twin sister were taken from their mother, Helen Morgan Tsosie-Ben, at birth.

Rose and her sister each weighed only one and a half pounds at birth. Their mother, who was fourteen years old at the time, believed the hospital was going to keep the infants until they were big enough to come home. Instead, they were taken out of Navajo country without their mother's knowledge. They were adopted by a Mormon family in northern Utah.

Their mother searched for her children for thirty-three years. By the time they met, Rose's father had already died. In 1984, Rose returned to the reservation to spend one and a half years as a missionary. Her mother, now sixty, had sixteen children, twelve of them home births. She is grandmother to twenty-two children.

Rose Johnson/Tsosie is a speaker and storyteller for both adults and children, drawing on her own life experiences and the legends of her people. She has been a consultant, administrator, and proprietor of a clothing design business. She was chosen for the International Who's Who of Professional & Business Women in 1993 and is a board member of the American Indian Center of Santa Clara, California.

She related her story of her return to her people to Lois Crozier-Hogle and Darryl Wilson.

Being adopted into a non-Indian family, we had to learn about American Indians just as the other children did. It took me thirty-three years to go back to my own people. I cherish the period I spent as a missionary, teaching on the Navajo reservation. My heart was open, my mind was open, and I wanted to grasp as much as I could.

The people I cherished the most were the children and the old people. The old people because they were very patient. They were very kind. They knew the experiences that I never had, they shared their lives and traditions. The children, their hearts were open, they loved coming and teaching us the Navajo language, Native foods, the different ways they knew were "the right way," although they did not live the traditional way.

The *Saani* (a respected grandmother or elder) were the ones who would teach us the old ways. They gave us the real insight to being Navajo. They would say, "I want to show you something," and we would make bread their way. They taught us not just about life, but about how they lived. They shared as much as they could—a lot of them didn't speak English and believed their children should speak Navajo.

I think the hardest thing to relate to outside people is how much the traditions are part of them. *Ho'zho* in Navajo means that you are in balance with yourself and with nature. To an outsider's eyes the land is barren, and yet there is a beautiful life there.

I think the hardest trial has been the changes the government has put the Navajo and Hopi people through recently. The Hopi land is in the center of the Navajo reservation. The government has relocated many families in the Joint Use Area into nontraditional homes. They said, "Okay, we've built a beautiful new home for you, but you can't keep sheep, cows, or horses here. Don't do your traditional weaving or baskets, because we are giving you a paycheck. We know this is going to be better for you."

The U.S. government still has the upper hand, I feel. They still hand out the paychecks and expect the Indians to obey their rules. They don't realize that this had been the way Navajo lived for hundreds of years.

My mother lived all her life in the traditional ways. She's always lived on the Navajo reservation. It would be hard to be put off of land that you've lived on for hundreds of years. It would be hard to be told, "You cannot herd sheep anymore." And yet, at the same time, the people are still beautiful. The Navajo people still believe in hope, they still have dreams. They still want their children to come home and speak Navajo.

Some young people are returning, yet a greater percentage are walking away from the reservation. It's really hard for the young people because their education level is not at a standard to get a job. A high school diploma is an accomplishment, so it is hard for them if they go outside of the Navajo reservation and an employer says, "No, your education is not enough."

It's a vicious circle. Some feel that if you're going to be a full Indian, you can't be outside of that realm. If you go outside that realm, you're going to get hurt. And if you get hurt and go back to the Indian way, you're going to be hurt again because the Indians will be expecting you to be different because you chose to live outside of their lives. When you go back into the circle, it's changed.

For myself, there have been so many "ifs" in my life. For instance, the man who was most responsible for me meeting my natural mother—the man who knew my family and where they lived—was killed in an automobile accident after I met her. My mom had faith for thirty-three years. I know she had a lot of "ifs" in her life too.

When I returned to the Navajo reservation, I had no idea I would *ever* find my real mother. I got information about her, and then got permission to visit from my mission president. When I went up to the door of my mother's hogan, I didn't know if she would accept me or not.

When I knocked, a young woman, about twenty-two years old answered. I asked if Helen Morgan lived there. She said, "No." There was an awkward moment. I thought, "Oh, no, I have come all this way."

As I looked around inside the hogan I saw a picture. It was one of my sisters—and she looked exactly like me when I was younger! Then the young woman said her parents were gone and would not be back for a long time. But ten minutes later we heard a pickup drive into the yard and the girl said, "Oh, they're back already."

I went outside and saw a man in the front seat and a woman on the passenger side. The woman was just sitting there. I went around to that side of the pickup. She rolled the window down about two inches and stared at me. My Navajo interpreter asked if she was Helen Morgan Tsosie-Ben.

She nodded her head. My interpreter started talking. After several minutes of talk, I asked him to ask her if she gave birth to twins in the Keams Canyon Hospital in 1950. She cried and rolled down the window. She pulled me to her and we hugged. I couldn't cry, all I could do was think, "This is really happening!"

Mother got out of the pickup. She took me by the hand and led me into the house. She told the girl that I met at the door, "This is your sister, who has been lost. She's come home." We hugged each other. She cried.

Soon my brothers and sisters were coming from every door and from every direction. I discovered that I had fourteen brothers and sisters. Many of them were crying, too. Later we went into another hogan, where an older woman was weaving a rug. She smiled at me when I entered the room. She knew me. Beyond the shadow of a doubt, that *Saani* knew me—and yet we'd never been introduced. It must have been because I look like her grandmother.

My mother searched for thirty-three years. She had *faith* for thirty-three years that she would find her lost babies. I learned that when she and her husband left the house that day, he said, "One more day. This is the last time we will search for your babies. If you can't find any evidence today, don't ask me to help you search again."

They were twenty miles from home. They didn't know where they were going, but it was the last day and Mom wanted to find some evidence. Then she just said, "Turn around. Turn around and go back." I was getting ready to leave the hogan when they drove up. That's how close I was to missing my natural mother. That is the power of the faith that Mom had that one day she would find her babies.

Helen asked about "the other one," if she was still alive. I said yes and gave her a picture of my twin sister, Mary Annette. Later, I had Mary Annette call Mom and say, "*Yate'e'h shima nazonee*" ("Hello, beautiful Mother") in Navajo. This was just so she could hear Annette's voice.

When the time came, it was not hard for me to leave. It was not hard because I know that at any time I can go home. I know now that I am accepted. It did not hurt when I left because I am always welcome. I am a part of their family.

There is a lot of inner beauty in my people. It's not just the tradition itself, it's the whole life. It does not mean just from twelve to three o'clock, it means from childhood until you pass away. I know I've not been able to comprehend a lot of it because I was not raised in tradition, but I respect it.

When you live on the Navajo reservation, it is what you become. You are a living part of it. Your life is from the beginning. Your mother and father tell you different stories, they teach you certain words I can never learn how to say because they are part of the Navajo way.

I missed out on traditional ways because I was adopted. And yet I know. I have experienced some of it with the old people and I have felt it with the young when I taught on the reservation. You can't experience this feeling until you're down there. The families had so much to give, and yet they had so little compared to what we have here. The Navajo way is a very simple life, a beautiful and peaceful way of life.

Each time they give a dinner, they offer a part of themselves. When a baby is born and when it first laughs—there is so much meaning there. Whoever makes the baby laugh the first time has to give it a party. That is something we may be missing.

One thing that I feel sad about in non-Indian society is that when I tell people I love and cherish them, they think it is an act of physical possession. But to me it's something that goes beyond, it is eternal friendship. That's one thing about the Indian people—they give from within their hearts.

Many white people have been given so much—possessions, land, money—that they have forgotten what the real world is. We would be nothing without this land. We would be nothing without the plants, without God, without the sun. I don't see very many people appreciating what they have. I really don't.

An Indian prays. The first time I went down to see my mom and dad, for Thanksgiving dinner, they asked me to say the prayer. I said a two-minute prayer. After I discovered everybody was looking at me, I asked my sister, "Louise, how come everybody's staring at me?" She said, "That was a really short prayer. Some prayers last forty-five minutes or an hour."

To me, and Indian way of life and Mormonism are similar but there's some inner conflict in trying to find where they fit in. I think it was meant for my twin sister and me to live outside the reservation, because otherwise we would not have survived. At birth we were three pounds—total for two babies! So I know I've had to fight for my life more than once, and give thanks to God for blessing me.

The thing my sister and I cherish the most about each other is our inner strength. Both of us are survivors. We've had to gain strength within ourselves, and our love for each other helps us. Our testimonies and prayers are really what carry us through.

Janine Pease Pretty on Top

The Quality of Listening

Janine Pease Pretty on Top is president of Little Big Horn College in Crow Agency, Montana. She is a member of the Big Lodge Clan of the Crow people. Her Indian name means "One Who Loves to Pray." It was given to her at the age of four by Elizabeth Yellow Tail, a clan elder who lived to be 112.

Education has played a positive role in Janine Pease Pretty on Top's life from the beginning. Her father was an administrator and her mother a teacher on the Colville Reservation in Washington, where she grew up. Her great-grandmother donated the land for the first public school in the town of Lodge Grass, where Janine now lives.

She held various posts in Indian education on the Navajo and Crow reservations until 1982, when she launched Little Big Horn College with two trailers, an abandoned house, $50,000, and a mandate from her tribe. It is now a fully accredited two-year college, with many classes conducted in the Crow language. She continued with her own education, earning a doctorate in education from Montana State University in 1994.

She has long been active in local politics. In 1983 she was lead plaintiff in a voting-rights suit against Bighorn County, forcing a review of a redistricting plan that would have reduced Crow voting power.

The National Indian Education Association named her Educator of the Year in 1990. She is a trustee of the Smithsonian's National Museum of the American Indian, and in 1994 she received a "genius" grant from the Macarthur Foundation.

She was interviewed by Lois Crozier-Hogle and Giuseppe Saitta.

The strength of my spiritual background has to do with who the Crows are. My dad's point of departure was that all religious expressions were an important part of being connected to the Creator and the environment. There was no dichotomy set up for us there. I never distinguished between what was white and what was Indian. In my world all of it was one, and I'm real grateful for that.

My dad is very active outdoors. He was anxious to share a lot of how we know our ways of living—Old Man Coyote stories and the way things are organized from the Creator on down. He made sure we knew people who could communicate those relationships to us. My aunt, his older sister, was always happy to share the literature and the ways in which women demonstrate their spirituality and do their share to uphold the community.

My auntie lives next to the river in a valley with pine trees on either side. It's a beautiful area. Across from her home is a straight track where we had horse races. We would climb up there and look and imagine, and they would re-enact what happened there.

All my relatives are in this valley. There's a place where people were born, a place where they're buried. We know their character, their deeds, their spirituality.

When you drive with my uncle you never listen to the radio. He talks to you about what's happening and where you are. The other day we were up on the hill watching the morning come about. My uncle explained, "As you look in this valley, you need to understand that when I was a child my mother brought me here. She would say, 'Look over there, you can see your uncle, he's moving around, he's lit the morning fire.'" Now the people who live there are my age and you can see them moving around, going about their business. So not a lot has changed.

There's never been any real separation from the land for us. What we say about our home country is that this is what God wanted. We think of it as a huge lodge over a part of Montana and Wyoming. The four main lodge poles are our four main places.

There are places where I always go to pray. One is a place where you can see large vistas, where you know the family and tribe has been for a long time. There's a tremendous amount of connection to the Creator at that place.

I meet people all the time who have this rich sensitivity, no matter what their background is. But the freedom to have that sensitivity is a whole lot greater in the Indian community. It's respected and appreciated more than in other cultures.

I take my children out as often as I can to pick berries or walk. I have an affinity for rocks; I tend to go places where there are rock outcroppings. I think my children will be less fearful in general if they're at ease in the outdoors and the creation as a whole. I know they have a sense of home. We're in a very wealthy place. We have black bears, moose, elk, deer, antelope, birds, skunks, porcupines.

People look at our land and say we should develop it. But the Crows are really fond of it just the way it is. Some of them are into ranching, which is relatively harmonious to the way the land is and will continue to be. Lots of people are satisfied to keep the land as it is. That's our commitment. We're not interested in change when it comes to our whole way of living.

We have been able to bring the wisdom of people from other lodges to the Crows. We have people who are able to listen to the wisdom that is shared from other species. We've had a lot of wisdom from bighorn sheep, birds— it varies in every family according to the messengers: there is eagle, hawk, and bear medicine. I have a friend who has spoken with the bighorn. They just come right up to her and visit her. She's able to listen and ask questions.

A lot of our spirituality and power to survive has been based on the wisdom of Little People residing on our reservation. They're miniature people who dress and act like we do. They dress in buckskin and war bonnets, with all the trappings we used to have. They live in a remote area of the mountains and appear only to people who are particularly sensitive. They've had a lot to do with protecting our land. They've been very instrumental in the kind of spiritual understanding that is most holy and insightful.

One of the elements of the Crow religion is that the Creator has messengers. People would be sent messages through a bear. In the case of the Little People, the messages are related through them to the sun dancer.

We also have an active interest in vision quest. We have three or four sun dances in the summer, and ninety to a hundred people come to these. They are on a quest. You usually only know the ways in which those things happen within your own family, though.

Almost all the homes and families have a sweat lodge. The sweat lodge is a place where we remember all the parts of our home. We don't just pray for our house and children, but for the wetlands, the swamps, the hills and mountains, and beyond that, the birds and animals.

Most of the sweats have a buffalo skull symbolic of the animals that walk the land. They use an eagle wing to spread the incense. They say that once the rocks are brought in from the fire, you can hear them sing and speak.

In the course of the prayer, you travel through all these lodges and remembrances. For some families, that happens three or four times a week. It takes six to eight hours to gather the wood and build the fire. The men go in first, followed by the women, and then it's completed.

It's interesting how certain nations will guard this kind of relationship with the Creator and not share it. I've never understood why they do that. Everything I've told you, I'd tell anyone. I'm not divulging any kind of secret. Some tribes are more likely to be generous with that kind of knowledge.

We're faced with a lot of contradictions in our lives. We see consumer things on TV or when we go to the city. We've never had any kind of income as a people, but we see those gadgets, we want them, and then we feel sorry for ourselves. We think everyone should have a share in the pie, but we don't have a way to get that share with the growing gap in the American economic system between the haves and the have-nots.

A whole system of things discourages people and makes them feel bad about who they are. By the time you've had a discouraging schooling experience because you speak Crow, or you were sick and fell behind, it all accumulates and you begin to feel you'll never get anywhere. When you don't have strengthening elements from your spiritual background, it's just downhill.

We have a lot of fundamentalist Christians on our reservation and I think they're very anxious to cast any sort of Native spiritual life as works of the devil. It's really based on fear, which propels people away from the ability to be one with traditional concepts. They lose touch with the lodges and the whole creation. It creates a real separation, which tends to make life so much more shallow. We get students whose parents have died or who have gone into fundamentalist religion and whose connection to Indian spirituality is very minimal. They're more than curious about it, but they may be afraid they'll be studying the devil.

We provide a full range of classes at Little Big Horn College that include Crow Indian language, philosophy, thought, and kinship studies. Most of our students speak Crow as a primary language, but they've never really looked at their language in terms of the frames that come with it. Our whole world is framed by our language. It embodies so much of our culture that it's a real exploration of who the Crows are.

The choices we make in curriculum and administration reflect who we are. The things we study are important to Crow people, and probably not to anyone else—our migrations, history, and oral literature, which is taught by elders who come in the winter time. The combination of disciplines, the perspectives we take, the comparative studies we make, are important to us. It's a unique place, one of the only places in the world Crow people can say this is *our* institution.

As a college president I see the scholarship of our people as something that can contribute to the global knowledge. But the mainstream society relegates Native American intellect and scholarship to a kind of hobbyist position. It's a real source of frustration for me that the knowledge that's kept our people alive all these millennia can be reduced to such a low priority.

I often feel like I'm invisible to the larger society. The things I represent are relegated to a position so far in the past that they might as well not be there. It's like a curio, a museum piece, a throwback to some childlike form of life—you're alive and you're Indian, aren't you cute?

I'm seen as someone who should know what it's like to live in the 1880s, but pardon me, but I'm a woman alive in the 1990s. I'm completely as coping and as challenged as any woman around the world. Maybe I do have some insight on a century ago, but why must I be thrown back to that era? There's a lot of stereotypical confinement.

It's only heightened by the constant talk about cultural diversity. Somehow that only means the threat of certain economic pressures, rather than a function of the spirit or the land. I'm not sure that Americans appreciate that diversity, but I certainly do. There is a certain amount of freedom in this country to express that diversity with integrity, but the majority still tends to rule, and sometimes that is very injurious to people with less influence in terms of money or land.

There's a quality of living that a lot of America has lost or ignored. Privatism and individualism have gotten out of hand. They have eroded the quality of community living—the caring, the neighborhood qualities that are important to human living anywhere around the world.

The community with a solid relationship to itself is respectful of the land and all the parts of creation. But the mobility of Americans has severed the possibility of that healthy community. I don't think we were meant to be rearranged on a playing board every few years. Even with the disjunctions within our lives, Indians have a whole lot more community than many other people can dream of.

There's a listening quality to community. If you're truly a member of a community, you listen and interact. There's wisdom from the least-articulate communities that should be shared. There's some scholarship within our small towns—and probably also urban America—where those qualities still exist. We need to listen to and learn from them. A world economy like ours can drive destruction, and the quality of life from one community to another should be of concern to all of us.

Our teachers are not just in the classrooms, but they're the grandparents and the aunties and the uncles. Their strengths are conveyed and they can share the full personality. My children's grandfather is a tremendously strong hunter and runner, but he's also very intellectual. My son and daughter can experience long hours with him, almost like an apprenticeship.

I think that without those qualities, you have this real fear of another generation. There's a false confidence in what youth is. When it's gone, never having known someone of an older generation, there's a tremendous loss of identity. You end up asking what is left in life.

We talk a lot about youth, but we really don't listen to their vision. We have some wisdom in our tribe from visionaries who were only twelve or fourteen years old when they found their vision. One in particular said there needs to be a careful balance among the lodges in the universe—the sea creatures, the water creatures, the winged creatures, the human lodge, the rock lodge. We have to observe and listen and be educated by the other lodges. Only by doing that can we survive.

Chief Plenty Coups had that vision at fourteen years old. Tremendous insight there. It's not one of a scientific nature, although it has scientific qualities.

I'm thinking that if we had a better sense of community and family, we could have more listening—authentic listening, listening with integrity. We'd hear the voices that are not empowered by money, but by wisdom and knowledge and a relationship with the Creator. But now it seems that the world is only empowered by the people who have the money to project their wisdom. They may be wise, but they may also be stupid. They may be very, very unwise.

There are several junctures where my work and personal life touch with mainstream, non-Indian society. The environment that surrounds our reservation is a very confrontational one. We have troubles over land, law jurisdiction, limited opportunity, and the finite nature of resources.

We've had trouble over a number of generations, so we carry baggage wherever we go. It's not just me and you meeting, it's my grandma and her great-grandma and so on. Our memories are real sharp and vivid, because the past is as clear as the present—our language brings the past and present tense with it. We're always speculating on how what I am doing today will affect my children. It's a very loaded situation, very tense.

A few years ago I was convinced there was *no* common language in this country. And I'm not sure that there is, but I strive to find ways to bring communication about, especially at those pressure points that really make a difference. It's fine for folks three thousand miles away to be sensitive, but I'm talking about right here at the battle lines. I want some understanding. I want it now, and I want it twenty years from now. How can we engage in those conversations? Where are the corporations who are the real perpetrators? How urgent does the situation have to become?

We tend to be leery of environmentalists because they have their own agenda. Often it's not a sincere interest in Native American agendas. Environmentalists have already benefited from development. We're fifty, sixty years away from the same types of development that happened in neighborhoods of the white folks. They've had incredible advantages. Now they're turning to things that might happen on the reservations. We've never had the benefits of development, which the rest of society has ridden on. There's a class comfort there. Native Americans are doubtful about trusting people who are wealthy. They don't share the same survival experience. They want to conserve somebody else's land, but on the other hand they haven't conserved their own.

It's hard to create something, because what we see of white folks is crazy. But I do think there are qualities in both classes that should be shared— human, spiritual, intellectual qualities. If you don't know rich people, you think they're probably inhuman. But the challenges of the world are so great that we really miss out if we don't have interaction. And we really don't. Our communities are extremely separate, and they're becoming more separate all the time.

It needs to start with visiting. Span the distances between us, begin listening to one another. There are so few forums for people to meet. We need to search those out. It's difficult for people whose values and spiritual commitments are so different. You think you're using the same language, and you really aren't. We have talked for centuries, yet look at how much is diverging.

I try to work at communicating, listening. It starts with my enjoyment of visiting with my family—my children, my mother, my grandmother, my aunts and uncles and cousins. We tell each other stories, we relate things. I don't care a lot for movies or TV. I'd rather go visit.

This goes over into life in general and my profession. That is, communication is really part of our survival. Have we really said anything, have we really listened and gleaned any meaning?

IT MUST BE HEALED:
WALKING IN TWO WORLDS

"It's called healing the hurt," Arvol Looking Horse said of one facet of
the Prophecy of the Mending of the Sacred Hoop. The healers, psy-
chologists, and medical doctors here examine the sources and nature
of the hurt and what is needed for healing. As Betty Cooper attests,
reclaiming one's Native heritage while coping with the larger society
often means learning to walk in two worlds.

Betty Cooper

Walking in Two Worlds

Betty Nell Cooper was born on the Blackfeet reservation in northern Montana in 1938 and was raised among Blackfeet medicine
people. Her grandfather named her for her great-great-grandmother, *Yoo-sqip-a-Tokii*, who lived to be 115. The name means
"Yellow Flower Woman."

Her father worked as a cattleman, hunting guide,
lumberjack, sheepherder, and fisherman. Her mother was born to
Blackfeet parents and had twelve children, of whom Betty was
the sixth.

She experienced government boarding schools as a
child and was sent away to an all-Indian government high school
in Flandreau, South Dakota. She got married the first summer she
came home. In 1963, she and her husband moved to the San
Francisco Bay area with their five children. After they divorced in
1976, she returned to her education, earning a GED and an associate in arts degree in mental health work from Merritt College in
Oakland, with further study at the Armstrong Business School and
the University of Montana, Missoula.

The occupation of Alcatraz Island in 1969 motivated
a return to her Indian heritage. The main focus of her work became
healing substance abuse in the Indian community in Oakland. She
designed and launched the American Indian Family Healing

Center, a live-in program for young Indian mothers and their children. She was director of the center for ten years and became prominent in the Bay Area Indian community.

After thirty-one years in the Bay Area, she has returned home to the Blackfeet reservation in Montana. She is now director of the newly established Pikuni Family Healing Center in Heart Butte.

Lois Crozier-Hogle and Ferne Jensen interviewed Betty Cooper in Oakland.

My grandfather, Joseph Bullshoe, was really respected in the community, and his values have been handed down to me. He was famous for his wonderful racehorses. He and my grandma had a thriving ranch on the Big Badger, which is a beautiful river that runs across the reservation. They had Sunday races with friends and neighbors. The Blackfeet are known for our horses, and there are many legends about how those horses came to us.

We lived on Little Badger River, and all down the river were houses. Right above us was Old Man Good Gun, a medicine man. He loved having children come visit him. His wife, who was called Old Lady Good Gun, always cautioned us not to walk behind him, only to come to the front and speak to his face. I remember the smells—cedar and sage and sweet grass. He never slept on a bed. He had blankets on the floor. He said beds make you lazy, you want to stay in them too much. He had a little mat in front of him, and sometimes that's where he would eat his food. We would come and just stand there while he finished eating. We were in communication with him without ever saying anything.

Further up the river was Old Man Turtle, who was also a medicine man. Many times we were invited, with all the neighbors, to come in and see him do healing ceremonies when people were ill. He would sing and pray and drum over them, and use sweet grass and sweet pine for smudging and blessing the person who was ill.

We also had more fun ceremonies with him. This was in wintertime when there wasn't a lot to do because the snow was deep and it was cold outside. He'd sing, and all us kids would dance. We knew he was a very holy man, a very sacred man. Whatever he invited us to, we were more than happy to come. It was a way of life, and I feel it's what's made me who I am today.

I also remember George and Maggie Badarms. They always fed us. That's where I learned how good berry soup was, and pemmican, and fry bread— we called it grease bread. Maggie taught me about different roots and medicines. We'd all eat together in the early evening in the winter, around their wood heater, and then return to our homes.

They also connected us with what we call feather game dances. There would be sacred singing and prayer ritual, but also a lot of fun for us children. The feather games were a gathering by invitation. There are special songs that are sung, and dancing that goes with it. They are hosted by one member, who cooks the food and prepares the house by clearing the furniture out of one room.

The feather game songs are taught from one member to another. You learn them when you're young, and you carry them with your all your life. The ceremony is real private, so all I can say about it is that it's renewal. It's what has kept our culture together.

There were many, many people. My dad was a hunter, and if he got an elk or deer, he used to get Grandma Choates to come down to cut and dry meat. We used to cook meat right on top of the wood stove, and it really tasted good. And there was Old Lady Red Fox, who walked everywhere. She never wanted to ride in a wagon or a car. If one of us kids was sick or something, my mother would call on these people and they'd come over and doctor us.

I think that was the best place I could ever have been. A lot of it, for a child, is to watch. That's how you learn the sacred things they're doing. You watch and ask questions, and they'll fill you in. But they never tell you the whole story. Each time you learn more. By the time you're an adult, you know what it's about. It doesn't come from books, it is oral tradition that comes from actively listening and participating.

There was a tradition that the grandparents took the first- and sometimes second-born grandchildren and raised them. These were really special kids. The younger ones knew they had a traditional brother or sister who was guardian over the family.

When I was born, my great-grandmother wanted to take me, but my parents wouldn't let me go. I thought if they had, I would've learned so much. But I still have that role in the family. Somehow the traditions got poured into me more than my siblings. I felt so strong that that was where I really needed to be, and I was able to hold onto those values and maintain them in an urban setting. When I go home to Montana, I'll live no differently than I have been here. I'll live the same. Our Blackfeet spirituality and religious practices are an everyday way of life. A person lives the life.

Here in Oakland, we worry about our adolescents picking up too much of other cultures. I say to the Indian kids, "You *do* have elders, you *do* have role models in the community." They can feel in my touch that they are important to me. Like when I teach them the proper way to do things at a dance, the proper way to respect, to hear their parents out. Just being around, they're going to get it, like I got it.

Last year I took eight kids camping. I felt really strongly that these kids were just like putty and this world was shaping them into something that was not going to be Indian. So I talked to them, listened to them, treated them respectfully. And the last night, they just all drew together. They were so thirsty for someone from their own community or their own race to be with them. I told them, "You need to satisfy inside of you your own Indian identity. You need to know who you are as an Indian person. I don't ever want you to be ashamed of yourself."

I told them how I feel so good when I go in a room and see a bunch of Indian babies with their beautiful black hair. I took my adopted grandson out on the dance arena for the first time and whispered in his ear as I was dancing, "Listen to the drum, hear these songs, those are your songs." Even if he doesn't totally remember, he's going to have that bonding with the sound of the drums.

Today, 33 percent of our children who are adopted are placed in non-Indian homes. A lot of them grow up not understanding why they're the only brown kid in the whole school or the whole neighborhood. They pretty much become the pet Indian. Many times they are treated as a novelty or misunderstood or ignored.

In one workshop, I was talking to an Indian teenager who had been adopted. I told him he'd soon be eighteen and he could find out who his mother was and who his relatives are. In the Indian world, all you need to know is one relative, one name. Then one connects one with the other. Anyway, one of the exercises was to hug each other. A lot of Indian women were there, and as he went around in a circle hugging, the more they hugged him, all those years of wanting his Indian mother came out so strong. He began to cry, and the women knew, and they held him more. He said then he knew what was wrong, that he'd missed out on being an Indian. I told him, "You were absent, but not by your own fault. Now you can be in the Indian world because there is always a place for you."

No Indian child was left to grow up without somebody. If there was a death of a parent, then the brother or sister or grandparents took that child and raised it. Now, in an urban area, I tell the kids *we* are your aunts and uncles. You belong with us. We belong with you. You have a place. No one was mistakenly born. You were born because you were a special little spirit meant to be on earth. You have a right to be respected and honored.

When a whole society is not doing that, then you're going to have ills. When an Indian person comes in who suffers from alcoholism, I can see in their eyes that their spirit is gone—even if they're talking real smart talk, even if they've been to college and they're very articulate. They may be able to say words, but they're empty, they're not in touch with themselves. If we can have them sober, which we do here, then we can expose them to their own Indian values. They can search for themselves with support from other Indian people.

Alcohol was never a way of life for us. Indians were taught to drink in a most derogatory way. They knew if they got an Indian drunk, they could take anything from them. You have generations of alcoholism because Indians and liquor just do not get along. It is devastating to the person, the family, and the community.

But if you have Indian values, Indian ceremonies, an Indian way of life, I don't care what has happened to those people, they can turn their life around. I'm not the first person to say this, but what's missing all over the world is respect for the earth and love for one another. It's really, really missing.

We're limited in that we can't bring their tribe to them. If there's someone from their tribal background nearby, we bring them in. But we say, "When you return home, go to the elders and learn." They'll say there are no elders. And I'll say, "That's not true. There are elders, and you need to get in touch with them. They never teach anymore because no one wants to listen. If you're willing to listen, they're willing to teach you."

I feel really strongly about that. We can teach and live Indian culture. At the same time, the reality is that we have to live in today's society. So I talk to them about walking in two worlds—being able to walk proudly as an Indian, and at the same time take the world as it is and use its resources to live a good life. I tell them, "A good life is not one that anyone else chooses for you, but one that you choose for yourself."

You have to be careful not to cross into one culture too strong, though. You can get your Indian identity and develop a lot of hate for what has happened. When I see Indian people who live with hate for the non-Indian world, I try to tell them, "Don't dwell there."

To me, a balanced person can live in both worlds. We can hear a thousand words and only twelve will mean something. That's the way we have to take life. I always try to find out where my clients came from, what kinds of traditions they've been raised with, what they know about their tribe. I try hard to nurture those real tender values. They might zigzag back and forth until they can come to a place where they're able to take both worlds and live in them.

All of us were born in our time. In our ancestors' time they picked wild berries and vegetables and stored them for the coming winter. In my time we planted gardens and had root cellars. But from the time I was a toddler, I was taught respect for the earth and for animals, the four-leggeds. I knew it was the same respect my ancestors had for all animals. They handed down all the stories about having your totem or spiritual being related to an animal. That is a part of your strength.

Now I've taught my children the love of the earth, the love of animals, and how important elders are. In Montana, every part of the year was a special time. So even here in the Bay Area, I tried really hard to show my children that the changing of the seasons was a part of them.

When my son was a teenager, it was almost as if he was a young buffalo caught in the city. I used to send him back to stay with his grandfather on the reservation. Grandma had already passed away, so he had to cook for himself. He came back when he was thirteen and showed how he could make bread on top of the stove. But he also rode horseback and fished and hunted and spent time with his uncles and his grandfather. Today his connection with the earth is so beautiful.

Three of my daughters went to college at Berkeley. I know our young Indian people need education to live in this society, but I worry about how they may get brainwashed. My daughters and my son go through really trying times to learn all these things, but also not to lose themselves.

I tell them that we need to hang on to our culture and we need to know the songs. We need to know all the ceremonies, we need to know all the legends. We need to understand what our ancestors did and how today it's our turn. How do we fit into this world and yet keep our connection with Mother Earth and all living things? No matter what has happened, even if it's been very painful, you have a cultural background that is so strong, it's stronger than anything on earth.

My connection to my home in Montana, to my own people and my own tribe, is really strong. I'm anxious to be returning to them. I inherited some land out in the country through my great-grandparents and grandparents and down through my mother. I plan to build my own home out there.

I also plan to be very much involved in our Blackfeet ceremonies, our medicine ways. I'm going to be working with the Blackfeet elders on the south side of the reservation. They have a very honored and respected position, but I want that to be more active. I have many ideas of how to connect them back into the community. I want the young people to have access to the elders in what we call Councils of Old.

In our Blackfeet culture, the Indian woman has always had a very strong role. The greatest role was we were able to bear children. Indian men pay the greatest respect to Indian women, because we're the givers of life and the nucleus of the family.

Women have a way of, like Charlie Rich says, rolling with the flow. Women are able to pick up and take care of things, despite all odds. They are the minders of the home, the salt of the community. There is a saying: No nation shall fall until the hearts of the women are on the ground. That says it all.

Times have changed so much—Indian men have been far more disempowered than the women. I feel like society as a whole has reached in and torn out the Indian man's spirit. In the past, his role in our Indian society was so strong. I know it can come back through our Indian ways.

I know the answer to the direction we need to go is having ceremony in our lives. We walk the Red Road, we call it, and that's what we need to honor. We were given techniques and ceremonies by our ancestors to take care of the land when something is beyond our control.

Being in touch with the Great Spirit is not just something you do on Sunday, it's not just when you get up in the morning or kneel by your bed at night. It's every moment of your life. You are a part of the Creator, the Creator lives through you and speaks through you. Every day, every hour, everywhere, through all living things.

All mankind travels down the road of life, and we get to the fork in the road and decide which way to go—just like drinking. You know, someone may have had an alcoholic life, and they come to a point where they no longer drink. When they have a period of recovery, they have an awakening, a rebirth. They make the decision to travel the road that is good for them.

I feel that the human race is doing that. We are the creators, the creation. Our body alone is a dimension beyond science. I have really strong faith in mankind. I really feel that there's hope for each of us to be who the Creator intended us to be.

Sarah Hutchison

The Power of Story

Sarah Hutchison is an elder of the Oklahoma Cherokee people. She is an indirect descendant of Sequoya, the great warrior and linguist. Her sixth great-grandmother was the last Chief of War of the Cherokee, and her grandmother walked the Trail of Tears. Stories about Sequoya and other forebears are kept alive and passed down in the family. Every year she returns to Oklahoma to tend the sacred fire watched over by her clan.

Sarah Hutchison was born in Claremore, Oklahoma, in 1920, the second of eight children. Her father was a scholar, teacher, and accomplished athlete before going into politics and serving as county clerk for twenty-eight years.

She attended Oklahoma A&M for her undergraduate degree, received a master's degree in education from the University of Oklahoma, and completed graduate course work in family, marriage, and child counseling. Now retired, she has taught at all levels, including sixteen years at the University of California, Davis.

She also worked as a marriage and family counselor in association with the distinguished psychiatrist Walter Bromberg. The work of Carl Jung made a great impression on her, particularly his interest in American Indians. She has had visions and premonitions all her life.

In traditional fashion, she and her husband "Hutch" (Huell Hutchison) have adopted an Indian child and have taken nineteen children into their home for varying periods of time to support and counsel them. She was interviewed by Darryl Wilson.

I was born in 1920 at my grandmother's home. I weighed thirteen and a half pounds. My father and the doctor thought this was some phenomenon of strength, some sort of blessing. They said, "This is a strong one. She could walk the Trail of Tears."

Dr. Bushyhead's mother and my father's grandmother walked the Trail of Tears in the winter of 1838–1839. They were little girls age eight, and they walked 1,200 miles from Georgia to Oklahoma. The Old Ones told many stories about the Trail of Tears, and I grew up listening to all that history.

The starting point was in Georgia, and the ending point was Indian Territory, now Oklahoma. The soldiers rounded up the Cherokees and drove them with the saber at the end of their rifles. If the people slowed down, they were prodded. Their moccasins wore out and their feet became infected. Along that trail they ate one meal a day and began hammering caskets for the dead at eleven at night. They walked thirty miles a day and lost a quarter to a third of the people, out of a population of more than 16,000.

I grew up on an Indian land allotment my father bought from his brother. We lived in a house my father built. My father was a well-known man by the fact that he was brilliant, friendly, and a great athlete. He knew everybody around. He could cook and sew, like most Indian people can. He made wonderful kinds of foods. He planted the gardens and the fields. He hemmed the diapers when a baby was to be born.

My mom was sent to Carlisle Indian School at age fourteen, and she has all the scars of that experience. She has always been soft-spoken, gentle, kind, and beautiful. I wondered how she could be so beautiful and how she could sing so sweetly. I remember being very curious how she could whistle tunes through her teeth. She never spanked her children and she was never spanked.

The day I started school, my father gave me a lecture. He squatted down, put his hands under my armpits to lift me onto the horse, and said, "You are an Indian, you know. People will say bad things to you, they will try to fight you. But you're as good as any human being who ever drew a breath or ever will. Remember that. And when children at school pick on you about being an Indian, you have to fight them back. If somebody picks on you who is not your size, you tell me and I'll take care of them. There isn't a man on earth who can whip my laziest side—or my strongest side."

As he put me on the horse, I thought to myself, "Gee, now I've got to fight." I didn't have a chance to ask him *how* I was going to fight. Fighting, for us, is negative. But I had to, and I've been fighting ever since.

There are seven clans within the Cherokee Nation. My mother's is the Bird Clan, and my father's is the Wolf Clan. In the Cherokee tribe, we take everything from the mother. The women in the tribe hold a very superior role. I don't quite know how that came about except through the wisdom of both the men and women.

Democracy is an Iroquois idea. It is the foundation of the Constitution of this country. The big mistake, the Iroquois and Cherokee say, is that they left women out. That is so foreign to my own tribe. The women selected and impeached chiefs.

The Keetoowah was the part of the old government that handled religious and moral issues—the laws, penalties, and behavior of the tribe. It is no longer in existence, but there are still a thousand members of the Keetoowah band, made up of Cherokees who are of the higher degree of Indian blood. One of the two Keetoowah organizations in Oklahoma keeps the traditional Indian religion that is held on the dance grounds. I have gone to visit one of these near Vian for many years.

Everything is done in the Cherokee language. We can tell who is familiar with their culture when they line up to eat a meal on the 19th of July—Redbird Smith's birthday.[1] Women get on one side of the table and men get on the other side to put food on their plates. They will drop some tiny speck from everything they take for the Great Spirit. If people do not do those things, we know they don't know their culture.

Fall harvest is on Labor Day weekend. I have been there when eight thousand people have gathered. The traditional chief speaks from a book and there is some talking by medicine men. The book is written in Cherokee, and has in it all the visions the medicine men have had since 1820. It is a wonderful thing. As you leave, William Smith, the traditional chief of the Cherokee, says in a prayer, "When you go through that gate, remember that you are not alone. You are not alone."

Cherokees worship the sacred fire which never goes out. It burns eternally. I am told it has burned for three thousand years. It is a fire sitting on a table of ashes about hip-high. Seven specific kinds of wood are burned. It has a fire-keeper whose duty it is to keep the fire alive. Seven holy men are always around the fire when Cherokees meet there. Under every tree there is a Keetoowah watching the people's behavior. They are identified by the hats they wear. During the time the Indian people are there, no child, adult, or elder shall be in danger. You are to speak almost as if in whispers.

Around the fire is an area where we dance counter-clockwise. It is man, woman, man, woman. We start dancing about ten or eleven o'clock at night, and dance until dawn. I can hear them when I close my eyes . . . it is wonderful music. The dancers look almost unreal—like they are going somewhere, they are traveling. It is the rhythm and the song, and once in a while an elder will play a little drum very lightly as the people dance and the men sing. You go away from there filled, spiritually filled, ready for a good, hard year.

The Cherokee philosophy includes the purpose of all life—plants, and animals, and the earth. We have two mothers, the earth and our biological mother. We feel we have an umbilical cord attached to the earth. We Cherokees believe that we are here to protect the earth and all life upon it.

In my tribal life, the meaning of the Great Spirit is the prime element of reality. It is real to me. This reality consists of the relationships between the earth, the sun, the moon, and the stars and planets, which profoundly affect all of life from the least to the most complex forms.

This explanation I am giving is a shortcut from naming all the animals and all the microscopic creatures that slither and swim in the creeks and the rivers and the ocean. This, what I am telling you, is the "stuff" of my Cherokee prayers. I pray for many things, things the overculture may never pray for. I always have and I always will. That is my reality, and I feel it is the Great Spirit's wish.

I pass this on to my children by doing. Just the other day I showed Yuma, my five-year-old grandson, how the gourd plants have feeling. I can hold a pencil to a tendril, and in five minutes it will wind around the pencil. He watched and put his little hands out and cried, "Oh, grandma! Oh, grandma!"

These plants will shudder. If I touch them early in the morning they will shudder. They shudder when they are in danger and when they are excited. They know us and respond to us. One night a woman who was mad at her children was sitting here. She was waving her arms around, and the plants began to get excited. There was one that would move simultaneously with her hands. All you have to do is watch them.

Later, Yuma and I pulled up a potato plant that had started late. It had a few small potatoes on it. I gathered them and put them in a pot of water, instructing Yuma all the while. Then we ate them.

So it is by doing.

Indians speak in metaphor. Metaphor is gentle and indirect. The therapist can tell stories that the client will go away thinking about because of the tone of the voice. The method in which a story is told opens up the un-conscious, which is more knowledgeable than the conscious mind. It is profound!

Everybody raises, at times, a resistance. The stories are an indirect reference to their problem. People will listen to something else before they will listen to something about themselves. You see, actions and responses are what all plant, animal, and human life is about. To some people I say, "I don't know if I can help you, but I will try." That creates a response in them.

If they've had bad experiences, a good way to help them is to get into the unconscious mind. Hypnosis is used professionally today, but Indians have always used it. Medicine men used this all the time. There are other kinds of healing, too, like energy. That is wonderful stuff. Put your hands out—they tingle with energy from the earth. If you don't believe it, do this. [She makes a c with her pointing fingers and thumbs, moving the open part back and forth.] Just play with that for a while. The good energy that comes from you is a gift. I know Indian people who can heal someone by sitting across the room from them.

I helped a doctor with a young woman who was very ill by saying, "If you can get her to plant a seed and watch it grow, you will make progress, because she will develop a relationship with that plant." Or if a person is very ill, say with cancer, and has no plants, they can look out a window and watch a pigeon come and go, bringing food to her baby. They can develop a relationship with the bird. I have talked with people who say that was the beginning of healing them.

The earth heals, plants heal—if we let them. They know. They are here for healing. But I don't know if other cultures can develop that idea and attitude.

Many of our own people have learned self-hate. What happens when you put any group of people where they have no control over their lives? They do not feel part of the power, or their power is very negative and they mistreat the earth. Some of them are so negative it is very difficult to do much for them except to speak in metaphor and lower the tone of the voice. Speak softly. You have seen medicine men like that. Sometimes they say almost nothing, and they heal.

It is in the belief system. Many people have no belief system, and they react negatively to everything and everyone. I've had students in my classes who would frighten every plant in my yard. The problem is that no one respected them from the beginning. So they have no respect for themselves, for others, or for the earth. Then the self-hate of the Native American is extended from one Indian to another.

One of the things Indians can do is to recognize and give compliments to one another. You have to be careful about compliments, though, because Indians haven't had very many of them—even from their own families.

The damage can be healed, but you know, it is not a simple matter. The way you get to that is by opening up the unconscious mind. It is a strength. It has more information than the conscious mind. Everyone has an unconscious mind and everyone dreams, but few cultures cultivate that.

Making the earth better starts by being responsible: recycling, organizing a household. The ability to respond—that's what responsibility is. The initiative to organize a household. It can go by a simple little story. We all have great magic.

Today I watched some neighbors come and go by my house. They drove down the road, then they came back to get something. I watched them search madly for keys. They can't find anything. They don't know where things are and they are in a hurry to get on to someplace else.

Why didn't they do some thinking? If they sat down and organized the household, they'd be on top of the situation. If they organized their purse, that would help. They are being good to themselves then. It takes a very small amount of energy to put a glass in one place. It takes very little to sort things. But people are impatient. They want instant happiness, instant service—and they don't seem to care if the earth is instantly destroyed.

Organizing a household is one of the hardest things. If it's organized, you give a place to everything, a "magic place." If you put it back in its magic place every time, you will always know where it is. Magic is very simply stated but you don't have to state it. To use the word is to make magic.

You can have a signal for magic. Raise a finger. Then it goes unspoken. People don't want to be told what to do, even if it is good for them. Tell stories. If you say in a low voice, "I knew a guy who had magic . . ." If you tell it not *to* the person but in their presence, it reaches their unconscious mind.

It gets into structures of families. There are families who can best be described as having a rubber fence. You can bend it, move it, flatten, stretch it, do anything to it. In those kinds of families you will find incest, abuse, all kinds of things. There are no rules.

In a family where there is structure, there is a code of behavior. What the family does becomes ceremony. It has a purpose which benefits all family members. In these families you will find happiness.

I am proud of my behavior. I am living like I ought to. I don't want more, but I am conservative with what I have. I don't want a big car, I want one that runs. I don't want a big house, I want one that's clean. I like to get the dishes done and put things back in their place—be organized every day. That is the way I think the world ought to be.

I have not given up and I have not run away. I stood my ground, and I have fought for the Indians and for other citizens. When my dad put his hands under my arms and said, "You are as good as anybody and you have to fight back," that was hard to hear. But at age five I started doing it. And I am well practiced by now.

Honesty is a great word. Stealing land is not honest. With the loss of land, the umbilical cord gets severed for many Indian people and we have to run. There are great groups of Indians who live in the medians between the oncoming and ongoing lanes of the freeway. They are usually full-bloods. They have their own system of how to get food, how to get procurements. I am so ashamed of our country because it so often tells other countries what to do while doing nothing for our people.

We never believed we owned the land. It is here for us to use. We must treat it as we treat ourselves—be good to it. That concept is very different from the power of money.

It seems simple to me to see that the earth is in trouble. I have visited Indian senior citizens in homes and hospitals standing by a window weeping as they looked out at bulldozers ripping holes in Mother Earth. I have felt their warm tears on my face, and I have cried with them. It is a difficult thing for Indians to accept. It makes us feel bad because we are of the earth. It is our mother. It is our everything.

I've been told by some white people, "I die and go on; it's none of my business." They are irresponsible. They don't know how to be at peace with the earth. They can't get into their unconscious—and with some, it would not be advisable to open it up.

I don't know if the earth can be saved. But we must keep trying. We might not make it, but we are not Indian unless we try.

There is a mockingbird who lived here before he molted. He sang like a computer printout—perfectly re-created sound. I knew one that made the sound of a rotating sprinkler. I went out many times in the night to turn it off—and it wasn't on. The mockingbird had learned its sound.

There are so many things we can learn about the earth, about the world. How can people not love nature and earth? How can they not see it?

Note

1. A traditionalist and member of the Keetoowah, Redbird Smith led opposition to the Dawes Act in Oklahoma in the early part of the twentieth century. He fought to preserve tribal unity and identity in the face of the allotment process, which carved up tribal lands into individual holdings and severely reduced the amount of land held in common by the tribe, ultimately leading to the loss of vast amounts of land.

Terry Tafoya

At the Center of the Dance

Terry Tafoya is a psychotherapist and healer. His father's family is originally from Taos Pueblo, New Mexico, where he was born in 1952. His mother's people are from Warm Springs in central Oregon and speak the Sahaptin language.

He carries several Indian names. His Taos name Chiu'u translates as "Child of the Eagle." In Sahaptin, his name Xaiyama-yai Aswan refers to the concept and spirit of the golden eagle. In his grandmother's Salish language, his name Chut means "Brother of Life." The Warm Springs elders chose for him the name L'aos, from one of the last Columbia River Indian prophets.

Terry Tafoya was put into a manual-training high school in Oklahoma City but after high school pursued the study of psychology and English at the University of South Florida. He earned master's degrees in both education and journalism at the Institute of Indian Studies at the University of Washington. From 1975 to 1977 he was area director of the Indian Head Start programs for Alaska, Oregon, Nevada, and Utah.

He returned to school to earn his doctorate in psychology from the University of Washington. He became professor of psychology at Evergreen State College in Olympia and also served on the clinical faculty in family therapy at the University of Washington Medical School. In the late 1980s he was director of training for the National Native American AIDS Prevention Center.

Dr. Tafoya is now executive director of Tamanawit Unlimited, a Seattle-based international consulting firm. He serves on several national boards dealing with Indian health issues.

He was interviewed by Lois Crozier-Hogle and Ferne Jensen, with additional material from Giuseppe Saitta.

I can't think of anybody in my family who is not concerned about the community. It's a general assumption that this is our obligation, this is our responsibility, and we don't hesitate to do it. I remember my mom telling stories about our grandfather taking trunks of Indian clothes to pow wows so that if someone wanted to dance and didn't have an outfit, he would dress them.

I have so much respect for the family I come from. I love them very dearly. On my mother's side, I belong to the *katnim*—"longhouse"—at the Warm Springs agency. The spiritual tradition from that area is called the "seven drums" because they use seven drums as part of the ceremony. In Sahaptin, the language of the Warm Springs people, there's really no word for religion. When they have to talk about it they'll use the word *washat*, which means "dance."

It's a nice way of thinking about it, in the sense that to dance you need so many different elements. You need the music, the drums, the singing, the people, the dancing, a place to do it. It's how all these things dance together. When you live your life correctly, it really is a dance, a giving back and forth, where other people are intimately involved by the singing, the drumming, and the music.

In Sahaptin there's a word, *tamanawit*, which means "the path," or "the way." It's about how you progress on a certain pathway—a path of balance and harmony. The dance keeps its motion going. That's how I think about it. It's not just me, it's how we're all moving together.

So many of these terms are like a floor with no ceiling. You have a foundation of understanding them, but there's no ceiling in terms of what they mean.

A lot of the work I do in terms of therapy is using stories, and ceremonies or rituals when it's appropriate. It's not just my telling a story, but in doing so, giving people permission to tell their own story and to look at their own heritage and traditions, which they may not even realize are traditions. Sometimes people get so caught up in the beadwork and feathers that they don't understand that the everyday living is the culture.

In our tradition, every time you take a sip of water it's a religious act, because it's a form of purification. It's not big and fancy, but it still has the same spiritual meaning: to make those small everyday occasions of life into sacred ones.

Every time we tell a story it's a ceremony. In English, we translate it that when you tell a story you "wet it with your breath." You give it life, just as when you give water to a seed it blossoms.

A few years ago I did a presentation on Indian legends for the Oregon Indian Education Association. In our tradition, we don't tell legends during the summertime. You're only supposed to tell them between the time the frost is on the ground and the spring, which is when the thunderstorms start or the frogs start to sing.

The conference was in August, and I was in an awkward position. Three elders from Warm Springs walked in, whom I hadn't been expecting. So I said, "Before I start I want to publicly apologize to you, because I was raised to know this is not the right time to tell stories. But I want you to know why I choose to tell them. I use these stories in the healing process with patients at the hospitals, and with children. When I tell these stories and it's not the right time of the year, I get sick. This is the price I pay. When the world was in balance, all the taboos and traditions were set. What's happened is that the world is out of balance. It may be necessary to break some of the taboos in order to go forward to the other side and tip the world back into a balance. So I'm going to go ahead and tell these stories."

One of the elders, Alice Florindo, got up and said, "Nobody move." She passed paper money to all the people and said, "I pay off this boy's shame so that he'll be able to tell stories whenever he chooses." Since then, I've never been sick after telling the stories out of season.

What she did was a very traditional thing, what we call a "giveaway." She made a public ceremony of announcing that she approved of what I was doing. Later she came back and made me a Coyote doll, because a lot of the stories we tell are about Coyote. He was dressed in a traditional Wasco-style Indian outfit. She even put a small obsidian arrowhead in the little quiver on the back of his neck. It was one of the greatest honors I've ever received.

It's estimated that within two generations of white contact, up to 90 percent of the Native people died because there was no acquired immunity against European diseases. So, many generations of Native people have had to learn to deal with multiple-loss issues.

Western societies in general do not have the mechanism to deal with these bereavement issues. People may come to some of our workshops because they've lost someone to AIDS, but they also have unresolved grief losses over a grandparent or sibling or parent. It's as though we'll peel off those layers and the deeper levels come out.

It's interesting to think about the term "healing," even within the context of Western society. The Old English word "heal" is related to the word "whole," which is in itself related to the word "holy" or "sacred." In that sense, if we work with a disease like AIDS — or alcohol addiction for that matter—where there's really no cure at the present time, there can still be a healing.

A lot of times we're trained in a professional capacity not to discuss those things because it's not scientific, but I think that's what real healing is all about: healing of the heart. The hand may be involved, but the heart is definitely there.

Even though we might not be able to remove the symptoms, we can restore that sense of connectedness, in the four directions and on many different levels. And it's not just the person who's dying, it's also part of the family, the loved ones, the support system, that's dying. There needs to be a connectedness there, so that when you lose somebody it's not a sense of complete loss, but how it reverberates back within the circular system within that family, whether it's a family of the heart or of blood. Even when you lose someone, the circle may be expanded.

There's also a sense of moving through cycles. This has sustained a lot of Native people in dealing with multiple-loss issues of whatever nature. A sense that, just as you can watch the seasons turn around, there are losses that we all go through. There is also growth we all go through, reclaiming a sense of maturity, so that when death comes, it's not seen as the enemy.

I taught at a medical school for many years, and the idea is that you attempt to slay death. Chief Seattle said there is no death, only a change of worlds. You may lose that person, but you gain them on a different level.

Those are messages that a lot of non-Native people, or even Native people, don't always hear from their churches or hospitals or schools. A lot of times people aren't aware of the stories, the legends, the history, the ceremonies, the rituals that relate to that sense of community and wholeness.

One of our psychiatrists once asked me how I defined sickness. The image that came to mind was that of a spider web. If you're in healthy relationships, again it's like a dance, or it's like being in the center of a spider web.

A lot of the beaded medallions the old people give you are a circle. They'll tell you the center represents you. All around you are the other beads of connectedness—to other people, to air, water, and healing. If you look closely, you can see the pattern of connectedness. The more you back away from it, the more it resolves itself into a very complex pattern.

It may be that only the Creator can see the total complexity of how the patterns interact together. But it gives you that sense of your existence forming a very complex pattern, a web of existence. When you become ill, depressed or alienated, it's like a scissors has snipped off a strand of that web. You literally have to heal all alone.

A Rilke poem says, "I was an orphan and I was crying out so loud I didn't hear the stars and mountain call my name." That's such a powerful image to me. So many people don't feel connected any more. A lot of tribes—the Lakota, for example—will talk "to all my relations" to incorporate the idea that I'm not only speaking to my own people, but I'm consciously choosing to address the four-footed creatures and the ones that crawl, fly, and swim.

This is what we're taught in our tradition—you always have to be careful because everything you do causes this ripple that goes out in all directions, to the furthest star. If a spider web wiggles in one place, the ripples go throughout the entire web.

There's a time in Taos when you're not permitted to disturb the land because the earth is seen as being pregnant. You have to wear moccasins or shoes without heels. If you have boots, you knock the heels off the boots so you don't scrape the earth.

My friend Barre Toelken, the anthropologist, asked a man on the reservation, "Do you really believe that if I were to scrape my foot against the earth it would interfere with the growing of things?" The answer was, "Maybe it would, maybe it wouldn't. But knowing how we feel about such things, if you then chose to scrape the earth, it would show what kind of person you are."

When children are reared in the traditional way, this is so much a part of what they're taught. The world notices you, the spirits notice you, the Creator notices you, you're treasured. You're never alone. There's always some kind of comfort around you.

In Taos and Warm Springs, these traditions are still very much part of the living. At a certain point, every tradition is a new tradition. The oldest song was once sung for the first time. So never be afraid of creating new traditions or trying to create new songs. If they have power, then they will live on and become your new traditions. If they're not, they'll be washed away and they won't last.

There are things that some communities are willing to share with others, and some things they are not. I think the most important thing to share is the ability to see through different kinds of eyes. To be able to borrow other people's eyes, to see to learn and learn to see.

In the Christian theology, there's the idea that Christ is a pearl. No matter how you turn a pearl, it's exactly the same from any direction. A lot of Western science comes from the idea that if you try hard enough, you will discover that objective truth. It means this is the *only* way you can see, and any other way of seeing is flawed.

For a lot of Native American people, there's the idea of understanding life as a crystal. A crystal of quartz has different facets. Every time you turn it you discover a new facet. But one is not more valid than another. The crystal tapers to a single point, so while the facets may be separated in terms of understanding on one level, on another level they join together.

In Native American teaching you'll hear the idea of harmony. Not balance, but harmony. This is an important distinction. Harmony exists as a function of difference. If everything is the same, you don't have harmony, you have monotony. Harmony is different notes being played together— not in sequence, but simultaneously.

In our teaching, the spiritual traditions are differences that blend together. Imagine moving from close up, where you see your one little bead touching just a few others, to a great distance, where you can see that all those beads merge into one complex pattern. I think that's what harmony is all about.

A lot of our teachings contain the idea of transformation. In the Salish language of my grandmother, the one who changes things was called the *Dukwibał*, which would translate as "transformer" or "changer." This concept is what we talked about with Coyote, who changed the world to make it the way it is now.

That's the message I want to leave: the potential to change. It doesn't have to be the way it is now; it can be different. Some people try so hard to stay the same. I see many patients who are fixated with the idea that this is the only choice they have. That has never been part of the traditional teachings.

This is a wonderful time to be alive. It's also a very frightening time. What excites me the most is seeing potentiality. I see people stopping and asking if there's another way. Prior to this time, the model had been for outsiders like professors, administrators, and funding agencies to say, "This is the right way and we are distributing it."

So the reclaiming of heritage and tradition that's happening now is very exciting to me—not just for Indian people, but for all people. Up until this generation, there was a powerful message that the only way you could be a good *whatever* was to give up anything that's really you. Now there's finally an acceptance that you don't have to give up those things to be confident or skillful.

The kind of either/or thinking that says you can *either* be a good human being *or* a good whatever is incredibly dangerous because you get into seeing other people as the enemy. You can poison land with radioactive material because it's in the *other* place. If you see the whole world as being *your* body, then you don't put poison in the back of your neck.

In terms of what we can teach each other, the issue for me is that Indian people don't come empty-handed. And the message to white people is that they don't come empty-handed either. Eventually you have to go back to your own roots—I can't really teach you to be an Indian. White people have a certain way of thinking or seeing the world that's very powerful, as long as it's understood not to be the *only* way. It's one more note to be sung.

A lot of people are fearful when we talk about traditions being revived, created, celebrated. My family has been called, in a derogatory way, "blanket Indians." But we've worked hard to maintain the traditions of responsibility and obligation. People might think that means doing everything the way it was done before white contact, but that's never really been our teaching.

Times change. The elements continue forward. You take foundations of understanding and apply them to new situations. Now you see people doing beautiful work in silver using the traditional designs that were done in pottery. The design continues, but the medium has changed.

Traditionally, the way to make pottery strong is to take old pottery that's already been fired. The firing of pottery creates a crystalline structure. If you only use new clay to make a pot, the pot is not very strong. So what you do is take old broken pottery, grind it up into powder, and mix it with the virgin clay. The tiny crystalline particles of the old pottery strengthen the structure of the new pot. The resulting pot is much stronger.

Traditions are like that. We don't necessarily use the same vessel, but we take elements or components of that vessel and incorporate them and make the new one stronger. If we just start with virgin clay, it will never be as strong as the old.

My hope for Native Americans would be to be of one heart, though not necessarily of one mind. We need to see ourselves as part of a larger dance. In addition to being tribal people, we are also Native Americans, with relatives not only in the United States, but all over the world. That's a much wider dance.

In our language there's a term for people who are interpreters. It's translated as "echo." That's how I think of myself. When I talk about my grandmother, I think of old people who would say these things or use a certain phrase or image when they sang. That's the most exciting part of what I do—being an echo to the old people, many of whom have gone on.

It's nice to see the web expanding and moving out in many different directions. I'm an echo for the teachings provided by my grandparents, all my family, and the old people in my community—all the stories they shared, the songs, the dances. I don't think of these as things I own. I'm just an echo.

Kevin Foley

These Things Are Absolutely Essential

Dr. Kevin Foley (Rappahannock) is a clinical psychologist. He is director of the Leo Camp Alcohol Program at the Sacramento Urban Indian Health Project.

He earned his Ph.D. in clinical psychology from Sierra University in 1988. Working under the direction of Dr. Royal Alsup, Foley and a group of scholars forged new approaches to Native American psychology. He did his research on the healing effects of the Native American sweat lodge.

His research and practice have focused on validating Native culture and values. His interest in psychology began when he was working for the Hupa tribe's Johnson-O'Malley program, where he had a growing sense that the problems of Indian children in school flowed from their being subjected to a non-Indian system.

Kevin Foley is married to Kathy Morsea, M.D., with whom he shares many ideas about healing and spiritual development.

He was interviewed by Darryl Wilson, with additional material from Jay Leibold.

The Native people of this hemisphere have a totally different way than Europeans of perceiving reality and relating to people and nature. The way I see the clash is that the two peoples were not able to relate to each other. Columbus met people he could not understand. His cognitive thinking and reductionism were not capable of relating to the red race, whose wisdom comes through the heart.

He came with a European manner of thinking—looking at the land, seeing something that is unique, and seeking to obtain it as a possession. This is adverse to Native American thought. With Indian people there is interdependence and interbeing with everything in the universe. If an Indian person finds something precious, it is accepted as it is, rather than seeking more of it.

European values do not have an aspect of interbeing and interdependence. It's an alienated, isolation-type of thinking. If I don't see that I am a part of a rock or a tree, or a part of Mother Earth, I can objectify it and make it separate from me. In a sense, I can cut it out of me. I can control it, manipulate it, deplete it.

When an Indian person sees a buffalo or a salmon or a tree, he senses they and other aspects of the Creator's creation are a part of him. As a Native person, if I destroy a tree, I know I am destroying a part of myself.

Seeking more and more for oneself is a sign of pathology for Indian people. Indian people seek harmony and balance to keep healthy—balance within themselves, balance within the universe, balance with other people.

An Indian person may receive warnings or signs in their lives that tell them when they are out of balance. A warning could be on the body level as far as an illness or injury, or it could be on a spiritual, synchronistic level. A warning received through the body could be as subtle as getting a cold. A spiritual warning could be some event, such as a bird, or an animal in the house. This is viewed as being more than just a coincidence to the person.

It's difficult for Indian people to understand alienation as a part of a worldview. For us, the Western type of thinking is so foreign it would involve a painful psychological process to adopt it. This is where we get into a clash today.

One place where this clash happens is in our schools. I met one Native child who told me about an incident in his social studies class. He told the teacher that his People did not come across from the Bering Straits. He said, "We came to this world through a hole in the ground. This is the fourth world, and we have been here for millions of years." The teacher said, "How could people come out of the earth? There is no evidence of that. This is the reason why you Indians never get off the reservation, because you don't look at the facts."

It was evident that the teacher had a different value system than the child. The child was able to clearly state the origins and point of view of his culture, yet the teacher denied this child his worldview and insulted his people. The teacher was being destructive to the child's psychological well-being. This is a form of racism. We are seeing it today throughout the California school system.

Indian students have a difficult time in schools where individualism is valued over cooperation, where students have to raise their hands quickly with the answers and work independently, without sharing. Those are the values that get rewarded in the school system, and many Indians aren't comfortable with that. Often Indian children get ignored or pushed out of the school system. If some speak up against the abuse, they are punished.

Indians are living in two worlds, and for them to keep their values and live in the white world has been very difficult. It's difficult for Indian people to assimilate by working for themselves, for promotions, for money. A lot of these things still go against the values of Indian people.

A ritual can be a very simple task, such as placing tobacco on a rock or getting up in the morning and greeting the sun. What this does for the person is to acknowledge the unseen or supernatural aspects of the universe and humanity.

Ceremony is a specific activity or experience that is set up by the community for the community. It has a positive, healing effect upon the people. It is set up to assist the community through various developmental stages, or to assist the individual through different stages—such as harvest ceremonies for giving thanks, or ceremonies for initiation into man or womanhood.

These things are absolutely essential for Native people to continue, as essential as it is for white persons to go to college.

A good metaphor for what these rituals and ceremonies do is that they charge the battery. A Native person is taught that life has its ups and downs. Life puts stress on them. Everyone gets depressed, and everyone gets inflated at some time during their life.

Every Native person realizes that the goal for him or her is to seek balance, harmony, and peace. Every time a person steps out the door, they will go through some situation that may cause them to get out of balance, to feel out of tune with their internal values. Ritual allows them to experience the transpersonal and to get outside their usual egocentrism. It recharges their spirit and their hope for life.

Ceremony is something that helps people get in touch with the archetypal aspects within themselves. Archetypes are like seeds in the psyche of the individual. They are represented by characters in myths, legends, and dreams. They are analogous to genes, which are biological. Genes help a person to develop into his or her biological potential. Archetypes help the Indian person develop into their psychological potential.

In working with an individual, doing psychotherapy, I have to be aware of that person's tribal symbolism in order to help lead them toward the path of wholeness and healthiness. I need to know the symbol system, the legends and mythologies for a particular person. Of course, some symbols and archetypes are similar for all tribes. Something like the trickster is universal for American Indians, as is the Wise Old Man or Wise Old Woman.

There's also what Jung describes as the personal unconscious. A person will have symbols and archetypes that are personal to them. In a sense I help the person develop their own dream dictionary so that they can amplify their symbols and use them in their experience.

For instance, I met with an Indian teenager in juvenile hall who told me that he was very angry. His family was going through a divorce and he didn't realize how angry he was. A medicine person told him that he was running with smoke instead of walking with his two feet. He then got mad at the medicine man. He told his family that the medicine man didn't know what he was talking about.

Two days after that the boy was picked up by the police and put in juvenile hall. As he was lying on his bed with a lot of time on his hands, he finally realized that the medicine man was right. So he started praying and thinking about things he could do to change his life.

This case is unique in that this Indian boy really understood spirituality. The things that the medicine man told him connected to his unconscious. Even though he didn't agree with him at the time, they explained his worldview to him, and explained how he needed to treat himself with respect. Running with smoke for feet was how the medicine person described his condition. Smoke can be interpreted as smoke before the fire, or smoke of anger, or smoke of darkness. This young man was not in balance, he was not grounded to the earth and standing on his own two feet. He was in a cloud of depression, not realizing that he was taking his emotions everywhere he went and acting out of them rather than being in touch with his foundation.

Where a medicine person understands the psyche of an Indian person, they are able to give the person the type of treatment that they need. If a white counselor was to talk to that Indian boy and confront him on his anger, or tell him in a way that would be appropriate for a white boy, it would not have worked.

Ritual and ceremony are part of my practice on several levels. I encourage people to do their own personal rituals. I refer individuals and families to medicine people. And I inform people about local ceremonies and rituals, such as the Bear Dance or the Big Time. I encourage clients to participate in sweat-lodge ceremonies. In our clinic we have a youth crime-prevention component that has built and sponsored a sweat-lodge ceremony and has recruited an individual to come in and do the ceremonies. That has been a real benefit.

The other part I haven't touched on is that in this development we are going through, we as doctors and counselors also have to take care of ourselves in those spiritual ways. We can't be hypocritical and say, "We're recommending that you be more holistic about your healing and seek sweat lodges or sun dance or fasting" unless we know and practice it ourselves.

That's a common bond between Kathy [Dr. Morsea] and myself. We both have our own spiritual development. It enables us to do better work in psychology and medicine. We have to be conscious and aware of our own growth and work on our own dreams. We go to sweat-lodge ceremonies. We're preparing our sons for their own manhood ceremony.

We have to create our own way. That's essential. My training taught me that growth and development must occur along academic lines, personal lines, and professional lines. All three go together to build a firm foundation of who I am in the profession of psychology.

I see this as a very exciting time for Native people because we are, in a sense, healing the damage from the holocaust that has occurred throughout the past five hundred years. There is a lot to be healed, and these ceremonies and rituals and ways of being for our people are the ways we know can heal us. My job is to strengthen our people and allow them the resources legally and psychologically to continue the rituals and the ceremonies. In this way we can continue upon the healing path.

I came from a Ph.D. program that was unique in that it was developed for Indians. We had a lot of autonomy. We realized that there was a need for degreed Indian people to fill the positions that were becoming available in the mental-health profession. The school allowed us to develop our degrees in a way that would validate our culture and at the same time meet the state's requirements for licensing.

We were fully aware that we were pioneers in this area. We wrote about American Indian psychology by looking at those theories and concepts that helped to validate the Indian values and worldview. We borrowed concepts from Jungian and humanistic existential psychology, but the research we did was all brand new.

We have to borrow terms from other theories of psychology to explain American Indian psychology to the dominant society. But when we are in the room with an Indian person, we don't have to use terms that are intellectual. We talk more on the everyday level as far as what's happening with the person and having them come up with the insights and answers for themselves.

I am an optimist. I believe, as Martin Luther King did, we should "think globally and act locally." I act locally trying to heal the damage that has been done to my people and to the earth. In global terms, I believe that the American school system has to be changed by adopting a truly pluralistic system that acknowledges and validates all people of color—rather than continuing a system that is exclusively based on Euro-American values. The biggest problem that I see is that Indian people are still suffering from racism—although it is a lot more subtle these days—through schools and institutions, the legal system, and economics.

The last thing that I want to say is about validating the rituals and ceremonies of Native people. I am not talking about motivating non-Native people to mimic our ceremonies and traditions. That would not be helpful for them. People with roots in Europe have ceremonies and rituals that have been suppressed. I want to encourage these individuals to give life to those ways.

By validating the Native worldview, it is my hope to bring about peace and justice for Indian people and for all people of America. Bringing love and compassion into the American system is the only cure for the problems of today. Our major objective is to bring relationship back into all people's lives. We must have a healing of communities, a healing of Native people and, ultimately, a healing of the whole world.

Kathy Morsea

Running toward the Rising Sun

Dr. Kathy Morsea's heritage is Navajo on her mother's side and Ojibwa, Sioux, and white on her father's side. She is the mother of two children, and with her husband, Kevin Foley, participates in sweat-lodge ceremonies and California Indian dances.

Her focus has been on health care and health problems special to Native Americans. In particular, she has been studying the high incidence of diabetes. She hopes to practice family medicine and perhaps run a clinic on the Navajo reservation someday, where she would like to combine traditional forms of healing with conventional allopathic medicine.

Dr. Morsea received her M.D. in 1993 from the University of California, Davis, and will complete her residency in family practice in 1996. Before that, she earned a B.S. in environmental toxicology. In July of 1995 she was appointed medical director of Clinica Tepati, which delivers culturally sensitive primary care to the Latino community of Sacramento.

She was interviewed by Darryl Wilson, with additional material from Jay Leibold.

I am Diné, which most people know as Navajo. We inherit our clanship from our mothers and are "born for" our fathers. So I am *Tła'chi'nii*, or Red Running into the Water, born for *biligaana*, Ojibwa, and Sioux. My mother was born in Crystal, New Mexico, and sent at an early age to the Sherman Institute. She met my father there. They stayed in southern California, and that's where I was born.

I was born near the Sherman Institute. I remember how it reminded me of a prison when I was a child. It's now accredited as a high school, and it's a more attractive place to go.

My mother had a very traditional upbringing on the Navajo reservation. She learned to pray in the traditional manner, and Navajo was her first language. Boarding school conditioned a lot of it out of her, but not completely. She would tell me stories about how she had been healed by medicine people, and a lot about my culture.

I speak a little bit of my own language, what my mother taught me and what I have learned on my own. My mother didn't teach us much Navajo because she felt it was a disadvantage for her in school. After I grew up, I learned that kids in her day were punished at schools for speaking their own language. My mother was unable to talk about that.

I became very interested in science. I did well in school as a child, and that love of the scientific approach made me really question the things my mother was telling me. It's been through life experience and observation that I understand now what she was telling me was real. I've learned to believe in traditional healing and spirituality. I've had to redefine the whole thing for myself, to balance the scientific with the spiritual.

My mother was very happy about my going to medical school, very proud of me. My parents had high expectations. They weren't very well educated, but living off of the reservation, one of the benefits they thought their children would have was an education.

I see myself as an Indian woman who has both a spiritual side and an intellectual side, who values Indian ideas and traditions, and who values traditional Indian healing as well as allopathic medicine. I also need to keep myself balanced in order to adequately care for my patients. In other words, I need to be able to heal myself before I can heal others.

I believe I have a special dimension to add to the medical profession. It's derived from my Indian heritage and my life experiences as an Indian woman. I believe I can do my job well within the white-male dominated world, even though there are those who might not see me as equal to themselves.

I will definitely be working with a Native population when I finish my residency, but I don't believe it's necessary to go to a rural area to serve Indian people. Urban Indians have the same kinds of problems as reservation Indians in terms of poverty, hunger, increased rates of disease, and alcoholism. Relocating Indians from the reservation to the big cities, as the government tried so hard to do, did not solve the "Indian problem." Sadder still, urban Indians may have a harder time obtaining adequate health care, especially surgery and specialty care, because they don't live on a reservation.

I chose family practice because I like the idea of caring for a whole family, or at least people of all ages. It is also more holistic than other specialties.

I think that so often in various kinds of training like the medical field, there's a standard of "normal" held up, which is usually a white male. Everybody else is measured against it, and minority professionals must be careful not to get caught up in that. Once a resident in my program asked my attending physician, knowing that she had worked on the Navajo reservation, "How does drinking among Indians compare to normal people?" I said, "Excuse me, *normal?*"

There are a lot of physical differences between American Indians and the non-Indian population. Some of them have contributed to the higher incidence of many diseases that you see among us. I believe we can overcome these differences, though. To do this, we must incorporate as many of the old ways as possible into our modern lives. In particular, we must become more physically active and as closely as possible eat the way our ancestors did. But I don't mean fry bread—a Native American diet was actually very low in fat, and tremendously varied.

One of my professional interests is diabetes among Native Americans. About sixty years ago it was practically unheard of among Indians, and the medical community once thought that Indians were immune to diabetes. This is no longer true. Indians now have the highest incidence and prevalence of diabetes. In my tribe alone, the prevalence has doubled in the past ten years. Traditional allopathic thinking has it that diabetes occurs in those who are over thirty-five years old, obese, and have a family history of diabetes. But Indians have broken all the rules. For one thing, you can't explain going from practically zero incidence to the highest incidence and prevalence by genetics. And now young Indians, even adolescents and thin Indians, are getting it.

There is indirect evidence that our bodies regulate blood sugar differently than non-Indians, possibly because we are adapted to a high-protein diet. This causes our blood sugar to rise much higher than white people's when we eat carbohydrates. I want to emphasize that this is not abnormal. This is normal for us, and I am sure it was an advantage that helped us survive long ago. Fortunately, the rise in blood sugar can be attenuated by consuming a little protein before the carbohydrate. Also, it appears that rigorous physical activity during the adolescent years offers a protection against developing diabetes later in life. This latter evidence comes from studies of Native cultures in transition from the traditional to the white man's way of life up in Canada.

In my tribe, the Diné, the young people were admonished to get up with the crack of dawn. It was said, "Don't let the sun overtake you." You had to air out your bedding and run in the direction of the sun as far as you could, and then turn around and run back every morning. This was so healthy. Literally and metaphorically, you blessed and honored yourself. But the practice has largely been abandoned.

It is known in the allopathic medical community that exercise is beneficial, and even necessary, to successfully treat Type II diabetes, which is the type that Indians almost always get. It helps the body respond better to insulin, to overcome "insulin resistance," which is a factor in the development of the disease. For those who exercise faithfully, medication can often be reduced or even discontinued.

Another study that impressed me involved Native Hawaiians, who now have the largest per capita consumption of Spam and are plagued with obesity and diabetes, much like Indians. Their traditional diet once contained about 10 percent fat, while the typical American diet is 40 percent. With a switch to a Native diet and no restriction on the amount of food eaten, the people lost an average of seventeen pounds over three weeks. Their blood pressure dropped, and those who were once Type II diabetics on insulin had to cut their insulin dose by a third to a half after the first day to avoid excessively low blood sugar. This is an impressive result so soon after making a dietary change. Clearly it isn't necessary to lose weight before seeing a beneficial drop in blood sugar, as much current thinking goes.

I believe that in order to wipe out diabetes and prevent it in future generations, we must look to our old ways. We need to incorporate our native foods back into our diets, or at least eat a Native-like diet by cooking foods in the old way by boiling, roasting, and grilling. We should consume protein before carbohydrates. Specifically, eat a piece of jerky first if we can't resist that coffee and doughnuts.

We even had medicines, herbs that have a hypoglycemic effect, that we can make use of today. We also need to revive the great traditions of vigorous physical activity, to once again consider it a virtue to have a strong body able to withstand hardship and the fasting that is integral to our ceremonies. Scientists would say we need more studies to see if any of these traditions are worth going back to. They would want to distill the facts down. "Exercise is good," they would say, "but there isn't strong enough evidence to say that it prevents diabetes. Even if it did, maybe you don't have to get up at the crack of dawn."

There is a part of the scientist in me, but there is that Indian part of me, too. Sure, we have to do everything we can to guide our children to be athletes, but we should also encourage them to run toward the rising sun.

I'm in a real fast-paced learning mode right now, with so much information coming at me in residency. At the same time, I'm trying hard to maintain the Indian part of me.

An issue I struggle with is that I tend to listen to people without interrupting them. It is an Indian value—although not unique to Indians—and considered part of their healing process. But I face a time constraint because I'm booked with patients every twenty minutes. And there will be even less time in any job I do after residency. It's so difficult to address the needs of a patient's mind and body and also expect healing to take place in a twenty-minute interview. I have been told I have to become more "efficient." I've been teased, "Oh Kathy, you've got to stop listening to your patients."

Sometimes I see that a patient has a very strong need for more than an allopathic physician can offer. Then I encourage that person to look to his own culture. Some people, especially Southeast Asians, seem to be really surprised. But I know that many groups have folk healers they use and also may be using some herbs that have pharmacologic activity that can either complement or interfere with medication I prescribe. It's important to be aware of this and deal with it in a way that is respectful of the person's culture.

I don't consider myself a medicine woman, but for those patients who need a traditional healer, I see it as my job to refer. I view it as a collaboration, knowing that medicine people often refer their clients to allopathic physicians if they're unable to help them. I'm also learning about herbs that I could recommend to my patients who don't want to take pills.

I have participated in healing ceremonies conducted by medicine people of several tribes. In particular, my first experience with a Navajo medicine woman had a powerful effect on me. I felt like I had been transported to another time, another world. I came away feeling renewed, cleansed, and centered.

I worry about our elders dying off. They are taking with them a lot of their knowledge and culture, things that could be a basis for our survival as a people. They have gifts we can use for ourselves and share with the world.

Gifts that can show us all a way to survival. In another generation or two, they may be gone.

We need to value our elders, of course, but we also don't talk enough about valuing our children. We need to see them as sacred and treasured gifts from the Creator, not as personal property in the tradition of the dominant society. We need to look at ourselves as growing beings—growing spiritually and emotionally. We all have a place on this earth. We all have a purpose, which we must find and follow.

When you see a medicine person, you make motions forming what is essentially a medicine wheel. You bless your little medicine bundle. You bless the east, the south, the north, and the west, in a circle. You end with a line toward the east, the rising sun. This symbolizes a never-ending line where you face the east. Always on a path toward the east. Always toward the rising sun.

David Lucero

Healing in Two Worlds

David Manuel Lucero, M.D., was born into the Luiseño tribe in southern California. His grandmother was a Luiseño from Lake Elsinore. His wife, Margo, is from the Kumeyaay of the San Pasqual Reservation. They have four children.

Dr. Lucero received his M.D. from the University of California, Davis, in 1991. He now heads the Indian Health Clinic serving the Pechanga Reservation in Temecula, California. He has restructured the clinic so that he follows patients through the entire course of their care.

This interview took place in two parts. The first part was conducted by Darryl Wilson while Dr. Lucero was completing medical school. He articulates his ideas and hopes about returning to his reservation.

In the second part, Giuseppe Saitta interviewed Dr. Lucero after he had returned to southern California to practice family medicine.

Part 1

One reason I came to medical school was that there is a myth at home that if you get an education you automatically turn into a white person. I want to dispel that myth. I am as much Indian as anyone. I am one of the young folks who is learning my religion, my language, and my culture. I care about those things. I have earned a small amount of respect from some local people because they know how strongly I feel about the culture.

One thing I have learned throughout my education is that none of the things I was taught about my culture and how our world functions—spiritually and in our "ways"—has been shattered by what they taught me in school and medical school. If anything, my education has strengthened my cultural beliefs.

I think we need education to deal with the white man's society, because it is not going to go away. We need an education so that we can protect our insides, our country, our culture, ourselves. We need an education so that we can keep them at arm's reach and say, "That's as far as you are taking us."

Nature, that spirit that makes us what we are, is still there. They have not been able to reach into our being and steal our spirits and kill us. They can't! It's like a little spark, a little fire in all of us that can be refueled and built up. That is our self-esteem. I believe that the people who are having trouble aren't truly rooted in their identity as Indian persons, because that is where our strength really comes from.

But we still have the sickness plaguing our people because we've basically been sidetracked from our path in life. You can't separate sickness from the human body or from spirituality. It is all one thing. You can't fragment it off.

These are times to slow down, to get more in tune to what is around us. Take a breath. A good example is the rain. Rain is a wonderful thing. It cleanses the earth. It is a time to slow down. But people still drive just as fast as they can.

All kinds of things go wrong in the world because we are not listening. Before white men came, I'd guess that we didn't spend more than twenty hours a week in hunting and gathering. The rest of the time was used spending time with your children, with your family. Instructing them in the ways of life. We have been captured by the "need" for materialism, which keeps us hooked on the forty-hour week.

The old way used to be, you grow up, you live life, you search for who you are and what you can contribute to your community as a human being. That was taken away from us as Indian people. Growing up and having the freedom to believe you can do whatever your destiny is—I think I've been able to plant that seed of self-esteem within my children.

One of the things I would like to see Indian people do is educate ourselves about accepting our limits—having the freedom to accept who we are. American society demands to know *what* you are. Everywhere my wife goes, it is always, "What does your husband do?" Rather than, "Is your husband a good human being?"

As far as what we have to offer non-Indian people, we had a way of life once that was truly in harmony. We were taught what to use, how to use, not to overuse. Among my people there was no obesity like there is today, there was no diabetes. We were taught from an early age not to over-indulge in anything. Elders were highly respected, our children were protected: they were like gods, they were sacred. They were raised pretty much by elders, so the wisdom was passed on.

It was a beautiful cycle. Many of us have gone off track of that, but a lot of us hang on to it and re-institute it into our families. I think that's the greatest knowledge we have to offer, and it's just been ignored. Indian people today, at least my people, are so skeptical of non-Indians that we aren't the truly open people we were five hundred years ago. We're not the same innocent, loving, accepting people we used to be. We're different now, and that's going to be an impediment to sharing anything else we have.

Part 2

I had my earliest thoughts about going to medical school at age fifteen. As I got older, through adolescence and in young adulthood, I realized I had a family calling to help people. My relatives had been involved in traditional healing going several generations back, up until my grandmother and my father.

In young adulthood, as I was going through spiritual realizations and talking to the elders, I learned about my own culture. This helped strengthen my own desire for a way I could follow my true nature and become a doctor-healer. In today's society, that meant going to medical school. Using traditional medicine is still an avenue for me, but the mainstream Indian population relies on Western medicine for their therapy.

When I finished my training and returned to the reservation to practice, certain things were just as I had imagined them. I imagined coming into an exam room and seeing an Indian person, and then seeing them realize that they weren't looking at a white physician. I mean, there are no words to describe that sensation of how *I* know that patient feels so at ease, so comfortable.

I have one patient, a little girl. Her grandfather has long hair, but every doctor she's ever had growing up here was non-Indian. She was scared to death of the clinic, she screamed and kicked. So her grandmother was just astonished, the first time I saw the girl, that she didn't even whimper. They couldn't believe it, but then they realized, "Well, he resembles your grandfather." I mean, it was like coming and seeing a family friend in the clinic.

That's the best that I anticipated and received in coming back to practice. But at the same time, it wasn't the homecoming I expected. You know, there's a lot of politics involved in Indian health care and tribal leadership. Being Indian and being a physician, I have some influence now, and I think I threatened some other people's influence. I envisioned myself going back to the Rincon health clinic, but I wasn't offered a position there.

But the work is phenomenal. I had the advantage over other practition-ers of knowing where I wanted to go. I knew the population, I knew some of their problems, and I knew what we needed to do to make good holistic health care available to them. I'm upgrading health care at this clinic to the first-line, state-of-the-art primary care that you can get anywhere. That is something these people have never had before.

The one thing that going to school did to me—it does change the way you see things, so I've got to say that I'm a little bit off from my center, maybe, from where I was eight years ago. Maybe I've lost touch a little bit with my own people during my education, and I'm trying to get back in touch with them.

You're taught how to do particular things in a white education and they're not always the most prudent way in an Indian community. An elder told me once, "You're going to get an education, and you come back and we'll tell you how to use it." Now, in coming back, I need to ask them how they want me to use it. I'm also realizing, "Okay, the way I want to do it may be the right way, but it may take longer than I anticipated to convince them it's the right way."

My ultimate goal as a physician is to be able to blend equally the practice of traditional Native health care and Western medicine. The obstacles I have are getting the community used to me as a Western-trained physician, getting their confidence, and *then* exposing them to my Indian back-ground. I'm still quite a young person and I see that taking years to de-velop in our culture, though I'm always moving in that direction. It's slowly evolving.

People don't always realize that I don't rely just on my Western training. My greater faith is in my Creator and the power the Indian people have to heal themselves. I call on that all the time to help people. And you can do that without letting anybody be aware of what you're doing.

I envision in the future there's going to have to be some kind of partner-ship between private Indian dollars and public Indian health funds to upgrade the standard of Indian health care. I hope tribes have the vision to start providing for that. I think it will happen when Indians have had enough money for long enough and become educated enough to realize what they need to do.

We're not a very future-oriented people. We think a little bit in the future, but not five or ten years. That's something we have to start doing. We ought to think of economic, cultural, and spiritual longevity for our people. That's really pushing us, it's changing us a little bit, from where we were before.

It's my belief that to save Indian people, we need to be educated. Because we're going to be our own best advocates to save our cultures. From my own personal experience, if you're uneducated, the dominant society is going to pay you no mind. The state of Indian affairs in general, and of Indian people, if anybody really cares, will be left to the educated and the spiritually inclined leaders of our communities.

We have been taken care of, or thought we needed to be taken care of, for so long. We are reaching a critical mass where there are enough educated American Indians who can be leaders, national leaders, and who care enough about our culture to be spiritual leaders for our people as well. If we can put intertribal politics aside, I know we can make better decisions for our people than non-Indians.

At the same time, I hope more young people can withstand the pressures of education and not be bitten by the dollar—rather than coming home and serving their people. That's a big hope, and a big fear.

Our culture was dying out, and a group of us are trying to hold it together and bring it back to life. It's happening—young people are starting to learn the language, the songs and dances. I hope that our people can realize that our strength is really within ourselves and within our culture and identity as Indian people. If we realize that, we'll hang on to our culture, we'll revitalize our language and traditions, and we'll survive.

THE CHILDREN ARE OUR FUTURE

In 1868, at the signing of the treaty of Bosque Redondo, the Navajo chief Manuelito declared, "Education is the ladder. Take the ladder, my son, and use it." Now scholars and educators argue that education is vital to the very survival of Indian people. Few have put more effort into advancing Native education than William Demmert, who eloquently outlines the challenges. The next three interviews demonstrate how these challenges can be and have been met from Alaska to New Mexico to Maine. Author and teacher Cliff Trafzer provides a summing up.

William Demmert

Education Is Survival

William Demmert, Jr. (Tlingit) was born in Klawock, Alaska, in 1934 and grew up in southeastern Alaska. His father is Tlingit and his mother is Oglala Sioux. He comes from a family of fishermen who believed strongly in the value of formal education. The original family name was Kokesh. On the same day William was born, his great-grandfather Old Man Kokesh died.

William Demmert attended high school in Sitka. He earned a B.A. from Seattle Pacific University and a master's from the University of Alaska, Fairbanks. After working as a teacher, he returned to Klawock to serve as chief administrator in the public schools. He received his doctorate in education from Harvard in 1973.

From there he went on to become an influential leader in the field of education. He was one of the founders and directors of the National Indian Educational Association. Among other positions, he has served as state commissioner of education in Alaska; deputy of the U.S. Fish and Game Commission; and director of education for the Bureau of Indian Affairs.

Dr. Demmert has guided many initiatives for Indian education, focusing on the pivotal role education and language play in the survival of Indian nations. In 1990–1991 he co-chaired a U.S. Department of Education task force whose final report,

"Indian Nations at Risk: An Educational Strategy for Action," reflects his concerns. Currently he is Visiting Professor at the Woodring College of Education at Western Washington University. He and his wife have four children.

The following text combines interviews conducted by Lois Crozier-Hogle and Darryl Wilson.

We're basically a sea-oriented people. In the Lower 48 you hear a lot of talk about the land and Mother Earth. In Alaska we looked to the sea for our livelihood. A lot of our legends and the spiritual worlds have to do with the sea. I remember my grandparents talking about the land otter, the animal that moves between the two environments, land and water.

I grew up with a strong code of ethics as a youngster. I listened to my grandmother, who taught me some of the songs and the dances of an earlier age. My uncles taught me things about work and hunting and fishing and the use of the resources—these were my paternal uncles, since my mother is Oglala Sioux. We were taught never to catch more fish than we could use and never to kill more deer than we could use that winter or take care of immediately. Never to cut down trees just to cut them down. What you could not use, give back to the sea or land, because it will refurbish itself. That has stayed with me.

In the Tlingit community, the teachers were the grandparents and the aunts and uncles. That's traditional. Part of the Tlingit theory was that the aunts and uncles could be harder taskmasters. They could be as demanding as they chose, and your relationships with your parents could still be warm and friendly. In my whole life I can only remember my parents getting visibly upset with me two or three times.

It started, as soon as the child learned to walk, with a daily bath in the ocean. For the inland Tlingits it was a bath in the river. Then the boys spent a lot of time with their uncles. If the uncle was a carver of totem poles, they did that. If he was a canoe-builder, in old times, then that is what they did.

I spent every summer with my grandparents while my parents went out and worked or fished. From a very early age, my grandfather would sneak me out on the fishing boat. I started fishing commercially with my uncles at age nine. I spent a lot of time with them, working, playing, hunting and fishing. When I was thirteen they said, "You are big enough to go fishing with your dad now." My father expected me to know everything he knew about the working of the boat. When I was fifteen, he and my uncles showed me how to navigate from Klawock to Seattle and back.

One summer when I was fishing, I fell off the stern of the boat. No one was looking. As I was falling, I grabbed the line that we use to tow the skip. I climbed aboard, then pulled myself up to the main boat. When my grandmother heard about that, she took me outside and went through a ritual with me that used devil's club, a plant in southeastern Alaska that is very thorny and grows very big. She said, "You have to go through this because of the accident. This will protect you and it won't happen again."

She was a strong believer in Tlingit values and practices. In the Tlingit community, we have a matriarch, and she was that person. The ownership of the lands passed through her line. The names the children received passed through her line and were the names of her past family members. That formed the unit family life moved around.

We continue to honor that tradition in my own family and in my extended family. One summer I brought my youngest son—who was born while I was a student at Harvard, and now is at college in Arizona—back to Alaska so my grandmother could give him his Indian name. She was surprised to see me because she didn't know I was coming. We sat down and talked for a while. She said in broken Tlingit and English, "Would you like me to name your son?"

She told us a story behind his name. It is the story behind the Takwanadee people of her clan, who belong to the Raven side of the Tlingit nation. The essence of the name she gave him is the story of a woman who nursed a woodworm. This worm became a giant. She kept it under the house until it grew too large to keep there or in the village, and she and her clan had to move north. The name represents the woman nursing the worm and the move north.

After we'd heard the story, we went back to my parents' house to unpack our bags. My wife opened her suitcase and laid out her clothes. On the top of her clothes was a bra. And on the tip of the bra was a little worm with its head up in the air—immediately following the story. Now what are the odds of that?

When I told my grandmother about it, she laughed as if to say, "What did you expect?"

My own name, Kaw-Goo-Woo, comes from the Eagle side of the Tlingit nation. It represents a marmot village. In these villages you have all the residents out feeding and doing their thing, and you have the sentinel, who keeps an eye out for danger. When danger comes they whistle and all the members of the village go underground. The sentinel goes in last. That is *Kaw-Goo-Woo*.

From the time I was young my grandmother told me it was very important for me to get an education, because a lot of the things that I was growing up with would change, and I had to be prepared to meet the challenges of the new environment. That was an attitude we grew up with. My grandfather and his older brother were among the very first to get a high school education. They were living in Shakan, an original village that is no longer there, and they went to school in Sitka.

The boat would pick up the students in September and bring them back in May. One year my grandfather and his brother missed the boat. So Old Man Kokesh said, "Take my canoe and go to school." They went up the coast and made it, but their parents didn't know that until they came back on the boat the next spring.

There were five brothers, and they all got their high school education. But my grandfather would not allow my grandmother, Sit-quay, to learn English. He wanted all of his kids to speak Tlingit. As a youngster I learned to understand and speak the Tlingit language. But I didn't really have the chance to practice it when I wasn't with my grandparents. My parents, of course, were forced not to speak the Tlingit language when they went to a government school. They felt I'd have to learn English in order to adjust to the new ways they were encountering.

I've always viewed myself as a Tlingit, even though I have Sioux blood. I know my home is always in southeast Alaska. I go back every summer. I have a boat and I go out and do my thing. I fish for salmon and halibut and other seafood. When I have the time, I put away enough for the year. I brought seventy pounds of frozen salmon and fifty pounds of smoked salmon back with me this year. I put away herring roe, berries, and other foods off the beach.

Wherever I've gone to work, I see that as a temporary move. I go back to Klawock, and I even go one step further. My grandmother's clan came from an island called Hecata, where they had the community house. A little place called Squa-ahn. On the charts it's called Indian Cove. I was one of the few fortunate enough to spend some time at that old village site.

I also see that as my home. But we've lost it. The traditional territory that my grandmother owned included a vast area in southeast Alaska. Back when the Bureau of Indian Affairs was moving people, my grandmother's people all moved from the island to the village of Klawock. Then the Forest Service went and burned all the community houses.

We still consider it our land. We've filed a claim to get access to it. We call it "the Garden Site." I used to go out there and help them dig the garden, keep it clean. I feel terrible about losing that place. As far as I'm concerned, they burned the clan house to force people out and eradicate any claim the Tlingit might have. Then they created Tongass National Forest, which took over all of the land.

One of the major problems we've had over several hundred years of contact with Europeans and other nations is the inability to exercise our rights as owners of the land and resources in a way that allowed us to develop our economies. That single thing has caused many of the problems we've encountered, including a loss of priority for education and continuation of the knowledge base that our ancestors and elders had.

At the same time, it seems to me that it's very important for people to recognize that American Indians and Alaska Natives are well, and that they still own land and resources as the first Americans. They welcome the opportunity to participate in the larger society as citizens, but that unique status as Native Americans is very important.

There are four reasons why Indian nations are at risk. One is poor academic achievement. We just are not developing the intelligentsia that we used to have. Our grandfathers and great-grandfathers were very smart people. And what have we done to maintain that? Not as much as we could.

There are some exceptions to that, but very few. We need to identify what is important to us culturally and traditionally and make that part of the education system. In our early history, the learning process was tied very closely to the mores and culture and language of the community. That's not true any more.

This is the second reason the Indian nations are at risk. The loss of language and culture. We are losing it faster and faster every year.

The third reason we are at risk is the constant pressure on the resources that we have left—land, water, timber, hunting and fishing rights.

The fourth reason is the changing nature of the relationship between the Indian tribes and the federal government. Too much depends on the "will of Congress" and on who the president is. Our leaders do not have the training that people in Congress or business and industry do. We can't compete with them until we train a cadre of people who have the skills to deal with them on their own terms.

Who's really going to protect you when the chips are down? Not the outsiders. It's got to be internal. We need to focus on the kinds of things that are important to our survival as Indian people. And that means becoming fairly self-sufficient communities. It means having doctors, lawyers, teachers, professors—even politicians. It might even mean having a president in the future. Until we understand this as a people, we are going to continue to lose.

It's important for members of the Indian community to be as highly educated and well trained as anyone—maybe *better* than most. I think universities across the United States have a responsibility to serve all of their citizens, and this includes American Indians and Native Alaskans. We continue to expand institutions that are limited to the Indian community. That's fine, that's good, but I think it's important for us to go to the Stanfords and Harvards and large state universities for part of our education. It's very difficult to build institutions with those kinds of resources by yourself.

To do this, it is going to take an understanding of how to maintain an Indian identity, Indian language, and Indian culture. It will take the ability to compete in the contemporary world with enough smarts to retain that identity, language, and culture. That means reaching all of these kids who've been conditioned by other members not to "become white," not to participate in the system. This negative attitude in fact sets the basis for the complete destruction of the Indian community.

Some students confuse arrogance with pride. A piece I read recently said that when you reach a certain maturity and status, you not only have responsibility, but you can afford to be gracious. A lot of us have lost that. We are no longer gracious or generous.

My grandparents were very generous. Our house used to always be full. If someone came to town and had no place to stay, they gave them a place to stay. We can pass this on to our children by demonstrating it, living it, talking with them. We don't do it as often as we should. You're off to work or school, and you don't spend long evenings with the family as much as you used to. I remember as a youngster sitting around with my grandparents, parents, aunts, and uncles, and they would tell stories or relate the events of the year or day.

The Tlingits have changed. Right up to my time, the changes were easier because they were tied to the kinds of things we did earlier. With my kids, the changes are more significant. My oldest son is a commercial fisherman in Alaska. But my younger son at Arizona only did a little fishing with his uncle and me. He spent most of his time in the summer playing basketball.

I've also seen change in Alaska that I haven't been happy with. Part of it has to do with exploitation of resources—timber, oil, fish and game, and the fact that people see Alaska as a place to make money and then leave. It would be much nicer if people saw Alaska as a long-term permanent home. But a majority of people who come to Alaska come to get rich, do their thing, and then go home.

There's an important difference between how Native Americans have traditionally looked at the land and the way Americans from Europe and maybe Asia look at the land. I remember holding hearings about the Native lands, as deputy commissioner for Fish and Game. One man testified that "if you give that land to the Natives (which they already owned, by the way) they're not going to do anything with it. They're just going to let it sit. If you let us take the land, we're going to make something out of it."

I believe in letting things lie in their natural state. That doesn't mean you can't use it—but don't use it just to use it. Only use it if you have to. What's wrong with letting the land sit?

Throughout my professional career, I have realized, as many others have, that the Native languages are a very important part of our cultural base. If that's totally lost, we will lose something that is going to be difficult to restore. One of the things I've been pushing for is a continuation of Native languages, both in schools and as a formal policy of the federal and state governments. Under the new reauthorization for Indian community colleges, the federal government has passed a language policy. Title VII, the Bilingual Education Act, now includes a clause to support the learning of Native languages. That's a major step.

I would like to see Native communities who believe their language and cultural heritage are important see that the education system is also important. I would like to see them prepare our young to become the best in whatever field they decide to work in, whether they're engineers, doctors, businessmen, or scientists. Then you can afford to spend time strengthening your language and culture—practicing those things that are appropriate for today, and turning those things that are not as appropriate but still important to remember into music, theater, or whatever you want to.

If we are going to keep pace with the contemporary world and retain our identity, we need the historians to write our history. We need playwrights to put our history into theater. We need our songwriters to continue developing the songs. We need our art communities to become self-sufficient.

Part of our problem is that not many of our people have the language base to do that. It takes a command of language. My grandmother had a command of the Tlingit language. My dad had a pretty good command of the Tlingit language. I don't really have command of the Tlingit language, and my children have even less.

It has taken me a while to recognize that there is a real deficiency, especially if we intend to retain our "Tlingitness." Our family structure is still strong because we have maintained close personal ties. But when my grandmother passed away, we no longer had the individual with the knowledge base to pass on the names within the tribe.

With her passing, we have seen the passing of an era. When my last uncle has gone, another whole era will pass. My brother and I were the last in my family to be trained by my uncles.

We have to get schools to recognize the importance of the language and cultural base. I've tried to get that started in Alaska. It doesn't matter whether it's a Native language or English or some other language, you have to develop a base. From that base you can learn other languages. If your home life is in English now, you had better develop it well so you can develop the Native language base. If you've developed a Native language, what you learn there can carry over into your learning of English.

I am pulling representatives from different groups together, along with some of the best language experts. I want to sit down and ask, "Okay, what do we need to know? And once we know that, what do we need to *do*?"

That is my mission over the next few years.

Edna Ahgeak MacLean

Keeping the Songs Alive

Edna Ahgeak MacLean (Inupiaq) is doing groundbreaking work on the relationship of language and narrative to the cultural identity of Native people, especially students.

She was born in 1944 and raised in Barrow, an Inupiaq community on the Arctic Ocean in northern Alaska. Her Inupiaq name, Paniattaaq, belonged to her uncle. It means "Little Daughter." Her maiden name, Ahgeak, means "Filing Stone."

Her father was a hunter. In 1959 he went to work for the Naval Arctic Research Laboratory to help put his children through school. She still has four brothers and a sister living in Barrow.

She attended the Wrangell Institute, a Bureau of Indian Affairs school, and from there went to Mount Edgecumbe, a high school for Native American students. She received a scholarship to attend Colorado Women's College in Denver, where she earned her B.A. After earning a teaching credential from Berkeley, she returned with her husband to teach at the University of Alaska, Fairbanks, where she helped to establish the degree program in Eskimo languages. From 1987 to 1990 she worked for the Alaska Department of Education.

She received her Ph.D. from Stanford University in 1995. Her dissertation focused on the structure of the language in the creation of Inupiaq stories and values. She has returned to Barrow, where she is now president of Iḷisaġvik College.

She was interviewed by Lois Crozier-Hogle, with additional material from Giuseppe Saitta.

My father was a hunter. He later became a carpenter, but prior to 1959 the source of family cash was hunting. Father hunted polar bears, seals, caribou and other animals. When he started working an eight-to-five job, he still had his huskies and went hunting during the weekends. He needed to. He enjoyed the outdoors. In the late sixties one of his friends went to Greenland. He came back with some Greenland dogs and gave father five huskies. They were huge.

I went to kindergarten through the elementary grades at the Barrow Day School. My Aunt Flossie taught kindergarten. Knowing she was my aunt made me feel great. At that time she used the Inupiaq language. But in third grade there was a teacher who didn't want us to speak any Inupiaq at all in the classroom. She picked on children who spoke Inupiaq. She would physically throw these children across the room.

One day she pulled my ear when I whispered in Inupiaq. My ear was bright red and my mother asked what had happened. She got so angry. She put my brother on her back, inside her parka, and stalked across the frozen lagoon to the school. She called for the teacher and said, "You and I are going down to the superintendent's office and I'm going to pull your ear!"

Mother was so upset! To have her do that made me feel good. Mother and the teacher became good friends after that.

My greatest satisfaction comes from studying my language and finding out about myself through the study of my language. When I was in college in Denver, I found myself doing a paper about a goddess in India.

I wondered what *my* people believed in. It hit me that I didn't know my own history. I didn't know the grammar of my own language. I felt really sad—then I felt angry. I could learn about other countries, but I wasn't able to take a course in my own ancestry and history. I ended up doing my term paper on that. That was an important moment for me.

I think that happens to a lot of Natives and Alaska Natives who have gone through some schooling. We spend a lot of time looking for our culture when it should have been with us all along. My work now is about understanding the process of acculturation. I have to know how a Native student might emerge out of the education process as a whole person. I have many nephews and nieces in Alaska, and I'd like to understand this process of life for them.

People are losing too much of the foundation of their cultural traditions, their language, their family. The changes that have occurred have come too fast in too short a time. The extended family has been cut off because the children have been shipped off to distant schools.

I'm helping people connect their Native language to English. I know my own language, the structure and the social uses of it. I'd like to develop a program to enable the kids to use English academically after the fourth grade. We need to make that connection. They would still use their own language, but also use English as a tool for learning.

When students can compare one thing to the next, I've found that's an exciting process for learning. If you have the Inupiaq language on one side, and English on the other, and you compare the structure of the two and the function of the words within each, it's an exciting way for students to understand how the languages accomplish some of the same things, but also accomplish different things.

The structure of our Inupiaq language, where we have inflectional endings at the end of our words, depicts the interconnectedness between the people, the animals, the land, and the ocean, as well as all the values of respect for each of those components of the universe. You see that reflected in people's attitudes toward the animals and the land. They realize that we have to take care of the environment. It comes out in the language.

For the Inupiaq, spiritual beliefs and a sense of connection with earth revolve around the whale—the activity of hunting and the necessity of being respectful of the whale. Our orientation is to the ocean and the ice. Our language reflects that. There are other Eskimos, Inuits, who are inland dwellers and probably have a different sense of connection to the land.

I have uncles who are whaling captains. Whaling captains clean the ice cellars before they go out, because the parka—the outer skin—of the whale is going to be stored there. The whale is going to give its body to us, and reverence for the whale requires that we put it in a clean place.

It begins in March. The women get together and start preparing the boat, the utensils, the equipment, and the tools that the men will be taking out on their expeditions. At this time the men start cleaning the cellars. People are very respectful in their thoughts and what they say about the whale. You're not supposed to boast. You don't say you're going to do this or that. The feeling is that the whale gives itself to the Inupiaq people. The spirit of the whale leaves the body of the whale—like the spirit of the human does—then continues on.

Songs are composed around the hunt, songs and ceremony to entice the whale. Individual songs are very powerful. Hunters could own songs to help them in their hunting. If a person sang a certain song to lure a certain kind of animal, that was his hunting song.

There are certain things the women have to do. Whaling takes a lot of money and energy. You must keep your boat in safe condition. The boat frame is made out of wood and is covered with bearded seal skin. There's a process to make sure the skin and stitching is done properly so the water doesn't seep into the boat. It's very laborious work done by the women.

All the food and gear amounts to about $10,000 to maintain a whaling crew for the season. After they catch the whale, they have a feed for the whole village at the whaling center. People are lined up for blocks. You give them different parts of the whale, plus bread or crackers and tea or coffee. That adds up to a lot of money, but it maintains a strong whaling tradition.

There was a lot of togetherness within the whaling center—they taught the hunting traditions. They made their weapons and tools and they told the legends. The young boys would listen to the older men, especially their uncles. This was true for the girls as well as the boys. They'd hear of their hunting experiences, the problems they encountered, and what they did in order to have a successful hunt.

The girls helped the women cook the meals. They would take the food into the whaling center, share the meal, and stay to listen to the stories. It was an egalitarian system—the men and the women working together. A woman I knew was on a whaling team, and she did the cooking. When it came time to launch the boat, she was one of the rowers. She said to me, "The only reason I never threw that spear was because I was so little."

At that time a lot of shamanism occurred in these centers. The missionaries saw it as an evil, pagan activity. The churches were relentless. When the Presbyterian church established itself, they started imposing customs that changed the position of women. There was a lot destruction of the Native community centers and centers for whaling crews.

The Inupiaq communities have always been very spiritual in terms of their belief in the forces of nature, influences that are not of the material world, and a tie to the other world. Christianity was received so readily because of teachings that were already in the Inupiaq religion. That feeling transferred over to the religious zeal brought by the churches. In Christianity they have the concept of the resurrection, a human coming back to life. That used to happen through shamanism, only the number of days differs in the Inupiaq tradition.

The spirituality is still there, but it's manifested differently. It was a way to connect with different worlds. Shamans had the power to travel into the ocean, and also to the moon. There are stories about shamans going down to the bottom of the ocean to visit the woman called Samna—in most of the English literature she's called Sedna. It means "the one down there, not visible."

There was a lot of healing, but there could also be harm done to people by shamans. They were a natural development in the Inupiaq world, in their relationships to animals and to other spirits. It was a way for a group of people to connect to those realms and phenomena they did not understand.

In our creation stories we have legends of the time when it was completely dark. People did not age or grow old or die until after Raven stole the light from a man and his wife in another part of the world. He flew away. As he was flying, the source of light got heavier and heavier. Pretty soon he dropped it and it exploded. And that's our source of light now. The name for the sun is *Siqiñig*. When you break that word up, *siqi* means "to splash out," and *ñig* means the result of this great splash.

Certain things—culture, tradition, and ceremony—are necessary to our existence. Some communities have been so stricken with drinking that their cohesion has been broken. They have to bring back culture and tradition and rely on that knowledge.

We've all had to go through a process of rediscovery. For me, it's meant putting energy into understanding the thought behind the language I spoke as my first, Inupiaq. If you can't learn the language but you know something about the thought behind it, there are certain concepts you can talk about. I can come to an understanding of what my ancestors believed.

We need to identify these concepts and have the children listen to them: "This is what it means when you say aġviqsiuqtut. It means 'searching for whales.'"

Then there's the art of telling the story and the narrative of the performance in the dances. *Unipkaat* translates to "things our ancestors chose to leave behind for us." On one level there's a structure of presentation that involves the audience and uses of words within the demonstrative system to direct the focus of the audience to certain images the storyteller is creating. On another level, as each event occurs there's a marker from a certain category of words. The climax of the story is usually marked with *kiisaimmaa*, saying, "Finally, this is the main event." Other markers show the epilogue or the ending.

Storytelling was a way of passing knowledge on to the next generation. Throughout the centuries the Inupiaq people have recorded their activities through song. Dancing was also a way of recording history. It may also be a way for a person to tell of his hunting experiences or whatever he's accomplished during that year. Several years ago, the Wainwright dance group went down and performed in Los Angeles. When they came back, they created a song and a dance about their experience flying from northern

Alaska to California. The actions of flying and things that they saw were incorporated into the dance.

The nonmaterial aspects of culture are very important to cultivate right now. I feel a real urgency to develop a curriculum in language, art, and music for the Inupiaq people. They must be able to see a dance that tells a story of a particular hunt or an event in the life of a hunter. A person may have a spiritual experience, so he writes a song about it. The song becomes part of his family's heritage. The daughter or son may then learn the song or dance and perform it in public. These things need to be done, and each family must continue this ceremony to make a strong culture and tradition.

Most of the schools are now run by the local district boards. The board members are Inupiat, and the schools are helping more in the area of dancing and teaching. Native people—our Inupiaq people—are at a point in history where they are able to decide what they want to emphasize. There's enough information now about what we should be doing within the schools and our communities to enable our children to be productive within that society.

The basic thing I've come to realize is that a person needs a strong cultural identity. In order to venture into something new and learn new things, they need a strong sense of their ties back to their ancestral knowledge and community.

In the schools we need to foster that through language and culture. Not just traditional knowledge, but using our stories and our knowledge of the environment and incorporating them into the science of the curriculum. If students have a knowledge of their own language and culture, they're more free to pursue other things—to go into chemistry or mathematics, astronomy, environmental science—and apply what they know from their culture.

Every tribe, if they have determination, can maintain their language and culture. Through the help of multimedia and electronic systems you can develop material that is ongoing and can be amended as the years go by. It can have different authors. You can enlist the help of different sectors of the community. These are tools we can use to make the process easier and faster. People can be authors of their own knowledge and incorporate it into the school system. It's a challenge, as well as a great big opportunity as far as influencing what your children know about your culture.

Joseph Abeyta

Look for Their Strengths

Joseph Abeyta (Tewa) was born in 1943 at Santa Clara Pueblo in New Mexico. He has been superintendent of the Santa Fe Indian School since 1976. He is married, and he and his wife have four children.

Joseph Abeyta was sent to Indian vocational boarding schools for thirteen years before his father convinced him to attend New Mexico Highlands University in Las Vegas, New Mexico. There he discovered his calling as a teacher almost by accident. He pursued a doctorate in education, receiving his Ed.D. from Harvard in 1973.

He was asked by tribal chairman Dell Lovato to take over and revitalize the Indian School in Albuquerque in 1975. Abeyta moved the school to better facilities in Santa Fe in 1979 and helped to build it into one of the premier high schools in the nation. It was the first Indian high school to be recognized by the secretary of education as one of 270 national schools "demonstrating excellence in education." In September 1994 it was recognized nationally for the second time in six years for its outstanding Title I program.

At present the school has around five hundred boys and girls in grades seven to twelve. A majority of the students are Pueblo, some are Navajo and Apache, and a growing number are from other tribes in Oklahoma, California, and New Mexico. Teaching positions at the school are highly coveted.

Superintendent Abeyta was interviewed by Lois Crozier-Hogle and Ferne Jensen, with a follow-up interview by Giuseppe Saitta.

The Santa Fe Indian School had its beginning in Albuquerque. The school provided an opportunity for Indians to do for themselves those things that the federal government had done for them up until that point. It was quite a challenge and was a result of a lot of congressional hearings and controversy in this country regarding all aspects of Native American life.

In 1975 and 1976 the Albuquerque Indian School was going through some difficult times. The school had deteriorated, the buildings were run down. It had become a dumping ground, a warehouse for the youngsters people didn't know what to do with.

By coincidence, our leadership, as well as the Bureau of Indian Affairs, was questioning the need for the school when President Nixon signed the Self-Determination Act into law. The Pueblo governors decided to look more seriously at it. I was given an opportunity to bring a group of planners together. We put together a program, went to the Bureau, and that resulted in our first contract.

In 1977 we started our school year with about 320 students. There were some pretty tough kids there. The dropout rate was about 50 percent. The turnover with regard to teachers and staff was just as high. The kids knew they were there because other schools didn't have a program for them.

The first task was to get some control. It's impossible to teach basic studies if you don't have a student population that is prepared to learn. We instituted a number of programs to develop a sense of trust between staff and students. We tried to assure kids that we were going to be there for a while. Their experience had been they didn't trust people. Social workers and so on would come out for three or four months and then get transferred. There was a lot of inconsistency.

During those first couple of years there were shootings, there were fights, there were rapes. The entire football team walked off the field because of the conditions we laid out for participating in extracurricular activities. I did things I didn't think I was capable of doing to establish some order.

Over time the program started to come together. We realized that the facilities were in such bad shape that we needed to improve the environment. We saw this facility in Santa Fe, and in 1979 we moved here from Albuquerque.

In the present program, the attitudes of the students have changed 180 degrees. The kids are aggressive and excited about education; they've got dreams and desires they feel can be fulfilled at this school. The staff is committed.

The community is also emerging in relation to the school. In the past a lot of Indian parents felt there was not a role for them. That was and is a problem in Indian education. The way you make significant change is to involve parents and develop an ability to listen and make them part of the program. At the Santa Fe Indian School we're open to community, we're excited about their participation and involvement. Over time that will be the factor that gives us life as an educational institution.

I went to an Indian boarding school for thirteen years. Then my dad said, "You're the oldest of the family, and since the day you were born your mother and I thought you were going to have a better opportunity than we did." I told him I didn't want to go to college, but he finally made me go for two weeks. At least it would give him the satisfaction of saying I tried.

So I went to Highlands University in Las Vegas, New Mexico. It was my first experience with a non-Indian community. I didn't want to be thought of as a dumb Indian, so I was afraid of asking questions. I just lay on my bed waiting for the two weeks to pass. I didn't even unpack my bag.

People have asked me how I wound up in education. The way it happened was I was in this big auditorium. The dean was instructing the students to follow the chairman for each major. I didn't have any idea of a major or minor because I was planning to leave school in two weeks. Then he said, "All the education majors follow Dr. Matlack." Everybody who was left got up, and I got up with them. That's how I got into education.

An individual from Santa Clara met me in the yard one day and said, "You're Joe Abeyta, aren't you? I know your father." I tried to pretend I had everything under control, but one evening he came to my room and saw my bed wasn't made and my boxes were under the bed. He said, "I thought things were going well. Are you going to class?" I said no. He pulled up a chair. He was rough; that was his personality. He said, "What's the matter with you? There's only seven other Indian students here and it's up to us to do well so others can follow us."

I said it wasn't my responsibility. He really got on my case. He said, "If you want me to help you, I'll help you. If you want to quit, go to hell."

So he came to my room every evening to help me. That first quarter I was on probation. My courses were so hard. He would study with me at night and get up early in the morning. We'd go to breakfast and study. I graduated from Highlands and that led to my first teaching job.

While I was in college, one of my roommates, a non-Indian, challenged me. "Joe Abeyta, why are you in this school? You know, my mother and father worked hard to make money so they could send me to school, and you, you government baby, the government's paying for you." This was in front of a class of thirty or forty other students. God, I was so devastated, I felt like crawling into a corner.

I recall clearly when I came home telling my dad, "It's so difficult at Highlands, because those people that are supposed to be our friends still have some real hostilities about Indian people." And I asked him, "Why is it that we have free hospitals and free schools?"

My dad said, "Well, they're *not* free. The fact of the matter is that your grandpa, your great-grandpa, your great-great-grandpa paid like no one else in this country has paid." He said, "Do you realize that at one point there were seventy pueblos in New Mexico and they've been reduced to nineteen? Do you have any idea what the population was three hundred years ago and what it is now? Do you have any idea how many people were put into slavery to dig the gold? Do you have any idea how many people had their legs amputated so they wouldn't run away? Because if you did, then you'd realize that there's been a payment in full."

My dad said, "Joseph, for goodness sakes, you shouldn't be embarrassed or shy. You tell your roommate that the water he drinks was *ours*. To this day there are agreements being violated. You tell him, 'I've paid. My grandpa paid for me. Paid for it ten times more than you'll ever pay.' And you take advantage of the opportunities you've got so that as you get older you'll be able to answer this question."

My relationship with non-Indian society has changed dramatically over the years. I have some clear memories from when I was a youngster that created a negative sense in my mind. There were a lot of people who let it be known that you were a second-class citizen. They had no qualms about laughing at you for being Indian. They'd say to old folks in the check-out line at the grocery store, "Indian, move aside."

Out of that experience came a sense of anger and even hostility. There was a point in my life, honestly, that I felt such anger that I just decided I was going to get my fair share. You know, the anger that I'm going to have a position at the table as an *equal*, to hold up those principles that my ancestors thought we were guaranteed when they signed on the dotted line or left their thumbprint.

That anger, as crazy and damaging as it was, was one of my motivations for succeeding. I've grown to the point where I understand more clearly that to accomplish good things for our communities there have to be alliances and relationships. There are decent and fair people who are genuinely interested in the concerns of Indian people, and we need to show them some respect.

I desperately want to be able to use the strength I feel, even for people who aren't good to me. I'm strong enough to deal with that. I still run across people who are hostile, but I like to be friendly and cooperative, because I realize that I've probably got more than they do in terms of an appreciation of what human beings are and what dignity is.

I have a hard time with educators who try to play God and say someone is better than someone else, who divide things and say who can and cannot come to school. I believe in God. God does good things. Every tree that grows, everything in this world that he's created is good. As you gain experience and accept that God does good things, it's pretty easy to accept that all kids are creations of God and therefore they're good people.

If you accept that God is good and the children he's created are good, it becomes the responsibility of the school to accept them all and work to the best of our ability to find and develop their strengths, and not dwell on the negative.

A lot of schools look at kids and evaluate them on their prior experience and expectations, and in the process lose out on the strengths and potentials of those youngsters. Because the youngsters don't have a forum or a place to speak, their needs go unmet. The purpose of the Santa Fe Indian School is to be able to recognize the strengths of our kids, to develop their potential and give them opportunity.

Not enough work has been done to understand how Indian kids learn. There are different learning styles. Wherever you look at Indian education, you'll find remedial programs, programs to change kids—programs that say we don't like you the way you are and we're going to change you. I'd rather accept that kids are good. Accepting the kid as a worthwhile person is very basic in an Indian education program.

Our students will tell you a critical part of our program is to get students to respect one another, to put into practice all the advice their parents and grandparents have given them—look out for one another, take care of one another.

There's a tendency for us as adults to impose on young people a set of requirements that are contradictory to how the world in fact works and how we run our own lives. I'm committed to the idea that before we implement more rules, students are going to be involved in that process. I've got concerns about the dining hall and kids going off campus to vendors on the streets. But before I make a final decision involving those rules I'm going to talk to those students.

The point I'm trying to make is that often decisions are made that impact kids without their participation, based on the assumption they don't know any better. Then all of a sudden I guess some type of miracle happens, and when they turn eighteen years old they're supposed to become adults—literally overnight. It's grossly unfair.

I think there needs to be an appreciation for young people early on. We need to work honestly and compassionately with youngsters based on the idea that we're the best examples they can have. We need to be accountable for the way we live our lives. Sometimes we tell kids one thing and then we go out and do the complete opposite ourselves. The kids aren't dumb; they see that.

Sometimes we sit back and say, "What in the world is the matter with the youth of today?" Well, to a great degree I think the problem is *adults*— we're inconsistent, we contradict ourselves continually, we send mixed messages. Then we have the audacity to ask why kids are in the turmoil they are now.

Part of the solution is respect: respecting the fact that they have minds, they have intelligence, and that they're going to grow up and become accountable for themselves.

I still live in Santa Clara. It's important for my kids to grow up here. I like the work I'm doing. This business is difficult beyond education. More and more I'm realizing that historically the support system for Indian people has been conditional. It was there as long as you knew your place and weren't a threat. Once you deviate from that and start thinking for yourself, people question if this person is a little out of hand.

There are some people who see the school as a threat. Last year our students got something like $280,000 worth of competitive scholarships, and in the past couple of years we've won a state basketball championship, two state baseball championships, and a cross-country championship.

I want to meet the educational standards of the state and exceed them. As the state tries to push their requirements, we've been good at telling them we don't like your standards and we're going to go beyond those expectations.

The attitude here is that this is an Indian school owned by Indian people. Seventy-eight percent of the people that work here are Indian. We're governed by an all-Indian school board. That gets into every aspect of our program. We teach math, science, physics, and English, but everything is from an Indian perspective. The students develop insight and a frame of reference. That's the power and strength I was talking about. You give me your kid, and he'll be different by the time he finishes here.

Our curriculum and calendar don't match that of the public schools. When we have assemblies, we open with an Indian prayer. We have a long Christmas holiday because the pueblos are involved in activities. We're not in school the end of October and first of November because Indian kids are honoring their dead in ceremony and tradition.

Last year we had a food fight in the cafeteria. The kids said, "Give us a break, it's the end of the year." I said no, we can't allow that because food has a special place in our lives. Some Indian people came from the community and lectured the kids about respect for food. The kids said they had never thought of it that way.

We've got religious leave on our campus. A kid can have a leave of absence if there's something going on at home. All we need is your tribal official to say you're needed at home. We don't even question it. We respect it.

God has created human beings and they're all good. Indian kids are good just like everyone else. Don't look for their faults; look for their strengths.

Photograph by Terry Foss, courtesy of the American Friends Committee.

Jerry Pardilla

People of the Dawn

Jerry Pardilla is a traditional member the Penobscot Nation, or Panawabskek (People at the White Rock Place). It is part of the Wabanaki, collectively known as People of the Dawn. He served as governor of the Penobscot Nation from 1992 to 1994 and as lieutenant governor from 1991 to 1992.

His family has been involved for generations with the Catholic Church on the Penobscot Reservation. Their religious beliefs have been a parallel of Catholicism compatible with traditional Native American religious beliefs.

At the time of this interview with Lois Crozier-Hogle, Jerry Pardilla was coordinator of the Maine Indian Program. He provided support to youth councils and intertribal youth networks. In the summers he worked with Indian youths at the intertribal camps sponsored by the Central Maine Indian Association.

He is now executive director of the National Tribal Environmental Council. This nonprofit organization, composed of eighty-four member tribes from across the United States, supports tribes' efforts to protect their lands and natural resources according to their priorities and values. He lives with his wife, Marla, a Navajo–Southern Ute, in Rio Rancho, New Mexico.

When I am invited to speak, usually I have some ideas that are in my head. But in the final preparation what moves me is that I want to speak spontaneously from the heart. That comes from the spirit.

Part of my background has been these parallel roads. My family was raised with the missionary Jesuits. We have a church on the reservation that is an overlay of Catholicism onto our special beliefs.

There are these two roads. I reached an age when I wanted to make very clear to my parents that this method of worship—reciting prayers by rote and reading a book that tells me how to respond—was not enough. It did not fully touch my heart, it did not allow me to establish my own relationship with our Creator. The word in our language is *Kchiniwesk*, or Great Spirit.

So I started to pray. A friend and I started praying and fasting. We talked to our elders, and they started to guide us. We said we wanted to know who we are. We don't believe what we see on our TV. We don't like what we're learning in school. We don't like the way we're being treated. We know there's something more, and we're going to find it.

So that really began the search that helped me come to an understanding about who I am and what my purpose is. Talking to the elders and my grandparents and medicine people. Endless hours of listening to them. Seeing what they did. And starting to experience that there is a spirit in all things. It's not a crisis of man versus nature. Really, we're part of nature. How dare we think that we can ravage this earth without it having a direct effect on us? We've learned it now, too late perhaps.

My elders said, "Take what you need, use what you need. When you go to gather medicine, don't gather them all. And when you go, you leave a gift because you're receiving a gift." So when I would go to see my elders, I would come with tobacco in my hand, or sweet grass. If they accepted what I offered, then we would talk. They had to feel me out, to see if I was sincere.

The teachings came to me in many ways, in legends and stories. You get little bits and pieces. You come in and start opening up. I really feel from my own experience teaching and fasting that not only as Indians but as human beings we have a responsibility to this earth.

My children have learned about this from a number of sources. Unlike me, they have a resource right here handy. I take my son to my ceremonies with me, and my daughters go to the womens ceremonies. I put him beside me and tell him to watch. I don't care where I am, if he has a question, he'll whisper it in my ear.

I bring him so he can hear our relatives and other tribes talk. I tell him, "This is no show. This is who we are, this is how we believe, and I'd just like you to notice. Someday it may mean a lot to you. You might want to go run and play, but just sit here." I talk to my daughters about things like that, too. I don't have to tell my children that I'm intensely proud of who I am and that no one can make me feel inferior.

It's a long time in coming, but now it's in them and it just goes without saying. I raised my children to feel and know their heritage. It's not just wearing leather and beads; it's a spiritual base. It's not an academic study, it's something that comes over time. It comes with responsibility.

In our communities, long before there were Christian missionaries, there was a "way" of life. It wasn't a regimented weekly visit to a church where you prayed for an hour and were absolved of what you did all week, then you could go back and do it again. Maybe I'm being too judgmental, but what I'm getting at is there was a *way*. There were certain people who emerged as leaders in ceremonies, who helped a community prepare for significant events in family and community life. Prayer was elemental to that.

As a pipe carrier today, I am a prayer person, and I participate in cere-monies. I'm not a missionary, I seek not to convert. Rather, I associate with people who believe as I do. I share right from my heart how I believe and pray.

The pipe isn't mine. I have the responsibility of caring for it. I cannot deny it to our people. I cannot put it under a bushel basket. Oftentimes it means traveling to communities who need prayer. They'll say come and help us. They'll send me tobacco and I'll go and pray with them and sing our ceremonial songs. The songs have been kept alive, and I feel very fortunate to know them.

I want to share them with the young people. I'll go into tribal schools and teach these songs. To see their faces light up when you come—I love the early childhood ones, the four-year-olds. I sit down there right in the middle of them with my drum.

I sing these songs, and they just slowly open up. Their parents tell me, "I love it when they come home singing in these angelic voices." They get up and learn to dance. I feel so good taking them by their little hands and dancing around with them. It moves me beyond anything.

I've been working in youth camps in Maine for Indian kids at risk. I've been pleased and shocked with what I've encountered. We have some serious problems. Not all of them are our own making, but we're caught in very difficult intergenerational cycles of alcoholism, abuse, and drugs.

In the exclusively Indian camps, some are in denial of who they are. When I speak in their language there's no response, and it's not always because they don't understand it. The children who are mixes—the ones who appear to be very little Indian—have an incredible crisis because they're not accepted by other Indians and they're not accepted by non-Indians. They're in this gray world.

Maine in the summer is a very beautiful place to be. You're at a lake and in cabins, and there is swimming, canoeing, and fishing. We start the day with morning ceremony. We want to downplay their identity as coming from a particular community and being cliquish. We're really all the same people. We introduce principles of the medicine wheel, telling them, "You will be an eagle clan and you will be in the east. You will be a bear clan and you will be over in the west. You will be a moose clan in the north. You will be a porcupine clan in the south."

We stand in a circle in our morning prayers. Then the kids go in their respective directions, and we open up with a ceremonial fire. We teach about caring for this fire, using very simple rules. We try to bring about prayer, and I sing a song from each of the tribes. When I come to the song from their tribe, a lot of the kids sing with gusto.

By the end of the camp these kids feel proud of who they are. In the evening we gather for a social—out west they might call it a pow wow. We drum and have a fire where the children can come and dance. In the beginning they are very standoffish. Then we start social dances where they dance as a group. Slowly they start doing individual dances. By the end of the week they request songs from their particular tribe. We feel the whole sense of instilling in them a pride of who they are as Indian people.

We're here for the long term. The effects of colonialism, racism, governmental policies, and persecution have been centuries in the making. We're not so foolish as to think that we can undo this in a short period of time. But we do have a voice. We will not allow ourselves to be ignored.

Change is coming, but it will not be a huge wave. We are diverse and I do not see a collective action. I feel more a movement to preserve and maintain elements of our individual tribal cultures.

Some of the changes are not always positive. I got up to share songs at a camp with some Passamaquoddy students. I asked them to help me, and they put their heads down. It was more than shyness. It was okay to be Indian in their own community, but they were very self-conscious among non-Indian people. I said, "Come up here and let's dance. This isn't a show, let's just have everyone dance together."

In our social dances we end with what's called a snake dance. There are legends and stories behind it, but the basic idea of the snake dance is that everybody gets together. Long ago, this dance began celebrations, but today it is usually the last dance. At the head is usually some respected person, and he has a rattle—unlike a rattlesnake, which has the rattle at the tail. They keep time with the drum. The purpose is that we are breaking up and may not see each other for months. We've all touched each other in some way in the time we've been together.

So when we dance, we interlock at the elbows and weave in and out and coil around while the song is being sung and the drums are playing. It's a time for everybody to be connected and touch each other and laugh and have a good time seeing each other go by as we're coiling and uncoiling. We're saying, "We'll see you again."

I was trying to have the Passamaquoddy students help me do this dance.

They were very apprehensive. I knew the source of this was that they were raised in an area where people discriminated against them. They didn't want to come out and show that, "Not only am I an Indian, but now I'm going to do a tribal dance." But after we finally got the dance going, they joined in. It was evident to me there is much work to be done.

At another camp where I was invited to drum and sing, there were two suicide attempts. It was devastating. We were on an island that was only accessible by boat, and we had to arrange to get the boys to a hospital. For these two to slash their wrists—it was mind-boggling to me. And there I was thinking that this was going to be a great time. Some of the issues concerning alcoholism and the host of problems in the communities were brought out, and the children weren't able to handle that.

So I've learned that when you bring up really sensitive issues, you need to have trained people who can follow up and help these young people who are hurting. How dare we even attempt to unravel all those hurts and pains if we're not there to help them through that?

In our daily lives we have ceremonies and prayers, and we give thanks to everything. It's a long ceremony, but we give thanks to the animals, birds, plants, winter, rain, moon, sun—and then there are phrases that take in anything that we may have left out. But we always keep the consciousness that we are only one part, not masters. We do not have dominion.

Earth is 75 percent water. People may think of land bridges like the Bering Strait, but I have the novel idea that water is the bridge for everything. It is essential to life.

Water, in ancestral times, was a way to travel. But it is also a life-giver. It flows through the body. Water is a bridge to life, spirit, and all else. If there is a cause, there is an effect. We may not understand all of the impact, but we will experience the effects because we are all related.

I feel a compression going on, though. On one hand, we have a strong sense of nature and an understanding that we're a part of it—that we're not above nature. I acknowledge that. I think that centuries ago this was really the way we could have lived.

But now in the modern world, we're caught in a vise. I drive a vehicle that burns fossil fuels. I use energy derived from dams that block the river that bears the name of our tribe. They've blocked the migration of salmon. That's one arm. The other arm pressing in on us is that when we Native Americans are seen as not acting in accordance with the notion that we should be caretakers of the earth, we're really condemned.

We're falling in between. We don't have the ability to go back and live our former way, mostly because this government doesn't wish us to do that. It wants us to live in the mainstream. But when we step forward today and say we'll do something that doesn't quite fit the stereotypical picture of us, we're condemned by environmental groups and a host of other people.

I tell them that they have denied us the right to our culture in the past, and now they are not allowing us to live in the present. It is the "noble savage" syndrome. They think in romanticized terms when they think about us: they want us to be noble, but they deny us the right to be either in the past or the present.

So we fall in between. How do we reconcile that?

Our leadership is considering a plant that will burn garbage and generate electricity. Some people are saying, "Hold it, this isn't the image that we expect you to put forward!" I'd ask them, "What image do you want? Do you want us to live in wigwams and have canoes? Then give us our land back and go away in your boats."

I'm being facetious. But we want what we could call a *clean* industry. It wouldn't be a paper mill that would spew pollutants into the air and river. As we look for factories or industry to invest in, we want ones that are beneficial economically and not harmful environmentally.

We can live in our modern world without having to go back and live precisely in the old ways. The values and belief systems are what I carry forward. There are obstacles, but we can still carry these forward today. The value of this land is part of us. When you walk on the earth here, you're walking on the spiritual home of my ancestors. That keeps me grounded—I'm not going to go and indiscriminately gouge out the earth and exploit it. I'm here to live with it. I know there really is a spirit in all things. That stone—it has a spirit, and I know it well. The water has a spirit. The air, fire, the elements.

One of the things we joke about is, who would ever have imagined we'd have bought and sold land like this? Who would have imagined that today we're even buying water? And who can imagine that someday we may be buying air? My ancestors scoffed at the idea of buying land: "Ha! We *occupy* the land."

Even though we live in a modern world, we don't have to ignore our background and our beliefs. But it's been very difficult because there are a lot of trade-offs. I'm deeply concerned about what hydroelectric energy means for Native peoples. It usually means flooding their lands and relocating whole peoples. Canada and the United States have to take into account the connection with the land. Forced removal is devastating to the spirit of the people.

I also have fear about pollution of the rivers and the fish we eat. There is an alarming rate of cancer in the Penobscot Nation. We're eating animals off the land, we're eating the fish, we're eating plants that grow along the river. And we're being poisoned by the waste that's put in the river by the textile plants, paper mills, and other industries. At one time the federal government was considering using Penobscot lands as a repository for nuclear waste, as if we were expendable.

I want my presence to be left on this earth as if I was placing my hand in a bucket of water. I'm here while I'm here. But when I retrieve my hand, when the ripples cease, there's no evidence I was there. I'd like to leave that with my children and my grandchildren for seven generations to come.

I want to leave for my children not just genetics, but belief systems. I know my great-grandfather as if he was sitting right here beside me. He passed away a few years before I was born, yet I know him. I've been raised with family stories and legends, and the values and memories of my grandfather are carried forward. When my children's generation has leadership positions, they'll make decisions that will take into account our beliefs and values.

Clifford Trafzer

The Children Are Our Future

Clifford Trafzer (Wyandot) is a teacher, historian, editor, traditional storyteller, and the father of three daughters. He is director of the Costo Native American Research Center and Native American Studies Program, as well as professor of history and ethnic studies, at the University of California, Riverside. He is also vice-chair of the Native American Heritage Commission of California.

As a child in Ohio, he never thought he would go to college. His family (including his Wyandot grandfather) moved from Ohio to Arizona when he was ten years old. At that age, his grandfather took young Cliff to the University of Arizona and told him that he wanted him to attend college. Jobs hauling freight and furniture, working in the fields, and helping in his father's upholstery shop during high school convinced him that his grandfather was right. He received B.A. and M.A. degrees from Northern Arizona University and went on to earn a Ph.D. in history from Oklahoma State University in 1973.

Dr. Trafzer has received numerous awards for his teaching, his scholarly works, and his children's books, including the PEN Josephine Miles National Literary award for *Earth Song, Sky Spirit* (1994). He is the author and editor of more than twenty books, including *Blue Dawn, Red Earth* (editor, 1996); *Grandmother, Grandfather, and Old Wolf* (1997); *The Kit Carson Campaign* (1982); *American Indian*

Prophets (editor, 1986); and *The Renegade Tribe* (1986). Many of his stories for children originate from traditional oral narratives.

He was interviewed by Darryl Wilson.

I think of myself as having a strong spiritual base, which was given to me during my childhood. It is a prerequisite for survival, both today and in the future. It is the real core of our being.

My spiritual beliefs come from my mother. I recall one night I was frightened by the darkness. She sat me down and we talked about the beauty of the night, the beauty of the sound we were hearing from the crickets. I remember seeing the lightning bugs down in the field below us. She told me that the earth is not really dark during the night, that we have the stars above us and it is a special time of a twenty-four-hour period that we can really see the stars. It is a time when we can reach out beyond earth.

She also taught me to love where we were living, a sense that Ohio had originally been a place of Wyandot people. My people had been there farming and using the woods and hunting close to where I grew up. So we had a real sense of closeness to the earth. Every year we had a garden. All the children had to go out and work in it. Mother would instill in us not just the fact that life needed that food to live, but that we had a responsibility to be doing this kind of work. A responsibility to ourselves, to the corn, the tomatoes, the potatoes, the beans, the squash—to the plant people we were putting into the ground.

She didn't drive home in a doctrinaire way that this was religion. But, in fact, it was. As we were planting the seeds, we were planting a part of ourselves into the earth. I didn't like working all of the time. I didn't like to hoe the garden. But I had to, and I learned from it.

Sometimes it is difficult to learn. We don't always get to do what we want. My mom and dad forced me to go out there and sow, weed, can, and store the food. We were working as a family for our well-being. But we also had a spirit about us. I learned about the importance of taking care of the earth, nurturing it and nurturing the plants. We took care of the earth so it would take care of us.

This may seem far afield from spirituality to some people, but that is the heart of *my* spirit—the stars, the sun, the earth, the moon, the plants. I recall my mother talking about the meats we ate. She would say these beings are alive and we had to give thanks. There was never a meal that passed that we didn't give thanks to the foods that we ate and to the Almighty for having provided these things for us.

Mother taught us about the spirit-people early on. She taught us that there was another level or plane all around us that we could not see, a level of spirits who were always there with us. They are like guardian angels, spirits of corn and beans and squash. They are spirits of people who have passed over. That, too, is spirituality. It is the Wyandot way to believe in the strength of dreams and visions that come to you.

The idea of spirituality is the heart of being Indian. It is the heart of Native history as well. I don't believe there is any understanding of us as individuals or Indian people without an understanding of our religious beliefs.

I want to make sure that my children have the same spiritual seeds planted in them. I take the girls out in the night and tell them that they were once stars, and that the stars are so beautiful that I wanted a particular star to come down and live with us. Those stars became our children. So they believe they are star-people. And I certainly believe they are star-people.

That interconnection between human being and the stars, sun, moon, and Earth is what ties our being with the creation and the Creator. We are all a part of the whole. We are not separate. We are as tied to the earth below our feet as we are to the sun that is shining on us now. We are a part of a whole that is tremendous. It is incredible!

When I was young, my mother instilled in me a sense of history, a sense of being. Being part of the earth. The way to transfer this is to give it to our children at a very young age. I do this by talking with them, sharing time with them, walking with them, telling stories and reading to them.

The children are our future. Those of us who have been honored by receiving an education have an opportunity put before us. We must not forget other people. Whether they are among our tribe or not, we have a spiritual obligation to reach out, to draw them into our circle, to help them with their education and their needs. We need to pick up the slack, to go beyond what a particular parent might do. We need to take it upon ourselves in a much larger sense. I do not turn my back on these children because they are not *my* children. They *are* my children, my brothers and sisters.

I am a strong believer in sharing what we have with others. Now, there are things of a sacred nature that should not be shared with people other than those of your particular group. But then there are the root literatures of our people that can be shared back and forth.

We have become so parochial that we are only concerned about our own history. We need to know about others, share in their stories. We need to come to an understanding of what happened to the Wyandots and Hurons, what happened to the Miamis and Muskogees. There are so many peoples. We need a broader understanding of both Indians and non-Indians, and of what has happened. We cannot find that in our history books, to be sure. History books are so Eurocentric. Columbus is portrayed as a hero, and little is said about the slavery and deaths of millions of people. We as a nation need to face up to that.

All people must have the feeling of value for themselves, for their people, and for their way of life. Nothing transmits that more than language. When the language is broken and destroyed by the Bureau of Indian Affairs or a church or what have you, something is really lost. We must work collectively to save and transmit languages. With language comes culture, understanding, art, religion, and music. We need to celebrate these things and look forward to their preservation.

I may not know a great deal about all of the traditions of Wyandot people. Certainly five hundred years ago, being Wyandot would have been much, much different than it is today. But you can pick up from other Wyandot people—such as Eleanor and George Sioui—a sense of story, a sense of song, music, and art. That kind of sharing can be done. I am not arguing in any sense for a "generic-Indian-thing," but you can draw on other peoples and other cultures to enrich your own understanding of Indian identity.

I don't think this is anything that is not traditional. I heard a story from a Maidu man not long ago. He told me about how catfish got thorns on their faces. That was because they once had spears and were going to attack an elk or moose. Then, lo and behold, I read the same story, and it was credited to an Anishanaabe person. You could probably go to the Cree country and hear it from Cree people, too. There is a great transference of stories and cultural beliefs that is as Indian as anything else.

It is difficult to change the views of adults, so we have to change the views of children. This would mean a new mode of education for Indian—and non-Indian—people. We have to deal with children on many different levels to get them to see the value of Indian literature and history—and to come to an understanding of the European perspective as well.

The beginning of the healing will be when the Indian people begin working with one another. We have a tremendous task in trying to get along with one another and let down factionalism, difficulties, and conflicts.

It is true with all of us. We are all born with a soft spot on the top of our heads. It is there so that we can communicate with our Creator. As we grow older, that soft spot grows harder and harder. We need to keep that soft spot open so that we can have communication with the creation and all of us within it.

I grew up in Ohio, the traditional lands of some Wyandot after some were pushed out of Michigan and Canada. On my mother's side, my family was forced out of Ohio, forced by the government into Kansas. In the 1850s or 1860s my people came back to Ohio to squat on the land that formerly had been theirs along the Upper Sandusky River. My grampa met my grandma at a pool hall. Grandma's father was in the trading business and grampa's dad was running the pool hall.

My understanding of my Indian identity comes largely from my family, from my grandfather and my mother. I spent the early part of my life searching for my Indian identity, what it meant to be a mixed-blood and how to reconcile both worlds. It is not at all an easy task.

I don't think that any place in the world was perfect. Before Columbus, the Wyandot and Huron people had enemies among the Iroquois, but still they had a good life. They lived as one with the plant and animal people. They lived as one with the earth. They had their traditional wisdoms, and some of them spent time thinking and being philosophers. They spent a lot of time with their families. They farmed and planted. They fought with their enemies.

I mention the dreaming and the family because the oral tradition was so strong prior to Columbus. There was so much history imparted to young people to help them find their way in life. People do this today, but it was done on a much greater level back then. With the harsh winters, having no TV or radio, people spent time very close together. Life was more intimate, more human. I try to impart this to my students so that they might understand the origins of Native American history.

People spent a good deal of time making a living. They kept their minds on the things that were important. You can only make a living if your mind is straight with the Creator. So we spent a great deal of time interacting with the plant- and animal-people, with the fish-people—and we spent a lot of time giving thanks to the plants for giving their lives for us. We spent a lot of time thinking about our relationship to plants and animals, and we didn't take things for granted.

I don't think we were materialistic. Besides not owning land, people did not try to accumulate great amounts of property. You might have pride in a beaded bag or your gloves or quill work or the kind of lodge that you made. But you also had items of power that you carried with you and always revered, like tobacco, arrows, wooden figures, or feathers. People did not spend a good deal of time earning currency in order to buy things. Instead, there was a larger life.

That is one of the major changes with white contact—coming into contact with manufactured goods where you spent a good deal of time trying to obtain furs to trade to the French, who then would provide you with guns or powder, lead, metal pots and pans, fish hooks, spears and things like that. That dramatically changed us. Indians had to play the game somebody else had made for them.

The conquest of America has not stopped. Euro-Americans blindly walk forward and continue with their old ways of doing things without giving any credence to the fact that there was and is a truly American people here: Native Americans.

All of the European nations came with an attitude. They did not come to be one with Native people or their environment. They saw something wild that needed to be tamed. This attitude continues in many different ways today. It is pretty harmful, not only for Indian people, but for the whole world.

Chief Seathl, as he was called in his day, gave an eloquent speech about white people not understanding that the very ground that they walk on is far more sacred to Indian people than it is to whites. The reason for this, he said, was that the earth held the remains of children, mothers, and fathers. It holds the bones of loved ones. The earth, he said, was more responsive to the touch of moccasins than to the boots of the white people.

Chief Seathl looked to the future in a semipositive way, saying, "We aren't going to forget who we are. We are not going to forget that this land is ours, first. We are not going to forget that the spirit people surround us everywhere. We are not going to forget that there are invisible forces here."

And there *are* invisible forces. It is those invisible forces that have helped us survive for all these years. These forces continue to work with us today. It is our obligation, as we live on this plane, as we are on this earth now, to transfer to young Native people a sense of spirituality. A sense of love of the earth, a sense of being Indian, and what that means today.

This is important in everyday life and in my scholarly work as an historian. Understanding the significance of spiritual relations of humans with the earth is a powerful factor historically, and one which I continually offer as a theme in my work and to my graduate and undergraduate students. Family and spiritual values are two themes that are not understood in the historical context, and I focus on both in most of my scholarly works.

We may lose heart now and then, but we must not lose sight of the work we need to do, whether it is our literature, protecting remains in the ground, sacred sites, religious ceremonies, or our scholarship. We must participate, we must remember, we must treasure, and we must transfer that on to the young people.

We must do these little things. We are not going to reach everyone, but if we make an attempt to deal with the larger community—especially with the children, to touch their hearts and minds in a way they have never been touched before—that is a great success.

My work in children's literature came about in part because I treasure the stories that have been shared with me. They don't belong to me, they belong to a hundred generations of people who shared them long before my birth. And the stories will be shared with generations to come. I want to share them with my children and all children. I want to do this to affect the ways in which children see the world—especially Indian children. Maybe one day this writing might inspire them, show them that they too can write and tell stories. That they too can learn more about their traditions and share them.

Some Indians tell children that education is not "Indian" and that they should not participate in it. I say that wisdom, knowledge, growth, development, sharing, vision, and looking ahead are all part of traditional Indian beliefs, and we should treasure them.

WE CAN HAVE NEW VISIONS

A renaissance of Indian artistic expression has been taking place, making links back to tradition, both keeping it alive and extending it. These expressions can also forge links with a non-Indian audience. Artist Roxanne Swentzell and writer Greg Sarris discuss meeting these challenges. Christopher Peters demonstrates the connection between traditional religious practice and the making of art. Finally, renowned scholar and writer Jack Forbes articulates themes found throughout this volume with an extraordinary glimpse of how all of this is woven into the fabric of his life.

Roxanne Swentzell

Hearing with Our Hearts

Roxanne Swentzell was born in 1962. She is from Santa Clara
Pueblo, an adobe village on the Rio Grande in northern New
Mexico. Her Indian name is O-gi-ghee Povi, which means
"Snowflake."

She is a highly accomplished artist who specializes in
sculpting human figures out of clay. Her work has been shown in
galleries and museums around the country and was featured in the
frontispiece of the Smithsonian history of North American Indians.

She lives with her husband and two children in a
two-story solar adobe house in Santa Clara, where she participates
in the pueblo's ceremonial dances and feasts. In addition to her
art, she is a farmer growing food for her family. She co-founded
and helps to operate the nonprofit Flowering Tree Permaculture
Institute, which experiments with sustainable living systems.

Her mother, Rina Naranjo Swentzell, is a Pueblo
Indian widely known for her views on Indian philosophy. Her
father, Ralph Swentzell, is a white man of German descent who
teaches at St. John's College in Santa Fe.

Roxanne Swentzell attended the Institute of
American Indian Arts in Santa Fe and the Portland (Oregon)
Museum Art School. She begins this interview with Lois Crozier-
Hogle and Ferne Jensen by relating her decision to leave art school
and go home.

People in art school looked at art very differently than I did. I got really depressed when I was in Portland because I felt that the people there had separated art from their lives and from everything around them. It became a dead world to me. I couldn't understand why people would do art just for art's sake. To me, art always had to come from a life experience—or what was happening around me. It seemed so strange to be walking a city street or through a parking lot and see the homeless on the side of the road, or see people crying. The focus of the art school seemed to be disconnected from these realities.

I could not pretend I never saw that, then try to make this piece of art-work that had nothing to do with what I had just witnessed. Making a piece of art, to me, had to be as full an experience of myself as I could possibly relay. If I was going through a lot of pain in my life, I couldn't possibly make a sculpture of a jolly guy, because my tears would ruin his smile. I've tried to say something I really didn't feel in my art, but it just looks and feels like a lie to me.

Many of the teachers at the Institute of American Indian Arts were white people who were trying to get Indian artists to make what the white people thought was Indian art. This caused a lot of conflict for me. I thought, "If I am an Indian then I'll automatically be making Indian art because that's what I am."

If we see through *our* eyes then whatever we are will come out. And that means whether I am an Indian or not. It doesn't really matter. What matters is that whatever appears from within us is true. I learned to listen to myself and not be so influenced by what other people wanted me to make. I am going to present the world through my eyes—and not as somebody told me I was supposed to.

My figures often look troubled because I am troubled a lot by how sad everyone is, how out of touch with themselves they are. The world is trying to show this to us. If a forest is dying, how does it tell you? It doesn't say,

"Hey, what do you think about not driving your car over me all the time?" It tells you by giving you clues and by a feeling you get when you are open to it and recognize the pain. If you're sensing a struggle or confusion of sorts, it is trying to tell you—if you're open to hearing.

People are showing the same signs of distress. All of us are trying to find love. That we are trying to all look like or act like some model on TV is a big sign to me that we aren't getting the love we need. We are getting desperate.

The art community didn't seem to understand that. So I came home. I am making a home, which is very important to me and to my children.

We're all on this earth together. This is our planet. Everyone is responsible to take care of this beautiful earth. I think the Native American people were among the last to give up that responsibility, the last to give up that sort of connection to earth—and I think they have, for the most part, given it up.

That's very sad to me. Some Native Americans have a lot of old ways of "seeing" that are really good, but I don't think most really understand what the "old ways" mean any more. They are just holding onto symbols and rituals because they know there was something there once. Hopefully, some-day they will know what it means. You can see how they are falling apart just by how they choose to live their lives.

Most of the people here at Santa Clara Pueblo don't have anything to do with the land, with the place, anymore. They go off to work from eight to five just like everybody else and they want their new car and their TV and their VCR. What they really want is to be middle-class white Americans.

I've watched this area and the Indian culture slowly disintegrating into white America during my lifetime. What that means is you go outside of your community for everything, and so you open the door for someone else to rule your life. Everything falls apart eventually if you put it all in that basket.

It can't stay the way it's going because nothing is in the hands of the people any more. Nobody has a center any more. Nobody grows their own food, nobody makes their own clothes, nobody builds their own houses, nobody takes care of their own family—they send their kids off for some-one else to raise.

I don't know if people have to go through the cycle of going clear to that end and saying, "Whoa! This isn't where it's at," before they come home again. Or, hopefully, they can take a short cut home. I think most of the people in this country have already gone way out there into materialism and they're saying, "No. It's not here. Let's find where it is." So they are looking at Native Americans and people like us because we have been spiritually in balance—or seem to have been there recently.

Some Native Americans are doing this, too. I find it in a lot of the younger generation of the Indians around this country. They have seen much of the white world and realized that it isn't where it's at. So some of them are trying to come back, at least to what is left of their Native culture.

They are trying to find where they belong, where they fit in. My generation is of the children who were raised in the white world knowing that we came from an Indian world. We were raised in the white world by parents from the Native world.

Some of us found that there was nothing out there in the white world. Some of us are now asking what our Indian culture holds for us. We want to get back to ourselves. That is our true home.

It is time for *everybody* to get back home, not just the Indian people. The whole world needs to get back *home*. But at the same time, remember that *home* isn't just another image or culture to get attached to.

That, to me, means being able to focus again, to not be blinded by the images we are given. We are all constantly being thrown suggestions of images of what we're supposed to look like, what we're supposed to *be* like, how we're supposed to dress, how we're supposed to live in this world.

Look around and you will start to notice just how much of the world is a subliminal message. I'm talking about images of all kinds from every culture—although many are from Western culture. Those images are poured into every world. That makes us all feel very unloved because all of us—white or Indian—aren't accepted for who we are.

What we need to do is see the world again for what it is, not through images created by someone else. And when we can see ourselves for who we are instead of as an image, we are loved again. And the whole planet is loved. You cannot hurt anything when you love it and it loves you back.

When there is respect for what things are, there is love. Then the planet will live again. I feel like we're so close to completely destroying it. We have to revive it again because it's almost dead.

Right now I think a lot of people are realizing that we can't keep going the way we have been. There's so much pain in this realization that it takes us inside ourselves. Hopefully, the next phase is to go completely inside where we can find ourselves again.

That may be painful, but we have to go through to the other side. It's a process. You have to go through the steps to get to the other side, to come out of the suffering of not being ourselves. I do not mean yourself with an image attached to it such as "Indian," "white," "banker," "artist," etc. I'm talking about yourself as an individual with the ability to be a part of this whole universe as *you* without a title attached, without a name or culture to hide behind.

When you take all of these off, what is left? That is who I want to reach. In that place there are a lot of feelings that are not moving and so are not allowing us to grow. You have to understand that things are dying, including yourself—perishing inside. And that's painful. You have to know by feeling and experiencing that, or else it doesn't change. When you understand *why*, then it changes. You've gone through the door.

I've thought a lot about all this because I've had to. I have a strong need to know why things are the way they are. My parents definitely encouraged me to think about "why." My mother was from the pueblo, and my father, being white, gave me a strong view of Western culture.

When I think of it, I can still hear Gregorian chants playing in my memories, and see Rubens paintings and Michaelangelo sculptures. Then my mother, grandmother, cousins, uncles, aunts—Pueblo dancers, drumbeats, Indian clowns, and feast days when we would run through the crowds catching the things they would throw. Then sitting on the ground watching the feet of the dancers, not realizing for a long time that the sound of the drumbeats were from a drum and not from their feet hitting the earth.

Those two worlds danced through my childhood. Maybe because I am from both worlds I can see what I see.

Times have changed very quickly among the Indians here, and the generations have very different viewpoints. For example, my grandma's "way" of looking at things is very much from the past. She puts herself down for it because it's not what white culture says you're "supposed to be." All of her children tried very hard to be in the Western world. They tried to teach their children values of the Western culture.

My mom is halfway. She's still got hold of that past, but is trying to live in the modern white world. And I'm over here stuck in the middle. Sometimes I feel like I wasn't given either world, because I couldn't be fully in the white world or in the world of the Indian. I was too white to feel completely Indian and too Indian to feel completely white. So I had nothing to identify myself with. When you have nothing to hide behind, you have to go inside of yourself. When you see yourself as an individual instead of a race, you have a view of your own.

I couldn't be here without them taking those steps, though. And hopefully my children will take the next step. I understand how it all has worked and why, and so it is all right, though I can still feel sorrow for all the pain that has been felt. My mother was hesitant to teach me about the Indian world because there was a lot of shame during her and her mother's time.

Then all of a sudden it was cool to be Indian. Yet it is just another way to kill the Indian. Pottery, dancing, "Indian art," all were made for the white man, not for the Indian. They were sold to the Western images of fame and fortune, while Native souls were left to starve as the white man starved his soul.

What was "Indian"? Either we're seen as savages that should be gotten rid of, or put up on some throne until we are fighting one another for the candies the white government hands out—fighting for the spotlight that reads "Indian."

Indian became another image and another thing for people to run after for a sense of importance. Because we had already lost a strong sense of ourselves, "Indian" could be defined by the white world. Competition for who is the "most" Indian seemed to be the name of the game, and the white world seemed to be the judge of the race. There became a kind of desperation to have attention from the white world and many things changed because of that. There became a kind of jealousy and greed.

And so we lose a little more of ourselves until we finally have no sense of who we really are. Then, I guess, when you realize that all those names, all those images aren't making you feel any better, they're just making you hungrier for more—you stop!

You have to find yourself again as naked—nothing to hide behind, nothing to pretend to be. You find yourself not through images but through your own heart.

It doesn't matter what culture you come from, it's going to be the same "way" that ties us all together. There will be a place for us in this world when we make a place for ourselves inside of us. There will be a wholeness but also a love for the self. There will be a kind of clearness because of the honesty that comes with not having images.

I love to watch people. My whole thinking is about people—how they relate to each other, how they relate to this earth. I need to understand people, to try to find what's in them that makes them who they are.

With my sculptures I try to reach people's emotions so they can remember themselves. Mostly I create human figures out of clay. Using gestures and expressions, I try to bring these little people to life—to communicate in a way other than with words. It's good practice to use the other senses besides just the mouth.

I'm trying to do that with everything I do. Everything we do has to be sacred. It doesn't matter if you're baking bread or making a sculpture— or walking, it's got to be done in the same manner. It's got to be done with love for yourself.

There is a kind of spirit and belief in us when we do a rain dance, for example. We dance knowing we are part of this whole world—or else we wouldn't believe we can help make it rain. It is believing in ourselves that enables us to be connected to this earth, and in so doing we have tremendous power.

To be in harmony with the earth, you must go inside and deal with yourself. It is not going inside to ignore the outer world, it is going inside to find the root of the problem. You deal with your pain, your grief, your frustrations. And when you go through the process of hearing yourself out, then there is a sense of understanding and peace or harmony.

In harmony you are able to hear the needs of the animals and the trees and the dirt and the children. You hear your own needs. It is listening and seeing and feeling. Everything is awake again.

If we go into the kiva for a ceremonial dance, there is a knowing, without words, that we are all important. We are there to do something that counts. We don't have to say anything because it is already known, already understood. It is a feeling and a slight turn of the head or a look of the eye.

The problem is that we have made the whole world and ourselves so trivial that we have no importance anymore. Many of our people got brainwashed into thinking they weren't important enough to make a difference while performing ceremonies.

This is for the pueblo as well as the entire world. I believe that everyone matters. If an individual comes home inside himself or herself and walks into the room, the ceremony is changed to fit that person because that person matters. If that person is true to him- or herself, then the change that occurs will be good and sacred. If not, there will be pain.

If we would realize we are all in the same boat, then we would be ahead. I hope we can all realize that we are very sad, blind people right now and that all of us are searching for what we long for—a place, a sense of importance, and love. And we deserve that "something," no matter who we are.

I would like us to be able to communicate with each other in a way that we never could before. It's just like talking to you. You are searching for love and I am searching for it, too. Because we are hearing with our hearts instead of our preconceived notions, we have just filled ourselves up.

I think it will get so that we can do that with anybody. We will be able to say, "When I cry I know she will understand why I am crying. When I laugh I know she will know I am not laughing at her. She will know I am laughing because I feel good."

And I can scream because I am hurt and you know why. Then when you cry in front of me I can say, "Go ahead, cry." At that time we will have peace.

Greg Sarris

The Truth Will Rise

Greg Sarris is a writer and professor of English at the University of California, Los Angeles. He has served as elected chairman of the Federated Miwok people and considers that part of Sonoma County, California, to be "home."

His ancestry is Coast Miwok, Kashaya Pomo, Jewish, and Filipino. He was adopted as an infant by a white family in Santa Rosa, California. As he grew up, he naturally gravitated toward the Indian youths and families of his neighborhood, including the household of medicine woman Mabel McKay. He did not learn of his Miwok and Pomo heritage until much later, when he searched out his natural grandfather in southern California. Once he discovered who his father — deceased a year before — had been, he was able to connect with his extended family in Sonoma County.

After a troubled adolescence, Greg attended UCLA. He lived in New York City for a time and then returned to Stanford University to earn his Ph.D. in modern thought and literature. He originated a "bridge" program for Native American and other students at Stanford, and continues to speak to and work with disadvantaged youth.

His book *Mabel McKay: Weaving the Dream*, about the renowned Pomo basket weaver and medicine woman, was published in 1994. He has also written *Keeping Slug Woman Alive: Essays Toward a Holistic Approach to American Indian Texts* (1993) and edited an anthology of California Indian writing.

In addition, he is engaged in chronicling the history of Sonoma County in a series of novels. His first book of fiction, *Grand Avenue*, was published by Hyperion Press in 1994. It has been produced by Robert Redford as a movie for the cable-television network HBO. Sarris is at work on the next volume, a novel that spans three generations.

He spoke with Lois Crozier-Hogle and Giuseppe Saitta.

We believe that truth is like a cork in water. No matter how much you or somebody else tries to push it down—especially another people, invaders—eventually it's going to float back to the top. Maybe Europeans are starting to see, maybe it's taken five hundred years to see that the cork is coming right back up to the top.

My family follows the teachings of Essie Parrish, the great Kashaya prophet, and Mabel McKay, the Cache Creek Pomo basket weaver and doctor. We have been true to the teachings and tried to keep our lives in order. That's been very hard for me because there's been so much anger. Growing up, I often felt I didn't have a home. I was mixed blood—too white for the Indians and not white enough for the whites. Where did I belong, who was I?

When you're angry you start pulling the wrong straws and you can get co-opted into untruth. You have to have faith in the teachings and faith that that cork will pop up. The signs that have been in the prophecies by our dreamers are all coming to pass. So we watch and wait for that cork to rise.

There seem to be a lot of Indians and non-Indians who don't understand really how the spirit works and what respect is all about. For us, the dreamer or prophet doesn't have it—they've been chosen by the Great

Spirit. The spirit works through them. We all have great powers that we've been born with, things that we are supposed to do. We're all buckets of water with corks in them, and we're all looking for our ways to let that truth come up.

Here's something Mabel McKay once told me. We were driving down the road once and she asked me, "Do you know how babies are born?"

I was thirty years old and I said I was well aware. She said, "You're stupid, you don't even know what I'm saying." She said, "The Spirit follows the parents for two years before it's born and it sees everything. It knows everything. Even after it's born, it knows everything. When the child is ten months or a year old, the knowledge starts to fall apart. It's like a mirror that gets shattered—your anger, your dependence on your parents, all those things close your whole vision. If you live long enough, and a good life, you're able to put it all back together again."

Then she said, "You know what you do in between?" I said no, and she said, "That's what you call living."

Patience, watching, respecting—that's what spirit means. There is spirit in all of us, everything on earth has spirit. And everything that has spirit has protection. That means it's potentially dangerous. If I were to stab you or rob you, even if you intend to hurt me, you have protection that's going to come back and hurt me eventually.

How did California Indians get along for twenty thousand years with little physical warfare? We have this system of ultimate respect. Nowhere else north of Mexico in pre-Columbian times were there such dense populations of people speaking so many different languages than in the areas now known as Marin, Sonoma, Lake, and Mendocino counties.

In my area, for instance, I might know the songs from my acorn trees. Those songs carry with them not only the blessing for the tree, but the power to hurt anybody who offends it. This engenders a divine respect for all there is. It tells you that you're not the only one with the power to hurt. Everything has that power. If you believe that, you'll have a very different attitude toward things. A tree will suddenly be equal to you, not lower than you.

Notice how antithetical that is to Western notions of man's place in the world. We have no problem with God or Jesus. Jesus was another prophet.

But the ideology that somehow we are here to rule separates and denies the power of anything else on earth. If you believe you're the center, you can't see or respect or give place to anything else.

I want to be careful about saying all Western ways are wrong or all Indian ways are right. Just because you're a certain color doesn't mean you're one way or another. But I think in general the West is out of touch. Europeans for a long time have had no sense of home, no sense of place. They've been wandering for so long. They see their home always, or only, in the sky—not on earth.

Indian people have a long tradition of place. With that place are rules, songs, intimate knowledge that the white people lost years ago. When you lose that sense of place and who you are, you make room for other things, such as greed. You get insecure, you fill your life up with material goods or certain kinds of obsessions. The history of the West is characterized by people who are obsessed with control.

When we were little kids, Mabel would say, "Don't pick up the rocks. Leave them there; say thank you. If something attracts you, just say hello and good-bye. Let it go; don't be greedy. There are things that might want to poison or curse you. They find where you're weak and greedy, and they work you. It's like a hole in your heart."

Your objective as a person is to become solid. As long as you have holes, if they come from anger or greed, there will be ways that negative things can get in there and work on you.

This is what respect means from my perspective. Every man, woman, child, plants, birds—all the creatures, all that lives and all that we cannot see—have as much power as I do, and are probably a little smarter than me. So I have to stop myself and constantly be reminded by creation how sacred my life is. And in turn, how sacred all of life is.

Many healers have said we're going to think about the earth in a different way. That's a lot of work. But until we heal ourselves, and the healing is from inside out, not much is going to be done. I see New Age people going around and hugging things. What does that mean unless you've explored inside? Words like "nature" and "love" are empty unless you've got a philosophy that envelops them. You must be aware of the history and stories and songs of a particular place. You must be aware of its power and rules, not just yours.

Nature writers like Thoreau say "love nature." But if you read between the lines, they're in a place of power. They talk about walking in the rivers and creeks—did they pray first? Who said they could walk there? The Indians never have a chance to answer back to these writers. The nature that Thoreau was living in had already been cleared of Indians.

I go out to nature and I wonder what don't I know. I constantly have to humble myself. Through prayer I get inspiration and the Creator talks back to me. It's more than just hugging a tree. If we clear our minds and hearts, that's prayer. We don't even have to go out in nature. You can be in Manhattan and find ways to fill your heart with other human beings. San Francisco and Manhattan are still nature, and so are buildings and cars.

It's important that we see Indians as relative spokespersons. Don't go to the Indian wanting a lesson and a quick fix. The purpose of our talking is that you'll have a better understanding of what constitutes *you* as a human being—not to find out how you can be more like an Indian.

Schools and teachers give you certain ideas of what Indians are. Even if they're well intentioned, they backfire. I don't run around in a loincloth, and I never saw an Indian do that. People who romanticize Indians only like to talk about the old stuff. They don't want to hear about the drunkenness and the anger and the problems that we have to heal. I want to be like everybody else. You *can* be like everybody else, but you can also have your heritage.

You can also begin to heal yourself. I teach that stories are inner things: you're interacting with a living story. The way the Western man is taught to read is to find the *meaning*, the *symbols*. Instead, I say no, a story is not something you figure out the meaning of, but something you carry with you the rest of your life to talk back and forth with.

Mabel McKay said, "Don't ask me what the story means. Life will teach you about it, the way it teaches you about life." It's a dialogue that you have. Interact with the story the same way you would with a plant or a person. What can you learn about yourself from it?

Children need to learn to read and encounter things in this way. It validates them as unique people. They can use their own background and who they are to develop their own relationships and knowledge. That's what I try to engender. A text has a life of its own. You respect it, you don't set out to dominate it or be dominated by it.

In the Kashaya-Pomo language, the salient feature is the verb. When you translate that to English, you lose a lot of the sense of the text, because English is a subject-oriented language. The text has a life, but in order for it to have meaning for us, we have to talk to it and let it talk back to us. That's very different from the way Western literacy has been taught.

One time I called up to the reservation to Auntie Violet Chappell. I was interviewing for jobs, and I went on and on about how they didn't understand me. She said, "How many times do I have to tell you—white man don't want to know 'he don't know.'"

She hit it right on the nose. Not just "white man," but so many people become threatened—as liberal as they are, they need a theory, a way to frame. They want to use *their* theories to talk about *our* literature. And I say no, I'm coming into the field with what *my* people taught me, what I know in my heart. I'm using my Native point of view to inform and talk back and forth with your theories, rather than your theories telling me what I am.

If I were to use *your* language to talk about me, it would never challenge you. But if I use *my* narrative forms, and the ways I understand these things are very different from the way you do, you're going to think, "What do you mean?" Then we're getting somewhere. The dialogue starts.

Many of my white students say they don't know what's in my class for them, they don't have any culture. I say, "Wait a minute, you do. In fact, what's wonderful is that by listening to us you can find out who you are. When you're in the center, in a position of power, you have no sense of boundaries. The danger is that you don't know your limits, you've never been tested."

On the other hand, if you're a minority person, you're always dealing with the margins. We wonder why minority kids are dropping out. It's because in many ways, they're taught that who and what they are is invalid.

If you're a kid on the streets and the schools and everybody else has told you that you're nobody, one of the ways you get to be somebody is to beat the crap out of somebody else. Then people are afraid of you.

I grew up around South Park and Lower Fourth Street in Santa Rosa and I used to get into a lot of trouble, as a lot of the kids did. When I talk to these kinds of kids now, I try to get them to question what they're doing. I say, "Why are you doing just what the white people want you to do? Why are you killing one another and yourselves? Go back to the classroom and tell your teachers, 'Hey, that's not our true history. Where are you getting that, teacher, and who are you?'"

Right now I'm speaking standard English, but when I go out and talk to these kids, I come at them on their level. I remember, I talk from the streets. I never forgot that language. And the kids can sense my passion, they sense there's a street man still in me fighting.

The teachings of Mabel McKay showed me I could fight back on my own terms. Instead of going around the way I used to, with a lot of anger and no words, wanting to hit somebody, I could use my mouth and the stories I've heard all my life. Mabel was the one who told me to come back up here. I used to come here as a kid, but I was out in the apple orchard getting stoned and drinking during the summers with my friends. I'm up here in a different way these days—I'm grown up.

The real job for me now is healing and trying to become a whole person. My father was a very angry man. He experienced a lot of racism and used his fists to get back. That violence will kill you. It killed my father. He was a boxer, and he drank and caroused and died early on of a heart attack.

I'm a product of his hate. I have to live with my insecurities about being an adopted child and my anger about what happened to my father. I have to accept and heal that. My father is not going to walk through that door. But I can become whole and use his legacy. My father gave his life so that I could have a story—not to replicate, but to re-create.

By learning how to box I became somebody, and people were afraid of me. That was because I had no faith in my words, in who I was. I didn't know my own history. But now I've found that my language and stories are valuable sources, they are *something*. I think it's so important to use the knowledge I have to tell the truth about my ancestors and what went on in the history of this county. I feel that's what I'm here for.

Sonoma County is my home, it's the source of my strength. This is where I'll always come back. I trace my ancestry back to my great-great-great-grandmother Tsupu, a Coast Miwok woman. She ran away from Petaluma to escape General Vallejo. His men used to molest Indian girls. At fourteen she walked barefoot all the way up to Fort Ross, which was held by the Russians and was a sanctuary for Indians. She married a Kashaya man, and if it wasn't for her escaping Vallejo's men, there probably would be none of us left.

You hear that Vallejo and the founders of California did all these great things, but they were raping and abusing the Indians. That's in our family stories, I *know* that. They made us ashamed. This is a historical pattern that happens again and again.

But the fact is that we are a great people who have survived. Our tradition survived, and that's something to stand up for. If our ancestors could get us this far, we owe it to them to keep going and learn from their teaching. That's words, that's more power than my knife or my fist can ever have. The words will last.

I want first of all to be a good writer. I want a broad audience to read my stories, not just Indians and a few whites. I am interested in American literature and the larger traditions—in using my traditions to inform them and make a marriage of the two. I want to write about universal themes, themes that reach a lot of people. If I work hard and have faith in my own stories, I think people will want to hear them. They're true and they're different; they're not the same old things we've heard about Indians.

What I'd like to do is to re-create through fiction the history of Sonoma County, starting with my great-great-great-grandmother, General Vallejo, and the missions, all the way up to this day. The history of this county is in my blood—Indian and Filipino and white, the mixtures of a lot of people. What made those people get along with each other, what made them not get along with each other?

There's a host of characters I grew up with that I'm fascinated by. Some are people in Santa Rosa who were kind of wild. I'm also interested in the old people, how they survived, and in making these old people human. One of the characters I always think about and want to write about is my great-great-grandpa Tom Smith.

There are many stories about him. He was a very powerful guy and led a fascinating life. He was also quite a womanizer. He's got kids spread from Fort Bragg to Lake County to Tomales Bay. He was a great medicine man, but at the same time he was very much a human being with passion. He got himself into trouble. He was married to a woman up here at the same time as he was with my great-great-grandma Emily Stewart down at Tomales Bay. Tom had a great system going—he had a woman in the north, in the south, and who knows where else.

I've got relatives all over this county, and all of us go back to this one man. That's the kind of thing that fascinates me, what happens from generation to generation. It's almost like the Bible. You take a few of those old Indians, and we all come from the ones who survived the horrible onslaught of the Europeans: the disease, the rape, the torture, all of that. There were a few survivors, and look what they did to keep us going.

I still have my fierceness, my strength, my passion. You need the passion, but for many of us in our lives there's dark spots. Rather than to strike the darkness with our fists, we need to word it with our stories.

In the old days, the old people used to say a good person is a person who spends a lot of his or her time thinking about the bigger creation. I hope we can start this dialogue and spiritual understanding of talking and being whole. That's what I work for. That's my path on the earth.

Christopher Peters

The Art of High Mountain Medicine

Christopher Peters is executive director of the Seventh Generation Fund, a national foundation that supports Native American renewal at a grassroots community level with grants, training, and technical assistance. He is Yurok and Karok, as well as Hupa and Tolowa.

He was born and raised in the northwestern corner of California on the Klamath River. For over twenty years he has worked with community development and grassroots organizations serving Native Americans. He joined the Seventh Generation Fund in 1989 and became executive director in 1990. He is the father of two girls, whom he enjoys taking backpacking.

He received a B.A. from the College of Agricultural and Environmental Sciences, the University of California, Davis, and an M.A. in counseling psychology from the Stanford University Graduate School of Education in 1973.

Christopher Peters talked with Darryl Wilson about the "World Renewal" traditions of his people and the discipline of high mountain medicine and prayer.

We have been referred to as "World Renewal People" by anthropologists. There are not many "World Renewal" tribes throughout the Americas who have a central focus on religious ceremony. The ceremony is addressed to the earth as fixing it or making it new.

We do this with the jump dance ceremony. This ceremony is group prayer. Everybody comes together in common mind and spirit to pray together for ten days. We also do the white-deerskin dance ceremony. These are ways of acting out world events. That is our orientation. It is in the blood.

I used to say that we are unique, but if you look at other Indian peoples throughout the Americas, there is that central philosophy of a closeness with the environment as a *way of life*. "Religion" is an insufficient word because ours is a way of life, like the Tao instruction of the East. It is not a religion, it is a "way." If we live a certain "way," we have certain relationships with the environment and certain connections with the spiritual universe.

Native people have only been subjected to a mechanistic thought process for one or two generations. We are not completely brainwashed into that type of thinking. We share a relationship with the universe. It is an instinctual relationship, not a process that is learned. It is not something where we can say, "If I live this way, if I do A, B, and C, I am going to come out of the end of the tunnel as a spiritual person."

It is something innate. It may be tempo, it may be rhythm. It could be an attitude, a philosophy, a concept—it is what makes up our spirituality. Certain formulas within our cultures enable us to draw that out.

Maybe it is prayer, or maybe it is more advanced in terms of medicine-making. The Native people in Northern California have an obsession for looking for the spiritual power where our life systems, our cultural belief systems, our educational systems, and our economic systems are based. This is formed around a spiritual search for medicine power.

The most precious items within our cultures are religious things.

A woodpecker head roll, a white deerskin. These are really precious items within our economic systems. Our pre-contact economy was tied directly to the ceremony process.

The uniqueness of northwestern California is that it is a linguistic triangle, three different language stocks. Over centuries we have maintained linguistic independence. But we share cultural-religious belief systems. The original populations were not so different than they are today.

The contact in Northern California with non-Indians has been for less time than the rest of California and the country—maybe 150 years. Most tribal groups went through a significant reduction in population during the Gold Rush, but in recent history there has been rapid growth in Native populations. We experienced a significant amount of atrocities over a short period of time and bounced back. We were deprived of religious systems for a time, but now they are reappearing.

It may never be the way it used to be before non-Indians came. We have lost a lot of knowledge and a lot of wisdom, but there is a process we have discovered, and that process is continuing.

A legend comes to mind. Two characters, Pohlikukwerek and Wohpekumen, are significant personages—spirit people, "gods." Pohlikukwerek had killed a human being. The sad emotion of the family over the dead person could have killed Pohlikukwerek and Wohpekumen within ten days. Through this spiritual connection the people sent mourning of such velocity that it could kill. Emotion directed at you, if you didn't take care of it, would affect you.

So Pohlikukwerek sent some dentalia money to settle up with the people for the crime. They accepted it. He was creating payment for death. He said, "It is a good law because it is of emotions." This controls how people live. You have to live right because of the attitudes, the mental processes, the emotions of people.

We are so sensitive to the emotions of others that it affects our physical being. There are good emotions and there are bad emotions within each of us. If bad emotions can affect you negatively, then good emotions can affect you positively.

Recently the eels have started coming into the river. It has been a really dry winter, and people have been waiting. Eels stay out in the ocean until there is a good rain. It takes high water to bring them in. So everybody was waiting for the eel run. It was late, but when it came you could feel people knowing that the eels were running. People were going to the mouth of the river to get eels, or waiting for them to come upstream. There was this fervor going through the community. Maybe it is not oral communication, but you know the eels are coming back. It was more significant years ago than it is now. The salmon, the same way. You know this is a good time for everyone.

Our ceremonies are in late summer when the salmon are running. We take care of the basic needs and then give thanks to the Creator. The ceremonies are the spiritual connection.

That connection, the world-renewal process, is tied to what we call high mountain medicine. It is a reaffirmation, illumination, or enlightenment that a person seeks for a lifetime. A lifetime of prayers, fasting, training, and sweating. Over time, traditional people move into higher levels of prayer—"seats"—through this process.

There are a number of prayer seats along the river. The more important ones are in the high country areas. The Burl's Peak area, then the Doctor Rock–Chimney Rock areas. These are where high mountain medicine people go for fasting and praying. They make the connection that unites them as individuals with all of creation and with all of their spiritual needs. This enlightenment and awareness-building brings total significance to the world-renewal process.

In medicine-making, we go to the prayer seat and holler. It is not shamanism, it is simply a good time of the year to go and holler. We go out into the seats to pray, to jump, to sing, and to holler. We holler for *Wa-gay*, the spirit people. We cry. It is a totally raw expression. We want something. We want it and we work on it. Our mind is set for it. If it is to fix the world over again, to make it new, to heal somebody, to look for a power, to look for a good exchange with the spiritual world, this is how it is done.

It is that primal utterance. Getting out the emotion. We get so intense with emotion. Like with Pohlikukwerek, where the sorrow of the mourning family was so intense that it affected him. He was sick. He was in a tree hiding. He nearly fell from the tree because their emotions were so thick.

In times of prayer and hollering our emotions are so thick, or so sorrowful, or so happy. We express it for ten days—and that is the only thing we do for those ten days. Discipline is the continuously driven thought. We want something so bad that we work on it for ten or fifteen or twenty days.

It is like an artist creating a piece of work. An artist may work on it for a month, two months. It is like poetry. You try to get every word right by scratching, writing, rewriting, focusing, focusing, focusing—then it is done. It accomplishes peace. You wouldn't have accomplished it if you had not put energy, heart, and spirit into it. It is the same way with high mountain medicine.

If you go and just look at things for a couple of days and enjoy, it doesn't do any good. But if you go up there and *work* for something, then eventually it happens.

To heal sickness, the medicine people would experience where the person is emotionally and feel their sorrow—sorrow to a point where they are helping the sick person feel. In this way, they get to the point of understanding deep sorrow. Our strong medicine people visited sorrow or loneliness often. So when somebody comes in with a really significant problem, the medicine people have to get to the depths of the person's feelings. Some they get to real quick, others it takes a long time.

With the World Renewal ceremony, we need to look at where the world is and start getting to that point. The world is in a sad place, and we need to visit that sad place and work with it for long periods of time. It is not empty mourning. It is a discipline. We must visit with the Great Spirit where she is and express our emotion. We must bind with her and help her "feel" in a spiritual sense. It will take thousands and thousands of people, massive numbers, being a part of the healing process.

I don't see medicine-making happening at the level that it should be. Years ago people actively pursued it. Today, with the distractions, fashion fads, television, a mobile society—there isn't that discipline within Native people to go through the process to attain the enlightenment.

I see Native people moving toward a more secularized religion. That process of affirmation and connection with spirituality happened at some time in the past, but we are replacing ceremony and ritual with a more common prayer.

Prayer is good, but that actual enlightenment, and the strong medicine process that binds man with the earth and the spirit—a vision quest or meditation—is not happening as much as it should be.

That process is a key. But before the process can occur, you have to have a way of life that will enable you to move into high prayer. A lot of people have tried it. It is hard.

The old people of the tribe who practiced this medicine years ago were extremely isolated. They lived lonely lives. They dedicated themselves to that type of spiritualism. Now Indian people don't make that kind of sacrifice.

If you look at the old traditional healers, you will find that some of them were kind of deformed. They practiced so much and did so much to heal other people that it affected their bodies. Some of them were affected in their minds, too.

If you could teach enlightenment through stories and legends, people might begin to think, "I can be happy with myself because I live this life and I have this relationship with the spiritual world that is gratifying to me in the most complete way. I don't need material wealth."

Certainly the generation that is coming now has to be taught this way. When our kids look at television nine hours a day, we wonder how much we are actually involved with them. Whoever programs television formulates how our children think and react.

The religious rights of Native people also must be protected. The authorities have been searching for ways to establish a law that says our religions aren't protected by the First Amendment on government land. They are more concerned with uranium or coal mining and all of the other minerals.

I think Americans have to look at the ethics of their religion combined with their own hypocrisy before they can begin to clean up the environment. They need to look at ethics within their belief system on a massive scale. But what is going to bring them to that? We are in a situation now where we have maybe fifty years before we reach a point of no return, where we can't fix the situation. We are getting really close to that point right now. There is a significant need to change.

There has to be an optimism saying, "Yes, we can do it. We can change the direction of development." If we don't get that, then we have to accept that we are going to die.

For a lot of non-Indian people, the optimism for living isn't there. Vine Deloria talks about people who believe in Armageddon. If that is rooted in their religious philosophy, if this world as we see it now is going to come to an end, then there is nothing for the future. We have to say, "This world is not going to come to an end. It is a living thing. It is a spirit. It is our mother. It is going to live on and on, forever and ever."

If people can come to the understanding that the world is not going to end, then we can start changing some of this thinking. But as long as the basic philosophy, is, "Hey, the earth is going to come to an end anyway, and when it does I'm going to heaven and walk through the pearly gates and live in eternity with God"—if they believe that, then they can go ahead and drill for oil, cut down trees, and destroy the whole ecosystem, like they are doing right now.

I would say we have a major task, as Native people, to change the white people. Because we are in this ship together. As much as I would like to say, "Let them do what they want to do," I can't. Because we have to realize that we are all in this together.

So our optimism is tied, largely, to our ability to change the mindset of the dominant society. That is a really significant task, if you consider the fact that for the last two hundred years the dominant society attempted to acculturate us—to make us think the way they think.

A small minority, a small percentage of Indian and non-Native people still retain optimism—a knowledge that we are going to live on and on. To continue for Seven Generations is one way to say it. But the thought that we are going to continue for One Hundred Generations or Ten Thousand Generations has to be put into people's minds, too.

Jack Forbes

We Can Have New Visions

Jack Forbes has been a leading writer and scholar in the field of Native American studies for over forty years. He is chair of the Native American Studies Department at the University of California, Davis.

His father was Powhatan-Renápe and other tribes, and his mother was part Delaware-Lenápe. Jack Forbes is working to preserve the Lenápe language, in which he writes poetry. He graduated from Eagle Rock High School in Los Angeles and received his B.A. from the University of Southern California. He worked his way through school in the dairy business, like his father and uncles, and also worked as a firefighter for the U.S. Forest Service.

He earned his Ph.D. in history, with a minor in cultural anthropology, from the University of Southern California in 1959. He introduced the first course in Native American history at the University of Nevada, Reno, in 1965 and was a co-founder of D.Q. University. He has been awarded a Guggenheim fellowship and has been a visiting scholar at Oxford and other universities in Great Britain and The Netherlands.

Dr. Forbes has written more than three hundred books, monographs, articles, stories, and poems. Among his groundbreaking studies are *Apache, Navaho and Spaniard* (1960); *Warriors of the Colorado: The Quechans and Their Neighbors* (1965); *Aztecas del Norte: The Chicanos of Aztlan* (1973); and *Africans and Native Americans: The*

Language of Race in the Evolution of Red-Black Peoples (1993). His most recent book, a collection of short stories, is *Only Approved Indians* (1995). (See bibliography.)

He was interviewed by Lois Crozier-Hogle.

My mother was a major influence on my life. She lived out on a farm when she was a young girl. They had a little five-acre place they called "The Ranch." They raised eggs and vegetables and things like that. She had a green thumb, so all my younger life I had the example of her love of trees and plants. She could never let a plant just dry out, always had to give it a chance to live. She was just wonderful with growing things.

We were quite poor during the Depression. My parents found an inexpensive half-acre south of El Monte and built a small house on it all by themselves. The area is all built up today, but we lived right next to a big field where they grew various kinds of crops. We had a lot of animals—ducks and geese, goats, a calf, and a big turkey named Winston Churchill who was like a watchdog. The baby geese would follow me around. I got very close to those kinds of animals, very close to them.

So that was my mother's influence—the love of beauty. She was a very kind person, very thoughtful, very spiritual.

My father was also a great influence on me. He died when I was about twenty-one. He was a very honest man, an upright man, a very hard-working man who believed in personal dignity. He was a great model for me in terms of his self-study and love of books. He wanted to study law, but his father's death when he was seventeen forced him to go to work in the Pasadena Ice Plant. He once took me to a used book store in Pasadena and we bought a British encyclopedia from the 1880s, with wonderful articles, for ten cents a volume. A bit racist, many of them, but nonetheless filled with detailed information.

He was a very kind man, too. He loved the outdoors. He and I used to take little outings to explore the countryside. I also had wonderful grandparents. They were self-educated people who loved the earth and loved growing things. My aunt and uncle had a magic yard. So I was very fortunate.

In 1943, when I was nine, my parents moved to the edge of Los Angeles, a place called Eagle Rock. We had a wonderful canyon behind our house and I spent a good deal of my time in the hills and that canyon. My friends and I would sit up on top of the Eagle Rock at night. It was very important to me. I used to crawl on my hands and knees through the brush, looking for new animals and things to see.

It is a very spiritual place. It hurt me when a lot of that was destroyed. They put a reservoir in the nearby canyon. I tried to sabotage their equipment by myself. You know, I was just a teenager, but it really hurt me to see the beautiful oak trees, and the pines and prickly pears and things I loved so much—the wildlife, the deer—decimated to make a dam. I'll probably never get over that. I was about sixteen.

I get a tremendous amount of satisfaction from nature. Nature heals. I like to run along the creek. It helps to mend whatever goes wrong during the week. There is a goose that lives down along the creek that I like to pet. I don't know why, he just allows me to pet him.

I also get a lot of satisfaction from creative work, from writing—both research, and fiction and poetry. I would be pretty unhappy if I no longer could do any creative work. My spirituality is not so much the inward type as it is of expressing inward knowledge outwardly. In other words, I am not a person who pulls away from the world.

Spirituality is very important for Native American people. But I have to say that there are good and bad Indians. There are Native people who are on a traditional path and are keeping their spiritual values, but there are also Native people who have taken a different road, sometimes a very evil road. So I think we have to be careful not to define Native Americans in a stereotypical way.

When I was in Holland I ran across a book called *The Last Indians*. It was only focused on the Indians in the rain forest who wore traditional clothing and were living in isolation from European influences. I think that is a mistake. Indians are still Indians, even if they are revolutionaries or if they are fighting in the Peruvian Army. We may not agree with what they are doing, but like any other people, they don't change their race because of changing their culture. They remain Native people.

Having said that, I do believe there is such a thing as a better way of life. And the better way of life is the more traditional way of life, where one lives in balance with nature.

I think it is very much of a mistake for Native Americans to adopt a materialistic and aggressive way of life. It is even more damaging for Indians than it is for Europeans. Europeans have lived for so many centuries in a Machiavellian kind of world that they have developed defense mechanisms in their family structures that help them survive. In many parts of Europe, for example, the extended family takes care of itself. They don't have feelings of responsibility for anything outside of the family. I think that mechanism may have developed from living for hundreds and hundreds of years in aggressive and brutal circumstances. You have to fall back on your kin, that is all that you can rely on.

But I don't think that's so good for Native people. Native Americans—even though the family is very important, and *some* Native people do not care about much beyond the family—feel we have to take responsibility for other things, including the earth.

That is our tradition, our way of life. When we fall away from that, we don't do well. For one thing, we don't have extended families that are as developed as some European or Asian families. So many Indians tend to break apart from everything when they take a materialistic path. They lose their sense of direction and identity.

To get on to a more positive note, I've always felt a sense of mothering and being loved by the earth and living things. I grew up with that sense of sharing my life with other living things—and with humans. Out of that grew a kind of religion, I think, a nondogmatic spirituality. It doesn't have anything to do with Christianity or other kinds of messianic religion.

I became convinced early on about that when I would hear people talking about Foursquare Gospel or Methodist or Catholic things. These seemed so hollow to me, somehow. They seemed to miss the point. Really, each one of us has our own personal religion. We are responsible for that to the Creator and the rest of life. We can't hope the Church will get us off the hook. We have to say, "I am Jack Forbes," and Jack Forbes has to take responsibility for his life and what he does in the world.

That is the way it is in many Native American traditions. There are a lot of communal ceremonies and activities, but I've never seen where they are mandatory. They seem to arise out of the voluntary coming together of the people in the community. Within these traditions, of course, we have examples of what to do. And new traditions come, new ceremonies develop, largely through dreaming. These come from the individual. The individual has the dream or the vision, a song or new dance, and then that may become part of the community's tradition.

Likewise, certain things may be gradually forgotten and set aside. So there is a constant change in the Native American's life, which is due to the harmony and interplay between the individual and the community. The individual is not suppressed by the community, but makes contributions— and the community supports the individual. It is a very different kind of thing from a lot of European religions where you have an authoritarian doctrine that everybody is supposed to follow, and if you don't agree with it you better get up and just leave because they're not going to respect your right to be different.

My feeling about Indian religion developed out of my own experiences. I didn't grow up in an organized community. Later I began to find out more about the traditional beliefs of my people and other Indians. I found them on the whole to be very beautiful and very refreshing, like a breath of pure air that made me feel immediately at home.

Indian people feel they play an important role in maintaining the well-being of Mother Earth and other living creatures. They believe that through ceremonies, as well as individual thoughts and actions, they can contribute to the beauty and harmony of the world. And that is a healing force.

In other words, when you have good thoughts and good prayers, you will put out influences that will affect other living things. You, yourself, are a source of power. Power is potentially found in everything. You are potentiality. And so what you do is important. If we do evil, that will have its influence. If we do good, that will have its influence. It begins within us.

You can't go out and just pretend you are going to be holy. You have to feel it inside. Black Elk made that very clear. He said the importance is in the meaning and the understanding of things, not in the ritual itself. Sometimes people today get hung up over whether the sweat lodge should face one direction or another, or whether the pipe should be leaned one way or another.

It is probably good to follow a particular tradition because it's a helpful form of discipline. But the most fundamental thing is what is in your heart. That's what really counts, that's what will make the difference in the ceremony. Our Delaware teachers have said the same thing.

So I do think we feel a responsibility toward the earth and other living creatures. We may not always live up to it, but we feel that way. A lot of times I will try to do little things. They may not be that important, but—there are certain trees and things I talk to, certain places I am particularly fond of.

I know the trees are very different from me in some ways. They are rooted to the ground in a different way than I am. They probably don't see in the same way I see. They may not hear the same way I hear. But I still feel I can communicate with them and they can communicate with me, so I try to greet them and make them feel good.

Another thing I do, which probably comes from my mother—I am always planting things. I plant acorns during that time of year. I plant pine seeds or nuts. Sometimes I help earthworms. If I see an earthworm out struggling because of too much rain or something, I try to get it out of the way of trouble.

Doing these kinds of things is not only for them, but also for me. Because I believe in the power of doing. In other words, you can talk all you want about how much you love animals or plants; your intention does some good, perhaps, but you have to bring it to actuality in *doing*.

We change ourselves by doing. I think this is so important in rehabilitating people who have gotten on a bad path. That's why the sun dance, the sweat lodge, running marathons, and so on are so vital for Indians.

You don't change yourself by saying, "I'm going to do good now. Yeah, I'm going to be more responsible and religious." You have to involve your body, totally, in *doing* certain things like sweating or protecting trees. By taking care of animals, or visiting an older person in a nursing home or helping to take care of one of your relatives. Suffering with someone when they are going to die. The things we can do are endless. When we *do* these things we change ourselves.

In the beginning, we may not do those things with a completely full heart or understanding. It may be even mechanical at first. "It's hopeless," you might think, "to pick up earthworms, or help a snake get off the road. I can't keep every snake off the road." And it's true, you can't. But it's not *only* for the snake that you are doing it. You are doing it to show yourself it is important to give your interest to something outside of yourself.

I think that one of the terrible things that has happened to Native Americans is being taken away from this tradition. Because when you are in the traditional way of thinking, your friends the plants and animals and the earth will heal you. They will give you strength and a sense that you are loved. You don't need other humans around you all the time because, in this kind of philosophy, you can have a mountain that is your friend. A powerful friend. Big and awesome, but a friend. So you can go off by yourself. You may experience adversity, but you have the strength to overcome it.

What happens with Indian people and other ethnic groups in modern industrial society, and in the schools that Indian kids are forced to go to, is that they lose this source of strength. They become alienated to the point where you can have Indian kids who are brutal. They may get involved in the logging industry, for example, to make their living. But it is not a good way to make a living—this is just my opinion—unless it is done properly. People in exploitative industries get into a situation of ugliness around them. The humans become just like the trees: they can be clear-cut, too.

Luther Standing Bear said that people who are alienated from nature will be living in a brutalized world. It makes me mad sometimes to read articles about ecology today where they don't mention a single Native American in the history of the so-called modern ecological movement.

Luther Standing Bear was writing all of these things in the 1930s, and much more fundamental things than most ecologists are writing today.

In any case, what has happened to a lot of Indian communities is that they have lost a sense of belonging to the natural world. Then what do they have left to belong to? Do they belong to the world of McDonald's and Burger King? To the world of VCRs and pop music and making money and alcohol and soft drinks?

The world of consumption is a very unhappy world. I don't know very many classes of people that have been able to be happy by consuming. Even the rich. But especially people of Indian background, because they're usually poor to begin with. When they become part of the world of materialism and consumption, their life is one of constant frustration. On the edge of poverty and on the edge of plenty. They get a check, they buy a lot of things, and all of a sudden they're poor again. Over and over.

I think that is one of the most horrible things that has happened to Indian people—the spread of an exploitative way of looking at the natural world. But still, fortunately, in almost every Indian community the old way of looking at things survives. The future must be built on that.

It's true that we've lost a lot, and we can't do everything our ancestors could. But we can recover and we can rebuild and have dreams again. *We* can dream ceremonies just like they did. *We* can have new visions. We don't have to give up just because we've lost part of our tradition and culture. We can still find the essential things in our life and make them work for us.

And they don't have to be perfect. It's just like learning to speak your own Indian language again. The first time you speak it, it's not going to be any good. You know you're not going to pronounce things correctly. People are going to laugh. Let them laugh. Unless you try, you'll never learn.

One of the things I hope for is that one of these days we will have a kind of a world in which there won't be large states. People can live in smaller communities in more democratic ways, in a kind of federalism based upon the principle of traditional Native American confederacy, like the Iroquois and Delaware. Where small communities come together to solve their problems, there are no big powers to trample on other people.

Behind that rests a couple of things crucial to Indian philosophy. One of them is the sense of humility. A sense that you are dependent upon the earth, that you are utterly dependent upon nature and other human beings. If you are truly humble, you won't force yourself or your ideas on anybody else.

The other side of that is respect. If you understand yourself and your place in life you will respect other human beings and other living things. Respect is what will build a world that is peaceful and democratic. Only respect. To take the time to solve problems in the way that they can be solved—by talking with people.

I am particularly interested in political independence for Indian people. This means having their own land and territory, a chance to live their own lives and preserve their own languages, to be free to follow a spiritual path.

A part of the rehabilitation process for Native American people is becoming involved in a spiritual movement, in tradition, and in working with non-Indians to save the earth. But the earth will not be saved until non-Indians as well as Indian people come to really believe and understand their oneness with the world around them. I think that is absolutely essential. We must teach people how to love. We must give them the right to love.

Unfortunately, the way a lot of people are raised now, particularly males, they think it is wrong to love. It's unmanly to love. The only thing manly is to be cold and distant, unattached. And I think women make a big mistake when they try to imitate the worst of men.

The way I look at the world, we are a living part of a living universe. Many Indian religions teach that the creation of the universe was a mental process or a dreamlike process. It was not primarily physical. The basic nature of the world that has been created is something we don't understand. Indian people don't pretend to understand the nature of the Great Spirit. That is why we don't have a theology. We don't study "God." That's impossible, from our point of view.

But some things are clear. One of them is that there is a principle of unity of the life around us. Not only do we have a common origin, but we are a part of it. There is no separation. The air that I breathe is the air that the trees have breathed. And the trees and plants breathe the kind of air I exhale. We are in a symbiotic, mutually embracing relationship.

People are starting to realize that we are "rooted" just like the trees. Our breath is a form of root, in that without the air, we are dead. We have to have that continuous back and forth flow of oxygen and expulsion of carbon dioxide.

We are also rooted through our pores and other body cavities. We are utterly dependent, as the old Lakota said, like sucking babies. We suck our mother's breasts all of our lives. We are utterly dependent upon the earth and air, we are one with them. Our bodies are made up entirely of them, nothing else. Mostly salt water, but the rest is made up of the animals, the plants, the grass, the air. We have nothing apart from that except our spirit itself.

So we are one with our environment. There is no boundary. We can lose our hands and still go on living. We can lose our legs and go on living. We can lose our noses, our hair, our eyes, our ears, a lot of things, and we can go on living. But if we lose the air, we cannot live. If we lose the water, we cannot live. If we lose the plants and the animals, we cannot live. So they are more a part of us than that which we call our "body."

At the same time, our body is also a universe. We are alive inside, not just with our spirit but with a lot of little creatures that are dependent on us in the same way we are dependent on the earth and the air. Without them, we would not be able to digest our food, we would have no immune system.

So I see the universe as a series of circles of dependencies. That is one of the reasons why the circle is sacred. We are a circle inside of a circle, and those circles go on and on and on and on, as far as anyone will be able to see.

EPILOGUE

As we look today at the whole picture of the American Indian in this country, it presents a microcosm of the American scene. We have paid a high price for the old attitude of "Manifest Destiny," with its emphasis upon the exploitation and ravaging of the given wealth of this beautiful land.

The attempt to obliterate the Indians is an unmistakable metaphor for what we have done to ourselves. Our future is in the redemption of their future, and theirs in ours. Will we choose to help liberate, or continue to resist and hold them down?

The difficulty of straddling two cultures and holding fast to the best values in each requires great strength and vision. Out of the suffering of Native Americans has come amazing growth and grace. Could this help to guide us in our future as well?

The real treasure, the real gold, lies not in exploitation of the earth, but within us. It is our hope that a new consciousness will arise in Indian and non-Indian alike, that a new understanding of what Jung called the numinous will emerge in order to realize the next five hundred years as a new way of living.

This book's purpose has been to increase understanding, for we know that only from understanding comes love. Is it possible we can learn to accept one another's best values and bring together the best in both worlds? This is our vision.

—LOIS CROZIER-HOGLE

BIBLIOGRAPHY

Works cited include books by the participants in this anthology; books mentioned in the interviews and footnotes; books consulted in creating this anthology; and selected works of and about American Indian oral history and autobiography.

Abbott, Lawrence, editor. *I Stand in the Center of the Good: Interviews with Contemporary Native American Artists*. Lincoln: University of Nebraska Press, 1994.

Allen, Paula Gunn. *The Sacred Hoop: Recovering the Feminine in American Indian Traditions*. Boston: Beacon Press, 1986.

Arden, Harvey, and Steve Wall. *Wisdomkeepers*. Oregon: Beyond Words, 1994.

Armstrong, Virginia, editor. *I Have Spoken: American History Through the Voices of Indians*. Athens: Ohio University Press, Swallow Press, 1971.

Bataille, Gretchen, and Kathleen Sands. *American Indian Women: Telling Their Lives*. Lincoln: University of Nebraska Press, 1984.

Bean, Lowell, editor. *California Indian Shamanism*. Menlo Park, Calif.: Ballena Press, 1992.

Broder, Bill. *The Sacred Hoop: A Cycle of Earth Tales*. San Francisco: Sierra Club Books, 1979.

Brown, Dee. *Bury My Heart at Wounded Knee*. New York: Bantam Books, 1971.

Brown, Joseph Epes, editor. *The Sacred Pipe: Black Elk's Account of the Seven Rites of the Oglala Sioux*. Norman: University of Oklahoma Press, 1953.

Brumble, David, III. *American Indian Autobiography*. Berkeley: University of California Press, 1988.

Capps, Walter, editor. *Seeing with a Native Eye: Essays on Native American Religion*. New York: Harper & Row, 1976.

Coltelli, Laura, editor. *Winged Words: Contemporary American Indian Writers Speak*. Lincoln: University of Nebraska Press, 1994.

Courlander, Harold, editor. *Hopi Voices*. Albuquerque: University of New Mexico Press, 1982.

Crow Dog, Mary, and Richard Erdoes. *Lakota Woman*. New York: Grove Weidenfeld, 1990.

Crum, Steven J. *The Road on Which We Came: A History of the Western Shoshone*. Provo: University of Utah Press, 1994.

———. *Native American Higher Education*. Albuquerque: University of New Mexico Press, 1993.

Deloria, Vine, Jr. *Red Earth, White Lies: Native Americans and the Myth of Scientific Fact*. New York: Scribner, 1995.

———. *Behind the Trail of Broken Treaties*. New York: Delacorte, 1974.

———. *God Is Red*. New York: Grosset & Dunlap, 1973.

———. *Custer Died for Your Sins*. New York: Macmillan, 1969.

Deloria, Vine, Jr., and Clifford M. Lytle. *The Nations Within: The Past and Future of American Indian Sovereignty*. New York: Pantheon Books, 1984.

DeMallie, Raymond. *The Sixth Grandfather: Black Elk's Teachings Given to John G. Neihardt*. Lincoln: University of Nebraska Press, 1984.

Eastman, Charles (Ohiyesa). *Indian Boyhood*. Reprint. New York: Dover, 1971.

———. *From the Deep Woods to Civilization*. Boston: Little Brown, 1916.

———. *The Soul of an Indian*. Boston: Houghton Mifflin, 1911.

Erdoes, Richard, and Alfonso Ortiz. *American Indian Myths and Legends*. New York: Pantheon Books, 1984.

Fire, John (Lame Deer), and Richard Erdoes. *Lame Deer: Seeker of Visions*. New York: Simon & Schuster, 1972.

Forbes, Jack D. *Only Approved Indians*. Norman: University of Oklahoma Press, 1995.

———. *Apache, Navaho and Spaniard*. Norman: University of Oklahoma Press, 1960; reprint 1980, 1994.

———. *Black Africans and Native Americans*. Oxford: Blackwell, 1988; Urbana-Champaign: University of Illinois Press, 1993.

———. *Columbus and Other Cannibals*. New York: Autonomedia, 1991.

———. *Native Americans of California and Nevada*. Healdsburg, Calif.: Naturegraph, 1969; rev. ed. 1982.

———. *Tribes and Masses: Essays in Red, Black and White*. Davis: D.Q. University Press, 1978.

———. *Aztecas del Norte: The Chicanos of Aztlan*. New York: Fawcett, 1973.

———. *Nevada Indians Speak*. Reno: University of Nevada Press, 1967.

———. *Warriors of the Colorado: The Quechans and Their Neighbors*. Norman: University of Oklahoma Press, 1965.

———, editor. *The Indian in America's Past*. Englewood Cliffs: Prentice-Hall, 1964.

Gifford, Eli, and Michael R. Cook, editors. *How Can One Sell the Air? Chief Seattle's Vision*. Summertown, Tenn.: Book Publishing Co., 1992.

Green, Rayna, editor. *That's What She Said*. Bloomingdale: Indiana University Press, 1989.

Hamilton, Charles, editor. *Cry of the Thunderbird: The American Indian's Own Story*. Norman: University of Oklahoma Press, 1972.

Haslam, Gerald, and Alexandra Haslam, editors. *Where the Coyotes Howl and the Wind Blows Free*. Reno: University of Nevada Press, 1995.

Heizer, R. F., and M. A. Whipple, editors. *The California Indians*. Berkeley: University of California Press, 1971.

Helms, Mary. *Middle America: A Cultural History of Heartland and Frontiers*. Englewood Cliffs: Prentice-Hall, 1982.

Hertzberg, Hazel W. *The Search for an American Indian Identity*. Syracuse: Syracuse University Press, 1971.

Highwater, Jamake. *The Primal Mind*. New York: Harper & Row, 1981.

Hill, Dorothy. *The Indians of Chico Rancheria*. Sacramento: State University of California, 1978.

Hill, Tom, and Richard Hill. *Creation's Journey: Native American Identity and Belief*. Washington, D.C: Smithsonian Institution Press, 1994.

Johnson, Sandy, editor. *The Book of Elders*. New York: HarperCollins, 1994.

Kaiser, Rudolf. *The Voice of the Great Spirit*. Boston: Shambhala, 1991.

Krupat, Arnold, editor. *For Those Who Come After: A Study of Native American Autobiography.* Berkeley: University of California Press, 1985.

LaPena, Frank (contributor). *This Path We Travel: Celebrations of Contemporary Native American Creativity.* Produced by the Smithsonian Institution. Golden, Colo.: Fulcrum, 1994.

————. *The World Is a Gift.* Santa Fe: Wheelwright Museum of the American Indian, 1988.

————. *Sunusa Stopped the Rain* (poems). Sacramento: Chalatien Press, 1979.

————. "Wintu." In *Handbook of North American Indians,* Vol. 8: *California,* edited by Robert Heizer. Washington, D.C.: Smithsonian Institution, 1978.

————. *The Gift of Spring* (poems). Sacramento: Chalatien Press, 1976.

Lesley, Craig, editor. *Talking Leaves: Contemporary Native American Short Stories.* New York: Laurel, 1991.

Lincoln, Kenneth. *Native American Renaissance.* Berkeley: University of California Press, 1983.

Lyons, Oren. Epilogue. In *Voice of Indigenous Peoples: Native People Address the United Nations, with the United Nations Declaration of Indigenous Peoples' Rights,* edited by Alexander Ewen. Preface by Rigoberta Menchu. Santa Fe: Clear Light, 1994.

————. *Dog Story* (children's book with illustrations). New York: Holiday House, 1973.

————, illustrator. Three books for children, by Virginia Driving Hawk Sneve: *When Thunders Spoke* (1974); *Jimmy Yellow Hawk* (1972); and *High Elk's Treasure* (1972). New York: Holiday House.

Lyons, Oren, et al. *Exiled in the Land of the Free: Democracy, Indian Nations, and the U.S. Constitution.* Santa Fe: Clear Light, 1992.

McGaa, Eagle Man. *Mother Earth Spirituality.* San Francisco: Harper & Row, 1990.

Martin, Calvin, editor. *The American Indian and the Problem of History.* New York: Oxford University Press, 1987.

Matthiesen, Peter. *In the Spirit of Crazy Horse.* New York: Viking, 1991.

Mayfield, Thomas Jefferson. *Indian Summer: Traditional Life Among the Choinumne Indians.* Berkeley: Heyday Books, 1990.

Momaday, N. Scott. *The Way to Rainy Mountain.* Albuquerque: University of New Mexico Press, 1969.

————. *House Made of Dawn.* New York: Harper & Row, 1966.

Nabokov, Peter, editor. *Native American Testimony.* New York: Viking, 1991.

Neihardt, John, editor. *Black Elk Speaks.* New York: William Morrow, 1932.

Perdu, Theda, editor. *Nations Remembered: An Oral History of the Five Civilized Tribes, 1865–1907.* Westport, Conn.: Greenwood Press, 1980.

Perrone, Bobette, Henrietta Stockel, and Victoria Krueger. *Medicine Women: Curanderas and Women Doctors.* Norman: University of Oklahoma Press, 1989.

Peyer, Bernd. *The Singing Spirit.* Tucson: University of Arizona Press, 1989.

————, editor. *The Elders Wrote.* Berlin: Reimer Verlag, 1982.

Philp, Kenneth, editor. *Indian Self-Rule: Firsthand Accounts of Indian-White Relations from Roosevelt to Reagan.* Salt Lake City: Howe Brothers, 1986.

Plenty Coups, with Frank Linderman. *Plenty Coups: Chief of the Crows.* Lincoln: University of Nebraska Press, 1962.

Sandner, Donald. *Navajo Symbols of Healing.* New York: Harcourt Brace Jovanovich, 1979.

Sarris, Greg. *Grand Avenue.* New York: Hyperion, 1994.

————. *Mabel McKay: Weaving the Dream*. Berkeley: University of California Press, 1994.

————. *Keeping Slug Woman Alive: A Holistic Approach to American Indian Texts*. Berkeley: University of California Press, 1993.

————, editor. *The Sound of Rattles and Clappers*. Tucson: University of Arizona Press, 1994.

Standing Bear, Luther. *Land of the Spotted Eagle*. Reprint. Lincoln: University of Nebraska Press, 1978.

————. *My People, the Sioux*. Reprint. Lincoln: University of Nebraska Press, 1975.

Suzuki, David, and Peter Knudston. *Wisdom of the Elders*. New York: Bantam Books, 1992.

Swann, Brian, editor. *Smoothing the Ground: Essays on Native American Oral Literature*. Berkeley: University of California Press, 1983.

————. *Coming to Light*. New York: Random House, 1994.

Swann, Brian, and Arnold Krupat, editors. *Recovering the Word: Essays on Native American Literature*. Berkeley: University of California Press, 1987.

Swinomish Mental Health Project, Jennifer Clarke, editor. *A Gathering of Wisdoms*. La Conner, Wash.: Swinomish Tribal Community, 1991

Tedlock, Dennis, and Barbara Tedlock. *Teachings from the American Earth*. New York: Liveright, 1975.

Thorpe, Dagmar. *People of the Seventh Fire*. Ithaca, N. Y.: Akwe:kon Press, 1995.

Trafzer, Clifford E. *Grandmother, Grandfather, and Old Wolf: Tamanwit Ku Sudat and Traditional Narratives of the Columbia Plateau*. East Lansing: Michigan State University Press, forthcoming 1997.

————. *Blue Dawn, Red Earth: New Native American Storytellers*. New York: Anchor, 1996.

————. Seventeen books for children, including: *Salmon Count* (1994); *American Indians as Cowboys* (1992); *The Nez Perce* (1992); and *California's Indians and the Gold Rush* (1989).

————. *Earth Song, Sky Spirit: Short Stories of the Contemporary Native American Experience*. New York: Doubleday/Anchor, 1993.

————. *Mourning Dove's Stories*. San Diego: San Diego State University Press Publications in American Indian Studies, 1991.

————. *American Indian Prophets*. Sacramento: Sierra Oaks, 1986.

————. *The Kit Carson Campaign: The Last Navajo War*. Norman: University of Oklahoma Press, 1982.

————, editor. *American Indian Identity*. Sacramento: Sierra Oaks, 1986.

Trafzer, Clifford E., with Richard Scheuerman. *The Renegade Tribe*. Pullman: Washington State University Press, 1986.

————. *Chief Joseph's Allies*. Newcastle, Calif.: Sierra Oaks, 1992.

Walker, James R. *Lakota Belief and Ritual*. Lincoln: University of Nebraska Press, 1980.

Waters, Frank. *Pumpkin Seed Point*. Athens, Ohio: Sage Books, Swallow Press, 1989.

————. *Book of the Hopi*. New York: The Viking Press, 1963.

Whorf, Benjamin Lee. *Language, Thought, and Reality*. Edited by John Carroll. Cambridge: MIT Press, 1956.

Wilson, Darryl. *Haya' Wa Atwen (Porcupine Valley)*. Berkeley: Heyday Books, 1996.

Wilson, Darryl, and Barry Joyce, editors. *Dear Christopher: Letters to Christopher Columbus by Contemporary Native Americans*. Riverside, Calif.: University of California Publications in American Indian Studies, 1992.

This boo

Printed on 60 lb Phoenix Natural
and bound by Edwards Brothers,
Ann Arbor, Michigan.

Designed and composed by
Elizabeth Towler Menon on
a Power Macintosh in
QuarkXPress 3.32 for the
University of Texas Press, 1996.